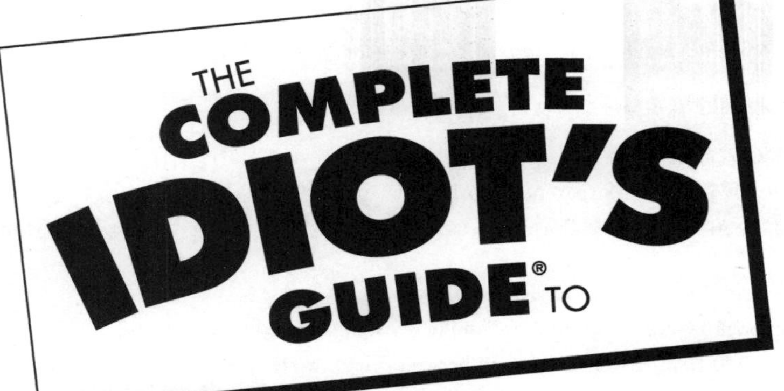

Sport Flying

by Dan Ramsey
with Earl Downs

ALPHA
A member of Penguin Group (USA) Inc.

May the Source of Life give you flight.

ALPHA BOOKS

Published by the Penguin Group

Penguin Group (USA) Inc., 375 Hudson Street, New York, New York 10014, U.S.A.

Penguin Group (Canada), 10 Alcorn Avenue, Toronto, Ontario, Canada M4V 3B2 (a division of Pearson Penguin Canada Inc.)

Penguin Books Ltd, 80 Strand, London WC2R 0RL, England

Penguin Ireland, 25 St Stephen's Green, Dublin 2, Ireland (a division of Penguin Books Ltd)

Penguin Group (Australia), 250 Camberwell Road, Camberwell, Victoria 3124, Australia (a division of Pearson Australia Group Pty Ltd)

Penguin Books India Pvt Ltd, 11 Community Centre, Panchsheel Park, New Delhi—110 017, India

Penguin Group (NZ), cnr Airborne and Rosedale Roads, Albany, Auckland 1310, New Zealand (a division of Pearson New Zealand Ltd)

Penguin Books (South Africa) (Pty) Ltd, 24 Sturdee Avenue, Rosebank, Johannesburg 2196, South Africa

Penguin Books Ltd, Registered Offices: 80 Strand, London WC2R 0RL, England

International Standard Book Number: 1-59257-317-7
Library of Congress Catalog Card Number: 2004115233

06 05 04 8 7 6 5 4 3 2 1

Interpretation of the printing code: The rightmost number of the first series of numbers is the year of the book's printing; the rightmost number of the second series of numbers is the number of the book's printing. For example, a printing code of 04-1 shows that the first printing occurred in 2004.

Printed in the United States of America

Publisher: *Marie Butler-Knight*
Product Manager: *Phil Kitchel*
Senior Managing Editor: *Jennifer Chisholm*
Senior Acquisitions Editor: *Mike Sanders*
Development Editor: *Lynn Northrup*
Senior Production Editor: *Billy Fields*
Copy Editor: *Susan Aufheimer*
Cartoonist: *Richard King*
Cover/Book Designer: *Trina Wurst*
Indexer: *Brad Herriman*
Layout: *Becky Harmon*
Proofreading: *Donna Martin*

Contents at a Glance

Contents

Appendixes

Foreword

Congratulations on selecting this book and exploring the exciting opportunity that it represents. If you're new to the world of flying—or, for that matter, if you're looking for a way to return to it—you've found a great guide to an exciting breakthrough that can put you at the controls of an aircraft, experiencing the thrill of flight, in less time and at less cost than ever before.

EAA worked with government and industry for more than a decade to ensure that our vision of a safe, affordable, and achievable way to fly became regulatory reality. We wanted to make the dream of participating in aviation—for no better reason than the sheer joy of flying—accessible to nearly everyone.

Many of EAA's 170,000 members know the exhilaration of taking wing and experiencing the world as an eagle. When you're at the controls—choosing your course, soaring high above, mastering the sky—the feeling is rousing and empowering. And now that sport pilot and light-sport aircraft are here, you can capture those feelings and *live* your passion for flight. Not unlike boating, RVing, motorcycling, scuba diving, or mountain climbing in terms of cost and training required, flying airplanes is now becoming the next great pastime for those who are *serious* about having *fun*.

EAA is working hard to build a world in which light-sport aviation will thrive, grow, and mature. Pilots and prospective aircraft owners need less expensive aircraft that meet safety requirements, as well as teachers and training materials to impart the necessary skills of flight. EAA is leading the way—engaging with other interested groups and individuals, including this book's author—to make sure these things happen.

Education and information are equally important elements of EAA's leadership, which is why we launched *EAA Sport Pilot & Light-Sport Aircraft*, the world's first periodical dedicated to this area of aviation. Each month, this magazine informs and entertains our members with a wide variety of articles showing them how to venture skyward and fly for fun. EAA has also created a sport pilot website (www.sportpilot.org), established a toll-free hotline for members, and participated in hundreds of aviation events and seminars on this subject nationwide.

By picking up this excellent book, you've taken your first step toward a great adventure in aviation. These pages provide the right information, use the right language, give the right advice, and point you in all the right directions to get your wheels off the ground.

And one of those directions most certainly is membership in EAA. We stand ready to be your partner through every stage of your journey in personal aviation. Joining EAA is the best investment you'll make in the pursuit of your aviation dreams. Call us at 1-800-JOIN-EAA.

Why does EAA care so much about light-sport aviation? Making the sky accessible has been a cornerstone of EAA's mission for more than five decades, because getting people involved and making their participation in aviation a reality are the essential ingredients in building aviation's future. Just ask famed aviation innovator Burt Rutan, leader of the SpaceShipOne team that launched the first successful back-to-back privately funded missions into space in the fall of 2004. His dreams in aviation, which he began cultivating as an EAA member 30 years ago, have led him, and the world, to a whole new dimension of personal flight.

When my father, Paul Poberezny, founded EAA in 1953, a then-new set of "homebuilt" aircraft regulations made affordable flight and ownership possible for a large population of postwar pilots who had learned to fly in the military through training paid for by the GI Bill. With the demise of GI Bill flight training in the 1970s, and the increasing cost of aircraft ownership, the growth of personal aviation slowed. To keep flying for fun within reach, EAA has led new efforts to sustain and increase opportunities for recreational aviation. These efforts have helped to bring you sport pilot and light-sport aircraft.

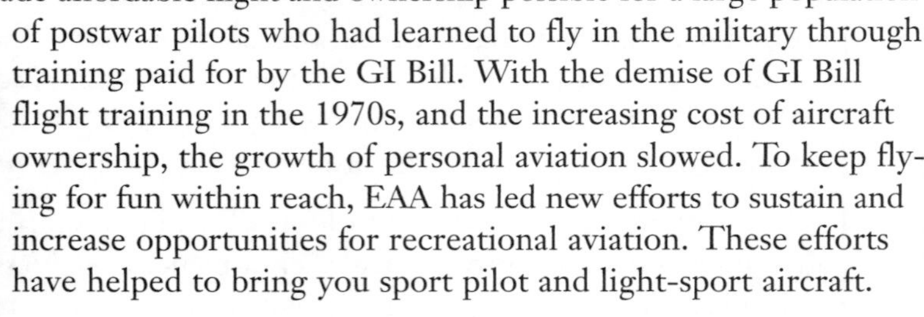

Why does EAA care so much about light-sport aviation? Read this book and you'll see. Join us in this exciting recreational activity.

—Tom Poberezny, president of the Experimental Aircraft Association (EAA)

Introduction

Twenty-five years ago, as I wrote my best-selling book, *Budget Flying*, private aviation was in a surge of growth. People were having loads of fun learning to flying. But just five years later, many pilots were grounded by a round of burdensome regulations, higher insurance premiums, and other rising costs. Some of the biggest names in small planes—Cessna and Piper—were facing layoffs and even bankruptcy. For the next two decades, growth in private aviation leveled off. Even the addition of ultra-lights and the recreational-pilot certificate couldn't quite get things moving again.

Then, on September 1, 2004, everything broke loose. More pilots went flying. More low-cost planes were becoming available. More people were having fun flying again. What happened?

The Sport Pilot and Light-Sport Aircraft (SP/LSA) regulation happened! The culmination of nearly 10 years of hard work by aviation associations and aircraft manufacturers, the SP/LSA rewrote the rule book to make pilot certificates easier to get and a new type of safe aircraft easier to buy. It was a new way of thinking about flying.

The premise? Not all pilots even *want* to fly high-performance aircraft in crowded airspace. Using common sense, the new rules made it much easier for noncommercial pilots to get trained and certified to fly plenty-fast planes under visual flight rules (VFR)—if it's clear enough to see, well, it's nice enough to fly. No flying at night and stay away from clouds. And you don't have to buy a plane that costs as much as a house! Based on this common-sense concept, private aviation leaders developed a full-blown proposal that, after much hard work, is now the law of the land. And I'm proud to say that *The Complete Idiot's Guide to Sport Flying* is the first major book available on this exciting new flying opportunity: sport flying!

This book is for experienced pilots, too! More than 100,000 ex-pilots can no longer fly because their FAA third-class medical exam has expired. Otherwise healthy enough to fly, they're grounded. The new sport-pilot regulations give them clearance. If they have a valid driver's license, they're probably healthy enough to fly! (If you're one of these pilots, remember that this book is intended for beginners.)

For updates on this book and additional information about sport flying, please visit www.SportFlyingGuide.com.

How to Use This Book

This book is presented in a very logical structure to make it easy to find things when you need them. Let's take a closer look at each part.

Part 1, "On-the-Ground Basics," introduces you to the recent FAA rule changes that dramatically enhance private aviation. You'll discover why planes fly and how to fly them.

Part 2, "Into the Wild Blue Yonder," takes you step by step through a typical flight course focused on earning your wings as a sport pilot. You'll soon gain confidence in your proven flying skills and enjoy your time aloft. And you'll learn what you need to know to pass your sport-pilot certificate on the first try.

Part 3, "Expanding Your Horizons," shows you how much fun you can have flying light-sport aircraft. You'll see how these new craft are airborne recreational vehicles. You'll also discover how to make a living by flying.

Part 4, "Choosing Your Sport Plane," focuses on how to select, fund, and share a sport plane that fits both your flying needs and your pocketbook. You'll discover ways of saving hundreds and even thousands of dollars as you discover the thrill of becoming "pilot in command" of one of many types of aircraft that a sport pilot may fly.

In addition, four appendixes include valuable resources that you must have if you want to discover sport flying. The first is "the rules" for the sport-pilot certificate and sport plane selection. Straight from the FAA's latest rules, you'll discover exactly what sport pilots can and cannot do. Want to know more? A comprehensive resources appendix is included to take you forward on your trip toward sport flying. Along the way you'll read and hear many new words, so I've included a clear-language glossary of words you should know as you take off on your flying adventure. Finally, a list of acronyms helps you keep track of the many acronyms you'll find in this book.

I've also included more than 100 photos, illustrations, and charts to help you discover the thrills of flight. Enjoy!

Extras

Along the way, practical sidebars show you the safe and smart way to do things, define words and terms you might not be familiar with, point out any dangers or pitfalls, and give you other bits of helpful information. *The Complete Idiot's Guide to Sport Flying* makes the trip easier—and more fun!

Stall Warning!

Sport planes are safe—if you pay attention! Here's how to fly safely and keep others safe as you discover the many thrills of sport flying.

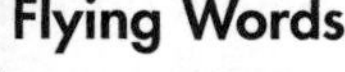

Flying Words

What does *that* mean? Here you'll find a concise definition of important flying terms in context. Also check the Glossary for more definitions to make things clearer.

Wing Tips

Here are some valuable tips from pilots, manufacturers, officials, and other aviation folks on how to get the most from your flying experience, as well as other related information you need to know.

Knowledge Test

You knew there would be a test! Throughout Parts 1 and 2 of this book I'll include concise tips specifically aimed at helping you pass your FAA sport-pilot knowledge and practical tests. You'll ace it, ace!

Acknowledgments

First, I must thank my technical advisor, Earl Downs, who has been flying for nearly 50 years and has earned just about every pilot certificate and rating you can think of. In addition, he's been an instructor teaching hundreds of others the thrill of flying. Besides operating Golden Age Aviation, Inc., Earl is the publisher of *Oklahoma Aviator*, and author of numerous articles on sport flying for *Sport Pilot and Light-Sport Aircraft* magazine, published by the Experimental Aircraft Association (EAA). Most important, Earl is a great guy who plays well with others. Thanks, Earl!

The Federal Aviation Administration administers the new rules for sport pilots and keeps our skies as safe as possible. Thanks especially go to Marion Blakey, Jane Garvey, Ron Wojnar, Jim Ballough, and Peggy Gilligan for all of your hard work!

Much credit for the new SP/LSA regulations must go to the Experimental Aircraft Association. It has been working with the FAA and others for more than a decade to bring the dream of flying to reality for thousands of new sport pilots. Specifically, I'd like to thank Tom Poberezny, Ron Wagner, Bob Warner, Dan Johnson, Bruce McCall, Mary Jones, Mark Forss, and the staff at EAA headquarters in Oshkosh, Wisconsin. Thank you for your hard work, EAA! And a special thanks goes to Dan Johnson who provided and identified the sport plane photos for this book!

Another prominent mover and shaker for private aviation is the Airplane Owners and Pilots Association (AOPA). It has worked tirelessly with the FAA and others to help make flying easier and safer. Thanks to all!

In addition, I would like to thank Debby McDowell of CH Products; Ken Kaplan and Pamela Olson of King Schools; Janet Jones of Sporty's Pilot Shop; Ed Downs of SkyStar Aircraft Corp.; William Connor of Tango One Aviation; Andre Cliché of Cybair Publishing Ltd., publishers of the *Ultralight Aircraft Shopper's Guide;* Paul Hamilton of Adventure Productions; Randy Schlitter of RANS, Inc.; Richard VanGrunsven of Van's Aircraft, Inc.; Bob Ellefson of Golden Circle Air, Inc.; Sebastien Heintz of Zenith Aircraft Company; and Jennie Trerise of Aviation Supplies & Academics.

And thanks, once again, to Mike Sanders, Lynn Northrup, Susan Aufheimer, and Billy Fields for their extensive skills and direction with this project. Lynn and Susan logged many hours of virtual flight time in developing and editing this book. They've earned their "wings!"

Trademarks

Part 1

On-the-Ground Basics

Flying is a blast! By simply following the proven and irrevocable laws of flight, you can soon be up in the sky looking down at all your problems and worries!

Once the domain of the rich or foolhardy, flying is now for just about anyone with a valid driver's license, some discretionary income, and a week to learn how it's done. Hey, that's *you!*

This first part introduces you to the new rules of the sky: sport flying. You'll soon discover how really easy—and safe—it is to go flying. You'll find out how planes fly and how to keep them flying. Most of all, you'll learn that *you* can do it!

Don't worry, ace! This first part will all be on the ground!

Chapter 1

The *New* Sport Flying

In This Chapter

- How the new sport-pilot certificate works
- Is sport flying right for you?
- Making plans to get your wings
- What you need to get started in sport flying

It's a fact: Learning how to fly has never been cheap. You have to hire an instructor and a training plane, take lessons, study for tests, pass those tests, buy or rent a plane, buy fuel and insurance, and find the time to get into the sky.

The new fact is: Flying is becoming cheaper than ever! On September 1, 2004, the Federal Aviation Administration (FAA) made official some major rule changes that cut the costs of learning and flying *by half or more.* Literally millions of wannabe pilots now can safely learn to fly. That includes *you!*

Flying Words

Sport flying refers to flying light-sport aircraft for recreation. Recent FAA rules offer the new sport-pilot certificate and define light-sport aircraft requirements toward making flying fun and safe.

This chapter introduces the brand-new sport-pilot certificate and light-sport aircraft designation, and what both can mean to your dreams of someday learning how to fly. Maybe you've already heard about the changes, but don't know exactly what they are and how they affect you. This is the real deal. Here's how you can do it.

The Wright Stuff

It was just a century ago that brothers Wilbur and Orville Wright discovered powered flight. On the windy dunes of Kitty Hawk, North Carolina, in December of 1903, the two bicycle repairmen were rewarded for hundreds of hours of planning, tinkering, and testing. The *Wright Flyer* flew for a distance shorter than the length of a modern airliner. But it flew!

Ten decades later, aviation has dramatically changed how we work, play, and move about the country. Without airplanes, cross-country trips would be made in days rather than hours. Overnight packages would take a week to arrive. Frequent-flier miles would go unused.

Today, there are three types of flying: scheduled airlines, military, and everything else—called general aviation (GA). What might be surprising is how big GA is! In fact, 95 percent of the 220,000 civilian aircraft in the United States are general-aviation aircraft. And there are lots of airports: 13,000 at last count, with just 2 percent of them served by scheduled airlines.

And there are lots of pilots; the latest count is more than 640,000 in the United States. The experts say that the reason there aren't more pilots is the perception that flying is unnatural and dangerous. The cost of flying enters the equation, too, but it is the fear of flying that keeps many people grounded. So here are the facts:

- Flight is a proven science that follows constant rules; the pilots who get into trouble are those who break the rules.
- When you get good training and follow the rules, flying is much safer than many other recreational sports we engage in.
- You can get a sport-pilot certificate in about a week of concentrated study and practice—or spread it out over a couple of months. (There's really no such thing as a sport or other pilot "license." It's actually a certificate, issued by the FAA at www.faa.gov.)

- The cost of earning your sport-pilot certificate is about the same as a nice vacation.
- Many sport pilot-qualified planes and the new *light-sport aircraft* cost about as much as a sport utility vehicle (SUV).

One of the latest of the new light-sport aircraft is the Jabiru Calypso.

Flying Words

Sport pilots are allowed to fly airplanes that meet specified weight and performance limits. New planes that meet these new regulations are called **light-sport aircraft** (LSA). Some older certified airplanes also meet these limits. Together, I will refer to them throughout the book as "sport planes." You'll learn more about the various qualified planes in Part 2.

In this and future chapters you'll discover that planes fly according to irrevocable laws of physics, you'll learn what knowledge and equipment you need to fly, and you'll find out how to keep it fun.

Understanding the New Rules

The majority of pilots today hold the private-pilot certificate. It requires at least 40 hours of training (with 60+ hours typical) and allows you to fly day or night, near or far, as long as you follow the rules.

One of the rules is that you must fly aircraft that have a current airworthiness certificate. That's a good thing—except that the type-certificate regulations for manufacturing these aircraft also cover planes manufactured for commercial use to fly lots of passengers many miles above the earth's surface. Getting a new aircraft design certified by the FAA can cost many millions of dollars. That's why there have been few new models introduced to the GA marketplace in decades. Most models are upgrades from ones that first flew 40 years ago. Even so, the latest models start at over $100,000 and go up—way up.

One of the exceptions to these rules is homebuilt aircraft. By following plans or building from a complete kit, you could legally build an airplane that didn't require a stringent certification. These are termed "experimental aircraft." The Experimental Aircraft Association (EAA) was born 50 years ago to serve this market.

About 25 years ago a new category of aircraft snuck in under the wire: ultralights. These are single-passenger aircraft intended for flying to nearby destinations. They use limited-power engines and basic airframes to take the pilot up for sightseeing. These aircraft do not have to meet FAA certification requirements. There are many fine examples of safe and fun-to-fly ultralights buzzing around the sky. No passengers allowed!

A dozen years ago, the FAA introduced a new pilot category with the recreational pilot certificate. It was intended to bridge the gap between ultralight and private pilots, requiring fewer hours of training but having many limitations. Unfortunately, it didn't work. Training requirements were cut by only 10 hours (from 40 to 30), but there were some limitations applied to the certificate that limited its usefulness. You can fly a four-seat aircraft but carry only one passenger. There are less than 400 active recreational pilot certificates.

Learning from errors is how pilots get to be old. The FAA also has learned and, with the help of the EAA and others, came up with what's called the SP/LSA ruling. It's actually two major rule changes, one covering sport-pilot certification and the other covering how the new light-sport aircraft are built. These rules are written to answer the need for lower-cost—but entirely safe—aircraft for pilots who want to learn as they go. For example, the sport pilot can be certified to fly a specific model type out of small airports. Once the sport pilot wants to fly into bigger airports, he or she must take additional training and get an endorsement, something like a permission slip. The sport pilot cannot fly at night but, if desired, the pilot can train for a private-pilot certificate that allows night flying. It makes sense.

Sport-Pilot Training

So let's go over the new rules. Sport pilots need the following training:

- A minimum of 20 hours flight time including 15 hours with a certified instructor and 5 hours solo (by yourself)
- Two hours of cross-country flying (more than 75 nautical miles)
- Pass the FAA knowledge test (30 questions requiring a 70 percent or better score)
- Three hours of training in preparation for the FAA practical test (called the checkride)
- Pass the FAA practical test
- Present a valid automobile driver's license or a third-class FAA medical certificate as proof of medical health

> **Wing Tips**
>
> Some folks think the most important new rule is the medical requirement for sport-pilot certificates. Private-pilot and higher certificates require an FAA medical examination and sign-off, intentionally restrictive to make sure airline pilots are in top condition. In most cases, the medical requirement for the new sport-pilot certificate is simply your valid driver's license. If you can drive, you can fly. The exception is for pilots whose third-class medical certificate has been denied, suspended, or revoked. In these cases the FAA requires reapplication for a new medical certificate.

With the certificate, the sport pilot can …

- Fly in non–radio-controlled U.S. airspace and certain radio-controlled airspace (with training and endorsement).
- Fly up to 10,000 feet above mean sea level (MSL).
- Fly with visual reference to the surface under visual flight rules (VFR), daytime only.
- Fly an aircraft that meets the following LSA guidelines:
    - Single-engine (non-turbine) aircraft with fixed (not retractable) landing gear
    - Two (or fewer) occupants, including the pilot

- 1,320 lbs. maximum gross weight (including the plane, passengers, luggage, fuel, etc.)
- Maximum airspeed of 120 nautical miles (about 138 miles) an hour
- Maximum *stall* speed of 45 *knots* (51 miles an hour)

- Have fun!

Flying Words

A **stall** occurs when wings lose some or all of their ability to lift the aircraft due to the wing angle. A **knot** is one nautical mile (6,076.12 feet) per hour, about 15 percent longer than a standard or statute mile. To convert knots into miles per hour, multiply by 1.15. To convert miles per hour into knots, multiply by .869.

The New Light-Sport Aircraft Rules

The airworthiness of light-sport aircraft falls under a new set of rules called consensus standards, established by the industry group American Society for Testing and Materials (ASTM) rather than by the FAA. It will be up to the aircraft manufacturers to follow the standards. They also will be responsible for letting aircraft owners know how to keep their planes compliant. An annual inspection of the aircraft for airworthiness is required. The new rules simply remove some of the bureaucracy from the manufacturing process and put more of the burden on the manufacturer.

What are the requirements for the new light-sport aircraft? Light-sport aircraft must meet the performance and weight limitations set forth for a sport-pilot certificate, mentioned earlier. I give more details in Chapter 14.

There are actually three categories of LSAs: fixed wing, powered parachute, and weight-shift-control aircraft. The majority of new sport pilots fly fixed-wing planes, and the principles are approximately the same for all three categories, so they are covered in this book. However, if one of the other two categories interests you, contact the FAA (www.faa.gov) or the EAA (www.eaa.org) for additional information. In addition, light-sport aircraft that land on floats can weigh 1,430 lbs., allowing an extra 110 lbs. for the extra equipment.

Several manufacturers currently are producing aircraft that qualify under the new LSA rule (see Appendix B), but some older aircraft and most ultralights already fall within these limits, so there are many planes from which to choose. I tell you more in

Chapter 14. Just to keep it simple, I am going to use the term "sport plane" (SP) when I am referring to any sport pilot-eligible airplane. I will use the term "light-sport aircraft" when I am referring to the new aircraft covered under the new SP/LSA regulation.

Some light-sport aircraft are those that were first developed for the ultralight market, such as this Challenger II.

That's the gist of it. The actual FAA rules are included in Appendix A and are described in more detail in coming chapters.

Knowledge Test

Want to read the rules for yourself? The FAA publishes and updates the Federal Aviation Regulations (FARs) that cover aircraft, airmen (pilots), airspace, air carriers, airports, navigational facilities, administrative regulations, and other heavy reading. You can (and should) buy a copy from the FAA or through aftermarket publishers and pilot shops (see Appendix B). All FAA regulations can also be obtained from the FAA at www.faa.gov.

Do You *Really* Want to Fly?

Let's get back down to earth for a moment. Before you get too far into spending money on flying, consider what you want to get out of flying.

For many pilots, it's the thrill of adding a third dimension to their visual prospective. It is being able to see their homes, workplaces, and even problems from a different prospective. Crabgrass doesn't look as important from 1,500 feet above.

For other pilots, it's the efficiency of cutting travel time and having more fun getting there. Even though a sport plane has limited performance, it can fly twice as fast as you can drive. Add to this that you can fly a straight line, so flying time could be less than half of an automobile trip. Still other pilots fly because they want to share their perspective with family and friends. They love taking kids and grandkids and neighborhood kids up in the plane.

Some sport pilots are simply looking for incremental training toward a career in aviation. Instead of paying up to $8,000 for a private-pilot certificate, they opt for the new sport-pilot certificate at less than half the cost. If they're hooked on flying, they will then earn endorsements and take tests to move on up in certification. Their sport-pilot logbook can be applied to requirements for any higher pilot certificate.

For some, the excitement of flying is enhanced with an open cockpit plane such as this Tiger Moth.

Wing Tips

Here's the bottom line: The typical GA airplane has a glide ratio of 9:1. If you are one mile (5,280 feet) off the ground and the engine conks out, you have nine miles in any direction to find a place to land. Much of your training will be toward knowing what to do—and how to avoid it. Relax!

Many wannabe pilots, however, aren't really sure why they want to fly. They just do. And they're not sure how they will use their flying in the future. They might start out by going to fly-ins and pancake breakfasts, then move to camping under the wing, and finally decide on turning their love of flying into a business or a career. For them, it makes much more sense to start with an inexpensive certificate and work toward higher ratings as interest and resources grow. That's the real function of the new sport-pilot certificate: to give people a safe and relatively inexpensive way to enjoy flying.

Getting Your Sport-Pilot Certificate

So what's it going to take to earn your sport-pilot certificate? Just like earning anything worthwhile, it's going to take some effort and some money. Fortunately, it's not like going to college—or trying to pay for college. I'll show you how to get your sport-pilot certificate in about a week for under $4,000.

First, let's take a look at the stages involved in getting your certificate. There are five.

> CAUTION
>
> **Stall Warning!**
>
> Since the terrorist attacks of September 11, 2001, the FAA has worked with other governmental and law enforcement agencies to dramatically reduce the opportunities available to use aircraft as weapons. The new light-sport aircraft weigh less and carry less fuel than a very small car. They also are slower than commercial aircraft and pose less of a danger than existing private aircraft. In addition, requiring a valid state driver's license for training allows for improved background checks of student pilots.

First, Pre-Solo

The first step in your certificate is getting signed up at a flight school or with a flight instructor. Here are your training options:

- Accelerated flight school: You come, you stay, you cram, and you fly away a week later.
- Local flight school: You study in the evenings, fly a couple of times a week, and earn your certificate in two to three months at an airport near you.
- Independent flight instructor: You rent or borrow a plane and hire an instructor to teach you what you need to know. The FAA certifies two types of flight instructors. One is called a certified flight instructor (CFI) and the other is called a sport-pilot instructor (SPI). A CFI may provide flight training for all pilot certificate levels. An SPI may provide flight training only for sport pilots. For the sake of simplicity, this book will call them all "instructors."

Which option is best? It depends on you. For some, the most convenient is to schedule vacation time and go for it. For others, taking a week off is out of the question, but weekend lessons will work. Still others have a plane and know a good CFI who can take them flying. The cost of local and out-of-town training will be approximately the same, except for overnight accommodations.

To help you estimate costs, consider that a typical trainer aircraft, wet (with fuel), will rent for about $75 an hour (something between $50 and $100 an hour depending on the model). Your instructor will charge about $45 an hour ($30 to $60 is typical). Figure on 15 hours of dual instruction (you, the instructor, and the plane) times $120 an hour ($75 plus $45) or about $1,800. You also need 5 hours of solo (you and the plane) at $75 an hour for an additional $375. Add another $500 ($200 to $800) for ground school and you have a bare cost of $2,675. However, you want to make sure you have some extra time to feel comfortable flying on your own, so plan an extra couple of hours with an instructor and a couple of hours of solo time to practice what you've learned. That adds another $390. It's up to about $3,100—well below half the cost of getting a private-pilot certificate!

Remember, that's just an estimate. If you already have a training plane, your costs will go down. If you can take only one lesson a week, you should plan on taking more hours of instruction to compensate for the memory loss between lessons. If you live in the Big City and need to travel to a small airport or you need to pay Big City prices at a nearby airport, your costs will go up.

My advice: Be a smart consumer, but don't be cheap. A $20-an-hour instructor might not be a good teacher. A trainer plane that rents on the cheap probably is. Instead, find a recommended flight school or instructor and fly only in well-maintained equipment.

There are many other ways you can bring down the cost of going up. In fact, Chapter 5 shows you how to fly at home in your own flight simulator for just a couple hundred dollars. You can practice whenever you want and even walk away from crashes. It's fun!

Knowledge Test

What certificate do you need to start flying as a student sport pilot? The answer is: none. You can start learning to fly and log flight training without any special certificate. However, you must meet all the training requirements and be at least 17 years old to get the sport-pilot certificate. A student-pilot certificate is activated for solo flight after you have been trained and tested by your instructor. After your instructor has endorsed your student-pilot certificate and your logbook, the student-pilot certificate becomes a license to fly solo.

Second, Practice Skills

Before you know it, you'll be ready to fly solo. Sound scary? Well, it's not, because you will be prepared. Your instructor will ensure that you meet all training requirements. He or she will administer a pre-solo written examination developed especially for you. You will receive special training just before you solo, and then your instructor will "turn you loose." You will probably have a touch of trepidation subdued by the knowledge that your instructor believes in you. You will be thrilled!

Once you have your sport-pilot certificate you can upgrade it with an endorsement to fly "seaplanes" such as this Kitfox on floats.

My first solo flight was July 10, 1980, at Evergreen Airport, Vancouver, Washington. That's when I *began* to learn to fly. Until that point, student pilots have one goal: to solo. After that the goal moves to passing the tests and getting their flight certificate. SPIs know this and work toward getting the solo out of the way as soon as it's safely practicable so the student will be ready to extend learning.

Your instructor will prepare you for solo flying and continue to teach you new piloting skills. Solo flying will be combined with learning new skills such as how to take off and land on short or unpaved (soft) airfields, and how to navigate away from your home airport on a cross-country trip.

Third, Solo Cross-Country

Once your instructor thinks you're ready to leave town safely, you'll get a logbook endorsement for a *cross-country* solo trip. That's a planned excursion of 75 or more miles with at least one turn in it.

What's involved in a cross-country solo? Logically, you must choose the destination (typically, the instructor will help you do this), chart a course, check the weather, and file a flight plan so folks know where you're going (in case they have to come looking for you).

You learn more about navigation in Chapter 9. For now, consider that there are four ways of figuring out where you are in the sky. You will learn all four methods, although you may rely primarily on one or two, depending on how your plane is equipped.

- **Pilotage:** looking out the window for landmarks that appear on your sectional chart (map)
- **Dead reckoning:** calculating and flying from point A to point B, then turning to a new heading and flying to point C
- **Radio navigation:** following various radio signals using instruments in your aircraft
- **Global positioning satellite (GPS):** using satellite signals to help you determine where you are, where your destination airport is, and how to get there

Flying Words

Don't let the term **cross-country** worry you. You do not have to fly from Los Angeles to New York. The FAA says that if you are logging cross-country flying for the purpose of obtaining a pilot certificate, the flight must be at least 75 nautical miles from one airport to another.

Fourth, Cramming for the Test

Your goal is to pass the FAA practical test for your sport-pilot certificate. Toward that goal your instructor will help you practice for the test, giving you at least three hours of instruction that will be very similar to what the experience of taking the test will be like. You'll be practicing …

- Takeoffs and landings.
- Turns and other maneuvers.
- Slow flight.
- Stalls.
- Emergency procedures.

Your instructor will be guided by an FAA document called the *Sport-Pilot Practical Test Standards* (PTS). You should have a copy as well. The FAA flight examiner will not attempt to trick you or to test you on any skill not described in the PTS.

Finally, Taking the Practical Test

Your FAA sport-pilot test is actually two tests. The first one is the written knowledge test which you took after completing ground training. Once your instructor has endorsed your logbook that you are ready to take the final sport-pilot certificate test, you will be ready for test two, the practical test.

A big part of the practical test is oral questioning. The examiner wants to be sure you really know this stuff and didn't just guess correctly to pass the knowledge test. The examiner will ask you to plan a cross-country trip to a specific destination. The oral testing will include showing your flight plan, discussing how you arrived at it, and answering questions about the weather, sectional chart, and other aspects of the planned trip. This oral testing will actually continue throughout the practical test.

Once convinced that you have planned the trip for safety, the examiner will ask you to start the trip. You will perform a preflight inspection of the aircraft, take off from the airfield (showing off your radio communication skills if necessary), and begin heading toward your destination, with the examiner in the plane with you. Along the way, the examiner will test your knowledge and skills. I tell you more about your checkride in Chapter 11.

Once you've returned to your airport—safely—the examiner will fill out the paperwork and you officially hold a sport-pilot certificate (or not). Should you worry about the outcome? Definitely not! Your flight instructor is staking his or her reputation on you, making sure you will easily pass this final test before your logbook gets the endorsement to be tested. So relax, enjoy the test, and enjoy your flight!

There's much more to say about the new sport-pilot certificate, light-sport aircraft, and the opportunities available. In fact, it will take this whole book to cover it. For now, envision the opportunities available to you for low-cost, high-safety flying. You can do this!

The Least You Need to Know

- The new sport-pilot rules are developed to offer inexpensive, yet safe, opportunities to fly.
- A sport pilot may fly any aircraft that meets the airplane limitations applied to a sport pilot.
- Light-sport aircraft (LSA) are a new type of plane designed specifically to meet sport-pilot limitations. They are fully functional planes that offer safe flight for what you'd pay for a sport utility vehicle.
- To get the most for your efforts, consider what you want out of flying.
- Getting your sport-pilot certificate is a simple process.

Chapter 2

How Planes Fly

In This Chapter

- A look at the parts of an airplane
- Understanding thrust, drag, lift, and weight (gravity)
- How flight controls monitor aircraft performance
- Flight instruments: What's happening as you fly?

What makes an airplane fly?

Money!

Actually, airplanes fly by following *irrevocable* laws of physics. In this chapter, you learn what those laws are and, more important, how to be a law-abiding pilot. Just as driving a car requires that you follow both the laws of physics and the laws of the road, so flying airplanes requires knowledge of the relevant laws. And knowledge is power. Knowledge can help you overcome the natural fear of flying. It can help you relax in the friendly skies.

Taking an Airplane Apart

An airplane doesn't look anything like a car—but they both work similarly. Beyond getting you from here to there, cars and airplanes have many of the same functions, even though the components look and operate differently.

So let's drive out to the airport and, when no one's watching, take apart a plane and your car to see how they are similar. It'll be fun!

Engine

Both a car and an airplane have engines that power them. Aircraft engines that power sport pilot-eligible aircraft can be *two-stroke* or *four-stroke*. It is common to find both air-cooled and liquid-cooled engines in lightweight sport planes. The car engine power is passed on to the transmission and then the wheels to pull it along the road. The plane's engine power is passed on to the propeller to pull it through the sky.

> **Flying Words**
>
> In a **two-stroke** engine, a piston travels up and down once in the chamber for each power cycle. In a **four-stroke** engine, the piston travels up and down twice in the chamber per power cycle. Two-stroke engines are simpler, less expensive, and less powerful than four-stroke engines.

Because you cannot pull over to a cloud if you have engine troubles, aircraft engines have redundant systems. For example, each cylinder has two spark plugs powered by two separate electrical systems (magnetos). You typically use both, but if one magneto system has a problem, you simply switch to the other and continue to an airport to land safely.

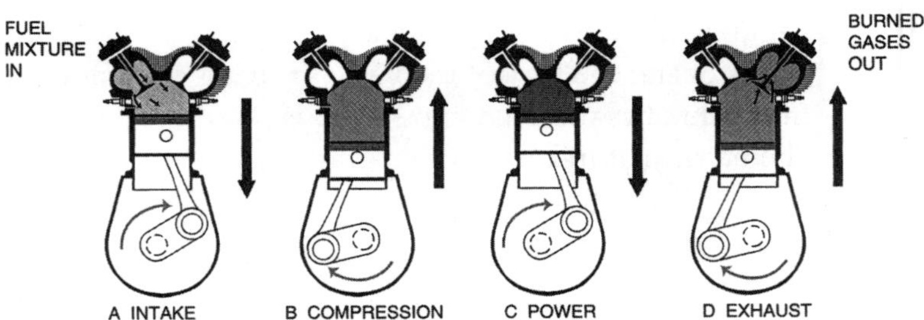

Four-stroke engine.

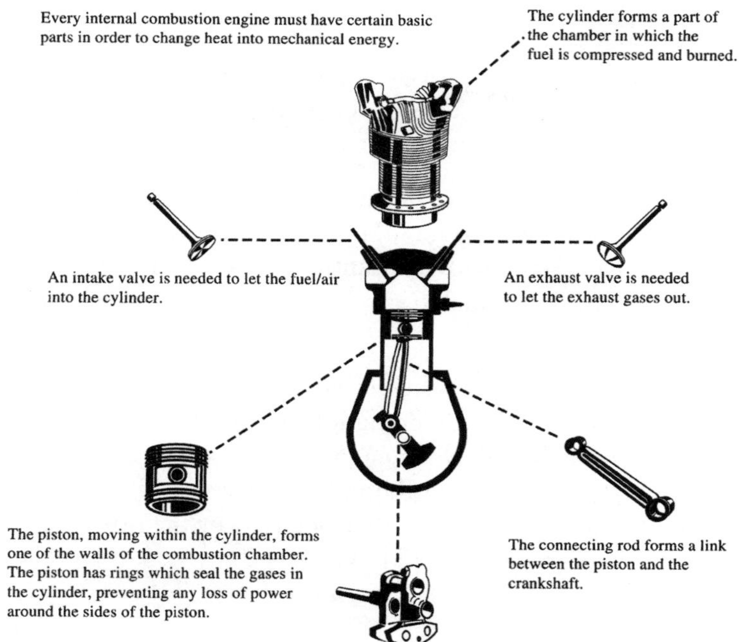

Components of a typical engine.

When you're ready to go to work in the morning you probably start your car's engine, count to three, and drive off, knowing that if there's a problem with the engine you can call AAA. However, there is no American *Aircraft* Association towing service, so you must take some time to check out your plane before flying off; it's called a preflight inspection and you learn how to do it in Chapter 7. Of course, the two most important things you'll check are the fuel and the oil.

Wing Tips

If you'd like to know more about how cars and engines run, read my book *The Complete Idiot's Guide to Car Care and Repair Illustrated* (Alpha Books, 2003), available at local bookstores and online at www.MulliganBooks.com.

Wings

If you've been to the airport—and I'm sure you have—you've seen a variety of types of aircraft, large and small, high-wing and low. Maybe some older planes with two sets of wings. What's that all about?

Wings, obviously, are one of the major differences between cars and planes. I tell you how wings work a little later in this chapter. For now, know that they have evolved in many ways since the Wright brothers first flew over a century ago—but they still operate about the same. The differences are small design changes to make them more efficient and easier to control.

Which is better: high-wing or low-wing? It's like the old Ford vs. Chevy question. It's really a matter of flying preference. If you plan on doing lots of sightseeing, high-wing aircraft make more sense because they allow you an unobstructed view of the ground. Low-wing aircraft give up some ground visibility for better visibility at pilot level and above. Many aircraft manufacturers make either one type or the other. A few offer both types. I cover this topic in more detail in Chapter 14.

Wing configurations.

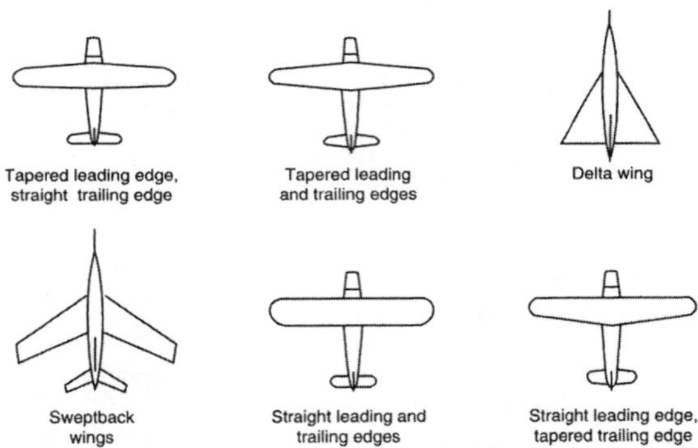

Tail

Cars have no real counterpart to the airplane's tail section. Boats do. A boat's rudder turns the stern one way and the bow goes the other. An airplane's rudder works in the same manner, turning the nose as needed to help guide the aircraft. In an airplane, this movement is called "yaw."

The plane's tail also has a horizontal rudder, called the "elevator," that lifts or drops the tail, thus dropping or lifting the plane's nose.

Landing Gear

An airplane's landing gear includes its wheels, though they are ineffective and a "drag" after leaving the ground. That's why some aircraft have retractable landing gears that move into the plane's underbelly so they don't slow down the aircraft. Sport pilots are permitted to fly fixed-gear airplanes only.

There are two landing-gear configurations. One has three wheels under the front half of the fuselage, called a tricycle gear. The other configuration has two under the front half and one near the plane's tail, called a "standard gear" or a "taildragger." Both are popular, though tricycle gears are more popular with those who fly into paved airfields, and taildraggers are more popular with those who land on grass or soft fields. Sport pilots are permitted to fly planes with either type of landing gear.

Understanding the Four Forces

Why are aircraft designed with these components and not some other configuration? Because these components are designed to take advantage of the four forces of aerodynamics. They work.

The four forces are thrust, drag, lift, and weight (gravity). Your car, however, doesn't have to lift anything to operate so it faces thrust, drag, and weight, only. Let's take a closer look at these four forces.

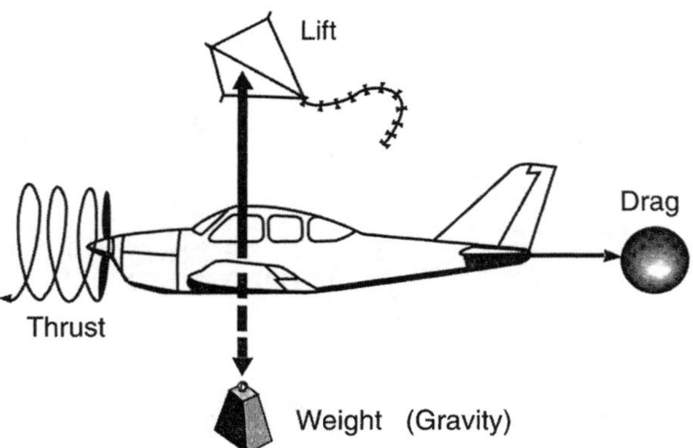

Four forces: thrust, drag, lift, and weight.

Thrust and Drag

Thrust is what moves your car or airplane forward. Thrust is applied to a car's wheels to rotate them and move the car along the road. Thrust is applied to an airplane's propeller to spin it and pull or push it through the air.

Drag is a real drag. We all know that a car has more drag when it is moving fast. That's why racecars are built sleek and slim to reduce the drag. Airplanes are similar—the faster they go, the more drag is created and the more thrust is needed to overcome it. This high-speed drag is called "parasite drag." However, slow speeds for cars and planes are different stories. Letting off the accelerator on your car slows you down and reduces the drag on your car. When an airplane slows down, the drag actually increases. In order to fly your airplane very slowly, more thrust is eventually needed. This is called "induced drag," which is caused by the increased lift needed to fly slowly. When we add up the effect of parasite drag and induced drag, the sum is called "total drag." Airplanes are designed to have a best speed that produces the least total drag for the thrust used. This speed is very close to your cruise speed.

Wing Tips

It speaks for the inherent safety of private airplanes that their average age is nearly 15 years and that there are thousands of planes built 50 or more years ago that are still flying.

Lift and Weight

Weight (gravity) keeps your car on the road whether it's sitting still or driving fast. Because it is firmly on the road it doesn't need lift. But your airplane does. Without lift, an airplane is an odd-looking car.

Lift changes during a climb.

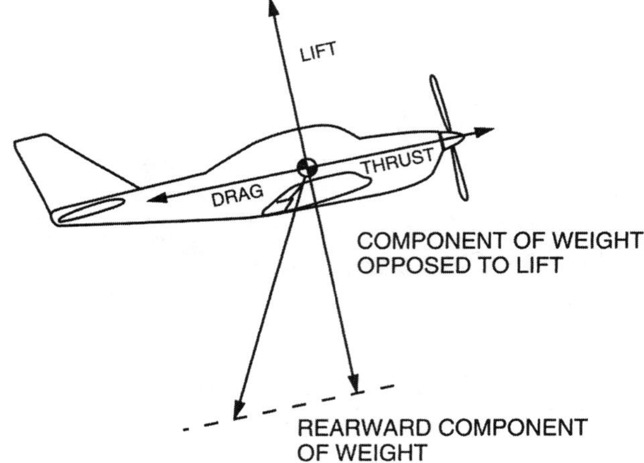

Lift is provided by the propeller and the wings. As the propeller pulls the airplane forward, air flows across the top and bottom surfaces of the wings. Physicist Jakob Bernoulli first described what happens: *Where air is faster, pressure is less.* Because the wing has a greater curve on the top than on the bottom, the air moves faster over the top than over the bottom. Bernoulli says there is then greater pressure under the wing than above it, and the wing is pushed up. That's lift.

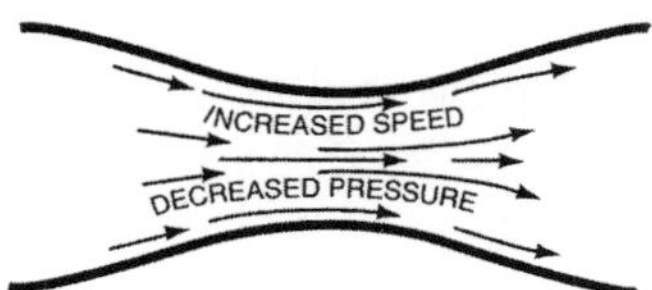

BERNOULLI'S PRINCIPLE, which explains how lift is created by an airplane's wing, is depicted in these three diagrams. A fluid traveling through a constriction in a pipe (above) speeds up, and at the same time the pressure it exerts on the pipe decreases.

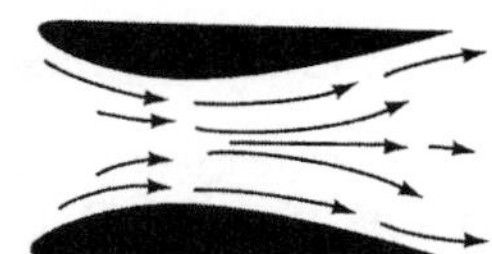

THE CONSTRICTED AIRFLOW shown here, formed by two opposed airplane wings, is analogous to the pinched-pipe situation at left: air moving between the wings accelerates, and this increase in speed results in lower pressure between the curved surfaces.

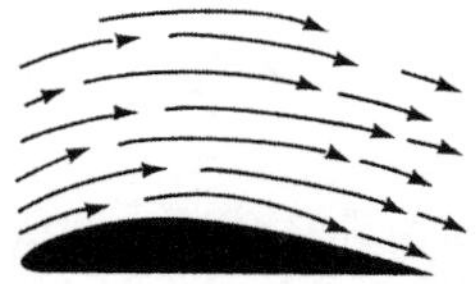

THE SAME PRINCIPLE applies when the air is disturbed by a single wing. The accelerating airflow over the top surface exerts less pressure than the airflow across the bottom. It is this continuing difference in pressure that creates and sustains lift.

The Bernoulli effect applied to aircraft.

You Have Power Over the Forces

In level cruise flight, the force of thrust is equal to the force of drag, and the force of lift is equal to the force of weight (gravity). The plane is in a state of equilibrium, sort of like an aerodynamic cruise control. In order to go up or down the balance of the forces must be momentarily unbalanced. To go up, the plane must be pointed up. But increasing the up angle of the wing adds drag, which means that thrust must be added to balance the forces. Just like a car climbing a hill, a plane must get more power or it will slow to a stop. The plane must be pointed down to go down. Decreasing the wing angle also decreases drag, and power must be reduced to rebalance the forces. Just like your car, your plane will exceed the speed limit if you don't let off the accelerator (called a throttle on a plane) during descent. Once you establish a steady climb or a steady decent, the forces are balanced again.

Summary of climbing and descending:

- To go higher, raise the nose (increase the wing angle) and add power.
- To go lower, lower the nose (decrease the wing angle) and reduce power.

In order to go faster or slower the forces must, once again, be rebalanced. Adding thrust causes your plane to speed up, but it also increases lift. This means that if you want to go faster in level flight (hold altitude), the nose must be lowered slightly (the wing angle must be decreased) to reduce the increased lift. Reducing thrust causes your plane to slow down. Lift is reduced when your plane slows, which means the nose must be raised (the wing angle must be increased) to prevent an altitude loss. Remember our old nemesis, drag? The slower we go, the more drag we get. So, thrust will have to be added again after you have slowed to the desired speed.

Summary of going faster and slower:

- To go faster, add thrust and lower the nose (decrease the wing angle).
- To go slower, reduce power and raise the nose (increase the wing angle), and then add thrust when the desired speed is obtained.

Equilibrium

Are all four of these forces ever in equilibrium? Does thrust ever equal drag and lift equal weight? Yes! Anytime the plane is not changing from one flight path to another, the forces are equal. That would be in straight and level flight, a steady climb or a steady descent, and when the speed is not changing.

Knowledge Test

In unaccelerated level flight, thrust equals drag and lift equals weight.

Using Flight Controls

Flight controls change the action of larger components: engine, wings, and tail. By doing so, they change the impact of the four forces on your aircraft. Your plane then moves faster or slower, higher or lower, and turns.

As you can see, it's important to understand the relationship of controls and their functions. Once you develop the skills to appropriately use controls, you will be well on your way to flying.

Throttle

As mentioned earlier in this chapter, the throttle controls the engine's—and thus the propeller's—speed. Think of the propeller as a spinning vertical wing.

The throttle is simply a fuel feeder. Pushing the throttle in (toward the instrument panel) works just like pressing the accelerator pedal on your car. The only difference is that the aircraft throttle isn't spring-loaded to return to its original position. On a car, you must keep your foot on the pedal. In an airplane, you push the throttle shaft in or pull it out, and it stays where it stopped.

Ailerons

What the heck is an aileron? It's a wing controller. It is a movable part of the trailing (rear) edge of the wing that can be moved up or down. Why? As you've learned, airflow over the wing surfaces gives the aircraft lift. By changing the shape of the wing with the aileron you can change the wing lift.

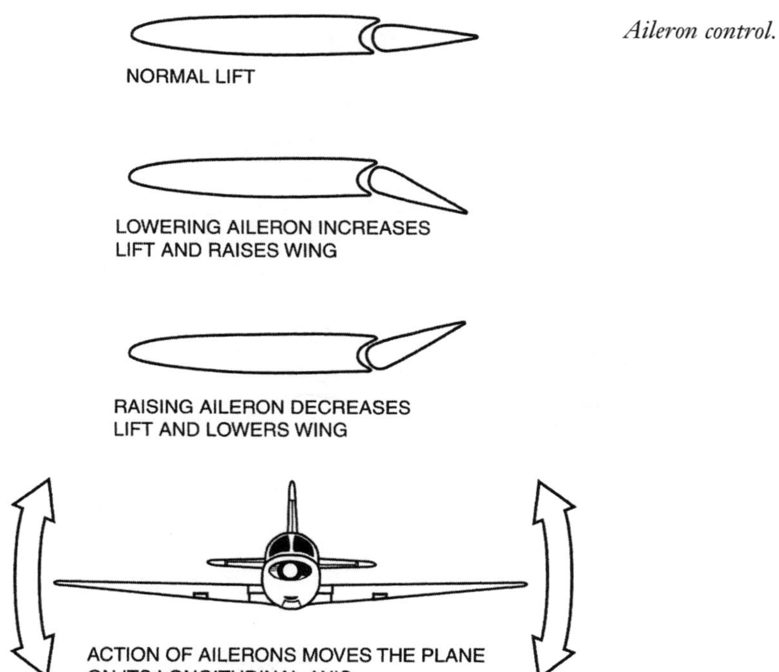

Aileron control.

Why would you want to change the wing lift? To bank (tilt the wings left or right) and turn the airplane. Changing the wing's shape increases or reduces lift. The aileron is efficient because it turns up on one wing to reduce lift and turns down on the other wing to increase lift. The result is that the wings bank and the plane turns in the direction of the lower wing.

The ailerons are controlled by the yoke, a flight controller that looks like half of a steering wheel. (Many planes have a joystick instead of a yoke, but they do the same thing.) Moving the yoke or stick to the left dips the left wing into a bank, and rolling the yoke or stick to the right dips the right wing into a bank. It's a very important flight control, and I'll tell you more as we go along.

You might see a second wing controller on the trailing edge of the wings, inboard or closer to the cockpit. These are called the flaps. They only go down. Their function is to simultaneously increase the lift and increase the drag of the wing. Why? It lets the airplane fly slower—a very important function when attempting to land an airplane. Flaps are controlled by the pilot and can be set to various angles. Some aircraft combine the ailerons with flaps in what are called flaperons.

Elevators

The plane's tail is actually two major control surfaces. The horizontal control surface includes the elevators, and the vertical surface is the rudder.

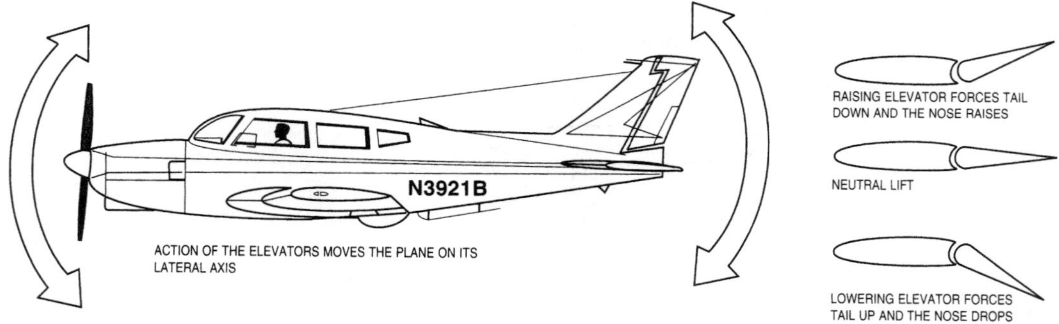

Elevator control.

As mentioned earlier in this chapter, the way to move the plane's nose up or down is to move the tail, specifically the elevators. There is an elevator surface on the trailing edge of each of the two sides of the tail. Unlike the ailerons, both move either up or down *together*. The cockpit controller that makes this happen is part of the yoke or stick. Moving the yoke or stick forward moves the elevators and the plane's nose down. Pulling back on the yoke or stick moves the elevators and the plane's nose up. Yes, some aircraft use a stick instead of a yoke to control the ailerons and elevators.

Rudder

The airplane's rudder is a vertical control surface that's part of the tail section. The trailing edge is movable from the cockpit. Turning the rudder to the left makes the plane's nose yaw to the left, and turning it to the right yaws the nose to the right.

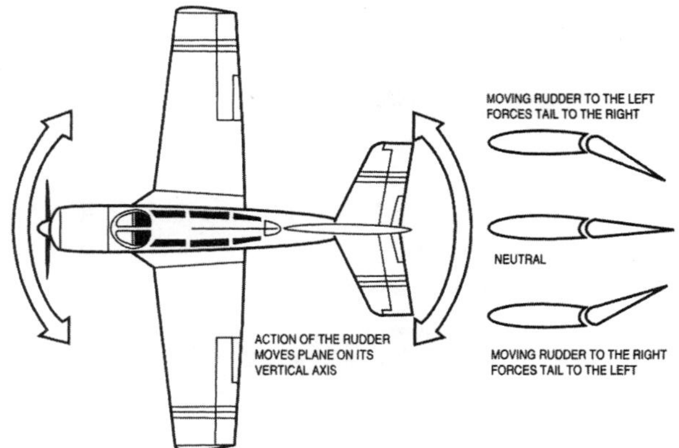

Rudder control.

The rudder is controlled using two floor pedals in the cockpit. Push on the left pedal to turn the nose left and the right pedal to turn the nose right. This action turns only the nose; it does not make the aircraft bank to the left or right. Ailerons control banking. You'll want to use the rudder pedals to move the plane's nose to compensate for any crosswinds while flying a straight line or landing.

Airplanes have a tendency to turn left, called the p-factor, due to the propeller's pitch or surface angle (asymmetrical propeller loading). This tendency or torque is greater at low speed, high power, and/or high angle of attack. Many planes include design features to minimize p-factor. As the pilot, you also can use the rudder to control yaw.

> CAUTION
>
> **Stall Warning!**
>
> Remember that the brakes (useful only when you're on the ground) are commonly attached to or located adjacent to the rudder pedals. Pushing them accidentally won't do anything while you're in the air, but press the brakes instead of the rudder on landing and you could have an accident report to fill out.

Coordinating Controls

That's how the aircraft is controlled. It might help your understanding to think of an airplane with three axes (pronounced AK-sees) or pivot points around which it can rotate. One of the axes goes through the wings, called the lateral axis of pitch; the tail goes up and the nose goes down (or vice versa) around this axis. The longitudinal axis of roll allows one wing to go up and the other down (or vice versa). Finally, the vertical axis of yaw is the pivot point around which the tail goes one way and the nose goes the opposite way. To relate these axes to the discussion, think of them in this way:

- Pitch is controlled by the elevator through the in-out movement of the yoke or stick.
- Roll is controlled by the ailerons through the left-right movement of the yoke or stick.
- Yaw is controlled by the rudder through the left and right rudder pedals.

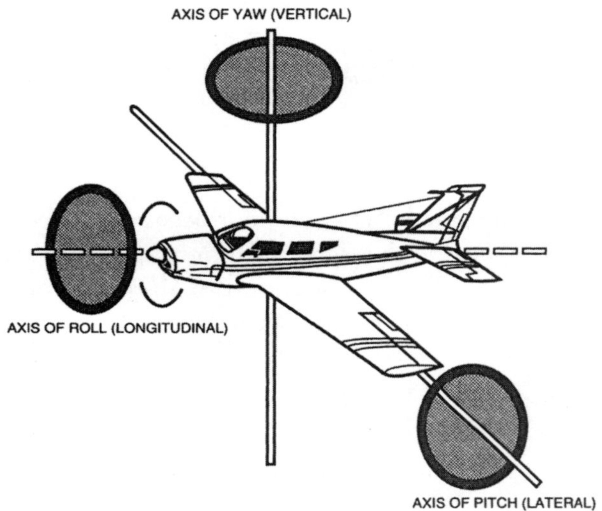

Axes of rotation: pitch, roll, and yaw.

In the real world of flying you will be coordinating two or more flight controls to make the plane do what you want it to do. For example, if you want to make the plane climb, you will add power (throttle) *and* pitch or move the nose up (pull back on the yoke to move the elevators). The real trick to flying is making *coordinated* changes on flight controls. Too much power or too little pitch will make the plane do things other than what you want it to do. Your job as a student pilot is to learn how to coordinate flight controls to get the results you want.

Many aircraft require coordinated use of ailerons and rudder to make smooth turns. For some models the rule is this: Anytime you move the ailerons, you should be moving the rudder on the same side (right aileron and right rudder, for example). The exception is during a crosswind takeoff or landing when the opposite rudder (right aileron and left rudder) would be used.

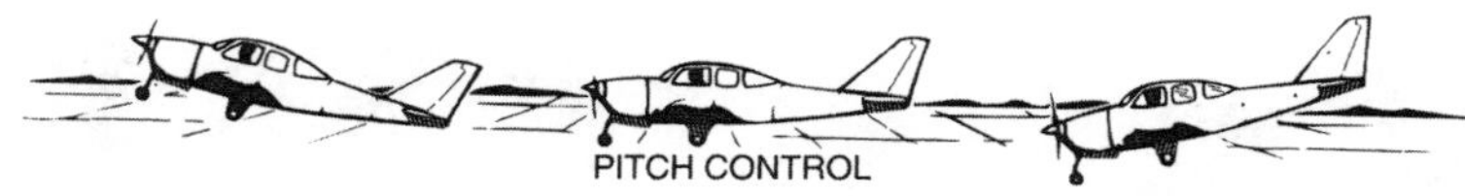

Pitch and bank control.

Knowing what you now know about the control surfaces of an aircraft, you can see that a change in the wind over the wings and tail changes how the controls will respond. If you're flying fast and pull back on the yoke or stick, for example, the plane will quickly respond to small motion of the yoke or stick. However, if you are flying slow, such as when you are landing, it will take more movement of the yoke or stick to get the same result. That's because there's less wind over the control surfaces. It makes sense.

Aircraft have something that cars don't: trim control. If you're flying straight and level, you can adjust the elevator trim control so that less forward or back pressure is required on the yoke or stick to hold the aircraft in level flight. Elevator trim is a separate control from the yoke and rudder pedals. Trim control stabilizes the aircraft and makes flying much easier. Aircraft trim control balances the various forces on the aircraft.

Reading Flight Instruments

That's how aircraft performance is monitored in flight. But how do you know how fast your plane is going, at what altitude, whether you are climbing or descending, and which direction your plane is headed? How can you ensure you are in control of a safe aircraft? You, the pilot, need feedback!

Sport pilot-eligible airplanes must be lightweight, and this results in aircraft that are simple in design and equipment. This simplicity carries forward into the flight instruments. Some instruments are used to help you fly and guide the airplane, while others are used to help you operate the airplane systems (engine, electrical, etc.). Let's just talk about the flight instruments for now. All airplanes must have at least three basic flight instruments: the airspeed indicator, altimeter, and the magnetic compass.

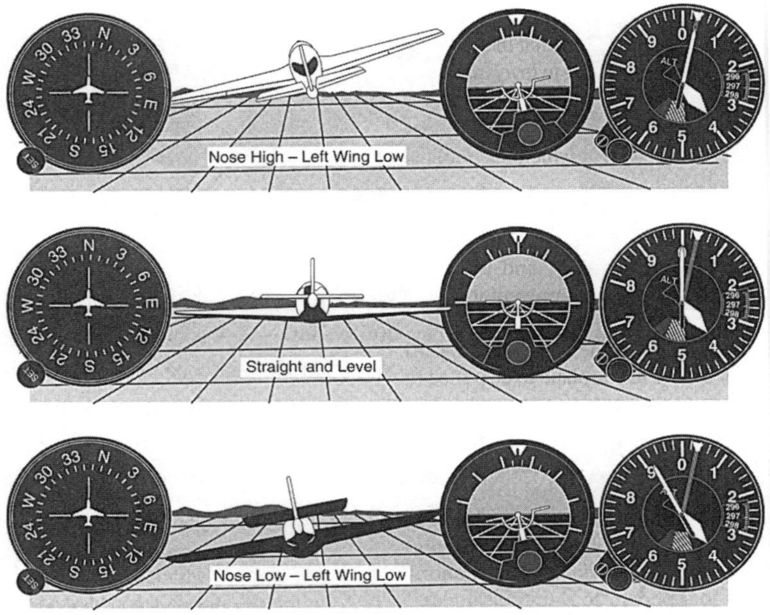

You control your sport plane using both visual references and instruments.

Airspeed Indicator: How Fast Am I Going?

The airspeed indicator is your plane's speedometer. It indicates what your speed is through the air in knots (nautical miles per hour). How does it do this?

Airspeed indicator.

The airspeed indicator compares the speed of air at the edge of the wing—actually at the pitot (pronounced PEE-toh) tube—against the static airspeed in a more protected location such as on the side of the aircraft. From these it calibrates the plane's speed through the air. Because air is thinner the higher you fly, there are some adjustments to be made to get a true airspeed. You learn more about these adjustments in Chapter 4. You'll also learn how to figure groundspeed by adding or subtracting the wind speed, depending on which direction it's coming from.

Knowledge Test

Airspeeds are sometimes referred to with the letter V for velocity, so they are called V-speeds. The most common are V_{SO} (stall speed with flaps down), V_{s1} (stall speed with flaps up), V_X (best angle of climb), V_Y (best rate of climb), V_{NO} (maximum cruise speed), and V_{NE} (never exceed).

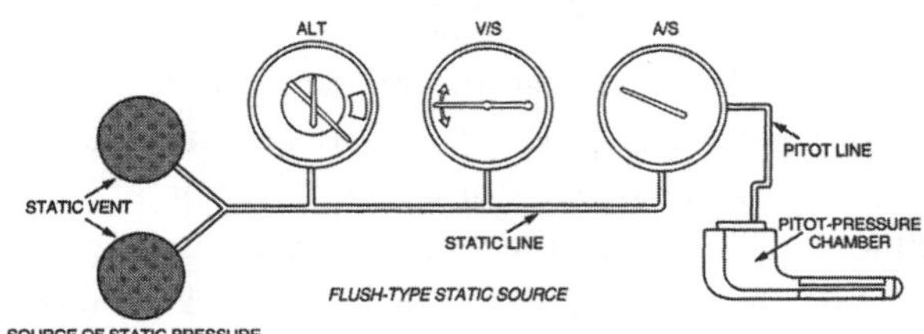

The pitot-static system measures the difference between air pressure at the front of the wing and at the side of the fuselage to determine airspeed.

Altimeter: What Is My Altitude?

It would be inconvenient—not to mention dangerous—to run a long, weighted string out the aircraft window to see how far you are above the ground. Fortunately, your plane has an instrument that measures the air pressure against a standard and tells you the difference in feet of altitude. It's called the altimeter.

Altimeter.

An altimeter is a barometer that measures atmospheric pressure. A barometer not only changes when a high- or low-pressure front moves through an area or when the temperature changes, it also changes when the barometer is moved higher into the atmosphere. At sea level under (rare) standard weather conditions, an altimeter will read 0 feet and the small window on it will indicate a barometric pressure of 29.92. If you then fly to a nearby airport that's at an altitude of 600 feet the altimeter will read 600 feet at 29.92.

Knowledge Test

The standard altimeter setting is 29.92 inches of mercury (Hg).

In fact, before you take off from an airport, you'll calibrate the altimeter by turning the adjustment knob until the airport elevation (posted somewhere near the main taxiway or found on aeronautical charts) is shown on the altimeter dial. The number in the small window—29.92, 30.40, or whatever—is the "altimeter setting" for that location at that time. It's your point of reference for your flight.

An important point is that the altimeter reading indicates the feet above mean sea level, abbreviated MSL. It is *not* the distance above the ground—because the ground level changes as the terrain below changes. For example, if you're supposed to fly over a location at 1,000 feet above ground level (AGL) and the map says ground level is 500 feet above MSL, your altimeter should read 1,500 MSL. We cover altimeters in more detail in Chapter 4.

Magnetic Compass: Which Way Am I Going?

The magnetic compass is about as simple as an instrument gets. A magnetized metal bar is balanced on a pivot point and points to north. Attached to the magnetic bar is a scale that allows you to read the heading of the airplane. A common aviation version of this places the scale in a container filled with fluid to help dampen out vibration and unwanted gyrations. It sounds simple, but it's what Charles Lindbergh used in 1927 to fly from New York to Paris.

Remember the question this chapter started with: What makes an airplane fly? The answer is … money. This brings up other optional instruments that might or might not be installed in a sport plane. These are the attitude indicator, turn coordinator, heading indicator, and vertical-speed indicator. Money is not the only issue when it comes to having your sport plane equipped with more instrumentation. It is important to remember that sport pilot-eligible planes must be lightweight. These instruments and accessories add weight.

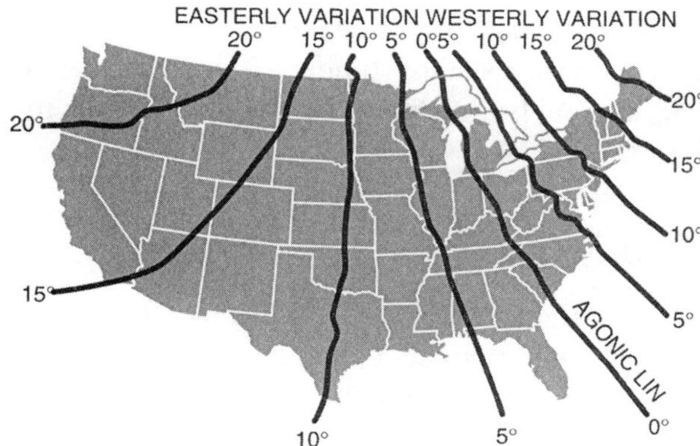

An isographic chart shows the magnetic variations in various parts of the United States.

Attitude Indicator: Am I Pointed Up or Down?

Sport pilots fly under what are called visual flight rules or VFR. That means you're supposed to be able to see the ground at all times as a visual point of reference. But what are you supposed to do if a cloud sneaks up on you and your visibility is cut? You can't see the ground or the horizon. You are flying blind.

First, you're *not* supposed to be flying anywhere near conditions where this could happen. Even so, it would be a good thing to know that you have an attitude-indicator instrument in your cockpit. It tells you whether you're climbing or descending or banking and by how much, in degrees. Good information!

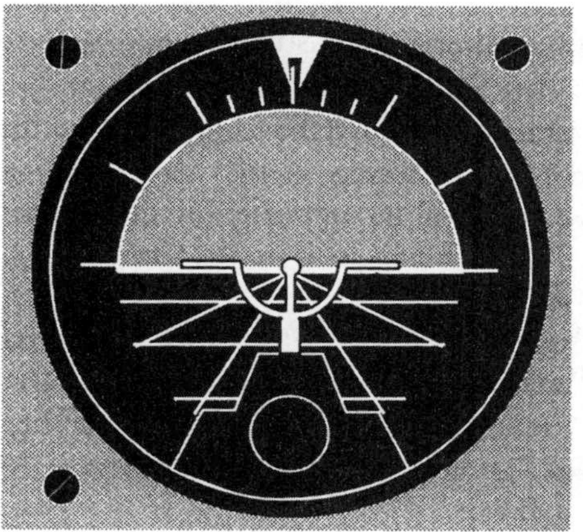

Attitude indicator.

Actually, the attitude indicator is very useful in flight because it indicates how much of a pitch up, pitch down, or bank angle you are making as you move about the friendly skies. You don't have to wait until a cloud envelops you before you use it. For example, you'll refer to it to climb or descend at a specific pitch angle—not too much and not too little. You'll also use it to make a shallow (under 20-degree), medium (20- to 45-degree), or steep (over 45-degree) bank or turn. Reading an attitude indicator takes some getting used to, but it's a valuable tool for pilots.

Turn Coordinator: Is My Turn Smooth?

For your comfort and safety—and that of your passenger—you must coordinate flight controls (as discussed earlier in this chapter) to make sure you not only bank (roll) the wings, but also move (yaw) the rudder for the most efficient turn. The turn coordinator helps you do this.

Turn coordinator.

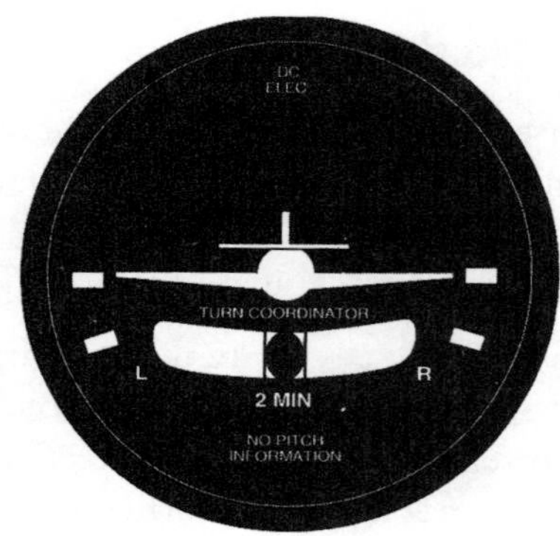

The turn coordinator is actually two instruments. The turn indicator component is another gyroscopic instrument. It helps you visualize that the plane is turning by showing you an airplane tipping its wings. Another part of the turn coordinator is the yaw indicator. It looks like a small carpenter's level you would find in a hardware store. Your job is to keep the black ball in the center of the indicator.

Together, the turn coordinator—also called the turn-and-bank indicator—helps you make smooth turns at a rate of 3 degrees per second. That means it will take 60 seconds or 1 minute to make a coordinated turn of 180 degrees.

Heading Indicator: Which Way Am I Headed?

All aircraft have a magnetic compass that tells you which way you're going relative to magnetic north. However, if you've ever used a compass, you know that it has many inherent problems. It has lots of drift and slop, swinging back and forth before it settles down—especially in a vehicle that's turning, climbing, and descending. It also is affected by nearby magnetic fields, such as the electronic gear in your plane. Airplane compasses have deviation charts on them to help you adjust for these problems, but the best solution is a heading indicator, a gyroscopic instrument that is more stable and easier to read than a compass.

Heading indicator.

With an image of a small aircraft in the center, a heading indicator is easier to interpret, showing you which way you are headed and the plane's relationship to other points on the compass. Many heading indicators have rotating markers that can be moved around the perimeter to help you remember which direction you're supposed to be going, called your heading.

Because a heading indicator is not a compass but a gyroscope, it needs to be manually adjusted (typically about every 15 minutes) to reflect the compass reading. Of course, you should make this adjustment only in straight-and-level flight when the compass is stabilized and not wobbling around.

Vertical Speed Indicator: At What Rate Am I Going Up or Down?

It's also handy to know at what rate your aircraft is climbing or descending. That's where a vertical speed indicator comes in handy. When it points to 0, your plane is flying level. If the needle goes up to 5 you are climbing at a rate of 500 feet per minute (fpm). The rate of climb or descent is good to know so you can calculate how long it will take to reach a specific altitude. For example, if you're flying at 3,500 feet MSL and you want to climb to 5,500 MSL, you can control the aircraft to climb at a vertical speed of 500 fpm for four minutes.

Vertical speed indicator.

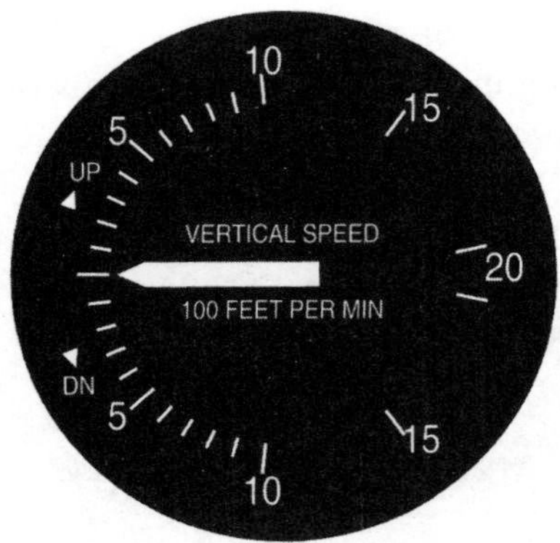

The vertical speed indicator uses changes in air pressure to take a reading. Unfortunately, there is a lag of a few seconds between changing vertical speed and seeing it on the VSI. However, with experience you will soon learn how your sport plane responds and will adjust your controls accordingly.

The Least You Need to Know

- An airplane has many of the same functions and components as a car or boat.
- The four forces of flight are thrust, drag, lift, and weight (gravity).
- Flight controls are engineered to help you control your aircraft with the least effort possible.
- Flight instruments give you feedback on your efforts to control your aircraft.

Chapter 3

Rules of the Air

In This Chapter

- The rules that keep pilots flying safely
- Knowing where you're going—and where you shouldn't be
- Figuring out where you are in the friendly skies
- What's included on aeronautical charts

Someday, the roads of America will be smoother. Buses and trucks will be tracked by radar and satellite. Fast cars will have their own highway. Sightseers will be able to wander wherever they want as long as they don't get in the way of commercial and fast traffic.

Aviation already is enjoying this structure. Commercial and freight jets as well as faster private aircraft follow instrument flight rules (IFR) to keep them from bumping into each other. Sport, recreational, and private pilots stay out of the way and use visual flight rules (VFR). In fact, VFR pilots aren't allowed to get near some IFR aircraft until they have proper training.

Of course, that's a simplification of what actually happens in the skies, but it illustrates that there are clear "rules of the air" to keep everyone safe. This chapter introduces you to those rules. You need to know them for your sport-pilot knowledge test. More important, you want to know them so you can fly relaxed.

How FAR Can You Go?

Who set all these rules? Because flying often occurs across state lines, it's a federal agency that determines and publishes the rules. It's the Federal Aviation Administration (FAA) that regulates who can fly, what they can fly, how they can fly, and what they must do to keep themselves and others safe.

It's the FAA that recently changed the rules of flying to allow the new sport-pilot and light-sport aircraft (SP/LSA) categories. They did so to encourage more people to learn how to fly safely. The skies are not crowded with aircraft, nor will they be in the foreseeable future. Let's take a look at how the FAA regulates the skies.

Federal Aviation Regulations

The FAA publishes and updates a document called the *Federal Aviation Regulations* (FARs). Published together with the *Aeronautical Information Manual* (described later in this chapter), it is referred to as FAR/AIM. You can purchase a copy directly from the FAA or Government Printing Office (GPO) or you can buy a copy from an authorized republisher such as Aviation Supplies & Academics (www.asa2fly.com). Many aviation suppliers, such as Sporty's Pilot Shop (www.sportys.com), sell this and many other FAA and flying publications.

Learning Your Part

The FARs include a number of parts (think of them as chapters), each dealing with one aspect of flying regulations. You'll often hear pilots refer to these parts and assume you know what they're referring to. For example, a "Part 103" aircraft is an ultralight because it is built and flown based on regulations in FAR Part 103. FAR Part 61 contains the rules for obtaining a sport-pilot certificate. You'll catch on to these references very soon. The FARs start at Part 1 and go to Part 198, but don't panic; sport pilots fall under only a few parts of the FARs.

Actually, the FARs are part of the U.S. Department of Transportation's tome: Title 14 of the Code of Federal Regulations. To be technically accurate, you will see what we call FAR 61 written in official parlance as "CFR14 Part 61." I am just going to use the terms pilots use and call all our regulations FARs.

One other valuable FAA document (there are many) is the *Aeronautical Information Manual* (AIM). AIMs are a more detailed discussion of things important to pilots. The AIMs cover air navigation aids, radar services, airport markings and lighting, airspace categories, air traffic control, and procedures, as well as flight safety and medical issues. Authorized republishers of FAA material often combine FAR and AIM into a single, thick (900+ pages) document that covers much of what you need to know about the rules of flying. Think of it as your flying bible.

One of the parts of the FARs that you will refer to most is Part 61. It covers airmen (meaning men and women), including the certification of pilots, flight instructors, and ground instructors. As a sport pilot you don't need to know everything that's in Part 61 because it also covers commercial pilots and instrument ratings, but you will be expected to know the requirements and limitations for the new sport-pilot certificate. To make things easier, the regulations covering sport pilots are reprinted in Appendix A.

You'll also refer to Part 91, covering air traffic and general operating rules. This part tells you who flies where, when, and how. That's important information! I'll include the components of Part 91 that regulate sport pilots in Appendix A.

Of course, there are many other parts to the FARs. They regulate how new rules are made (Part 11), aircraft airworthiness standards (Part 23 and others), airspace rules (Part 71), commercial aviation (Parts 119–139), flight schools and training centers (Parts 141 and 142), airport operation (Parts 150–169), and many more. For your sport-pilot knowledge test you should be knowledgeable about those regulations that directly affect sport flying, but you should also be aware of what rules other pilots fly under.

Wing Tips

Aviation uses a standard clock, called coordinated universal time (UTC), rather than regional time zones. The clock is in Greenwich, England, outside of London, and aviation clocks all around the world use it as a reference point. For example, the eastern standard time zone in the United States is UTC + 5 hours; 5 P.M. in New York City is 12:00 UTC. UTC is also known as "Zulu time." Really!

Following the Rules of Airspace

Once you've studied the rules of airspace for a while, it will all start to make sense. However, your first look at how airspace is designated might seem odd. Who designed this plan anyway?

Actually, the rules of airspace over the United States are those accepted around the world. The International Civil Aviation Organization (ICAO) set the rules for the world, and most countries have adopted them, including the United States. Your sport-pilot certificate doesn't authorize you to fly outside of the United States, but once you have a private-pilot certificate or higher, you can do so and the rules will be the same in every country. So let's take a look at how the sky is mapped.

Flying VFR

Earlier in this chapter I mentioned IFR and VFR rules. Sport pilots always fly by visual flight rules. No exceptions. However, you must share the skies with IFR pilots, so you should know what they're doing.

IFR flights are made by pilots who have earned an instrument rating on top of their private pilot or higher certificate. VFR pilots can't fly under IFR rules, but IFR pilots can fly VFR rules if they wish.

IFR could be called "assisted flying." The pilot gets information and directives from air traffic controllers who, using radar and other electronics, can "see" the aircraft—and hundreds of others—on their radar screens. An air traffic controller advises the pilot what to do to "maintain separation," or keep a safe distance away from other aircraft in the area. In addition, the IFR pilot is trained how to fly the aircraft using instruments inside the aircraft rather than visual references to the ground. Otherwise, how would commercial and business aircraft fly through clouds and land at airports during a rain or snow storm?

> CAUTION
>
> **Stall Warning!**
>
> Sometimes you'll see references to MVFR, or *marginal* visual flight rules. These cover visibility that is close to the minimums for VFR flying. Things could get better—or worse. Remember that your personal limits should be more stringent than the FAA's, and you shouldn't fly unless you are comfortable with the level of visibility where you are, where you are going, and the path you're taking.

Sport pilots cannot fly IFR! That doesn't mean, however, that they cannot learn about and take advantage of air traffic control or about using instruments. In fact, sport pilots are encouraged to keep learning. Many of you will become private pilots or even commercial pilots with instrument ratings. In coming chapters I tell you more about getting tracking from air traffic control (ATC), called a flight watch. Your flight instructor will give you some instruction on using instruments for flight in emergencies.

Keeping Your Distance

VFR for sport and private pilots means being able to see the ground and keeping away from other objects, including clouds. In a nutshell, here are the VFR weather minimums for sport pilots:

- Visibility of at least 3 statute miles
- Stay at least 500 feet below, 1,000 feet above, or 2,000 feet to the side of any cloud

Remember, these are FAR *minimums* for sport pilots. Your personal minimum, because you are a new and inexperienced pilot, should be greater. You could decide that if you don't have a ceiling (bottom of the clouds) of at least 3,000 feet and visibility of at least 10 miles, you're not going anywhere. Besides running out of fuel, the most common cause of pilot accidents is flying in conditions beyond their abilities.

Basic VFR Weather Minimums

Airspace	Flight Visibility	Distance from Clouds
Class A	Not applicable	Not applicable
Class B	3 statute miles	Clear of clouds
Class C	3 statute miles	500 feet below 1,000 feet above 2,000 feet horizontal
Class D	3 statute miles	500 feet below 1,000 feet above 2,000 feet horizontal
Class E		
Less than 10,000 feet MSL	3 statute miles	500 feet below 1,000 feet above 2,000 feet horizontal
At or above 10,000 feet MSL	5 statute miles	1,000 feet below 1,000 feet above 1 statute mile horizontal
Class G		
1,200 feet or less above the surface (regardless of MSL altitude)		
Day, except as provided in section 91.155(b)	1 statute mile	Clear of clouds
Night, except as provided in section 91.155(b)	3 statute miles	500 feet below 1,000 feet above 2,000 feet horizontal
More than 1,200 feet above the surface but less than 10,000 feet MSL		

continues

Basic VFR Weather Minimums (continued)

Airspace	Flight Visibility	Distance from Clouds
Day	1 statute mile	500 feet below 1,000 feet above 2,000 feet horizontal
Night	3 statute miles	500 feet below 1,000 feet above 2,000 feet horizontal
More than 1,200 feet above the surface and at or above 10,000 feet MSL	5 statute miles	1,000 feet below 1,000 feet above 1 statute mile horizontal

Layers of Airspace

So let's cover how the sky is divvied up. There are five categories of controlled airspace, plus one that's uncontrolled. The amount of control, as you can imagine, depends on how busy the airspace typically is. For example, dozens of aircraft are trying to land at any given moment at Los Angeles International or other large airports. That's very busy, and everyone must be in contact with air traffic control to make it work smoothly and safely.

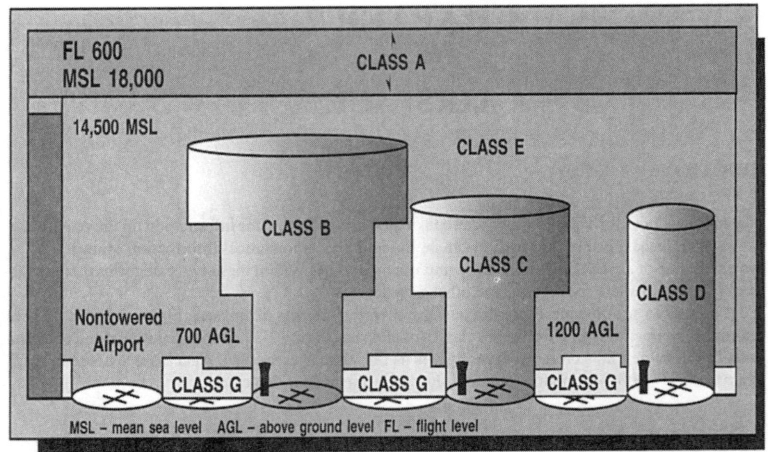

Categories of airspace over the United States.

The categories of airspace over the United States are:

- Class A
- Class B
- Class C
- Class D
- Class E
- Class G

Sport pilots can fly in Classes E and G airspace, only, until they get training and an endorsement to add Classes B, C, and D. As you will soon learn, sport pilots cannot fly in Class A airspace. Class F isn't used in the United States.

Class A Airspace

Class A airspace starts at 18,000 feet MSL and goes up to 60,000 feet MSL. Because sport pilots are limited to flights below 10,000 feet, you don't have to think much about this airspace—you'll never get there.

Who flies here? Commercial and business jets with pressurized cabins or a supplemental oxygen source. The air is thinner. If you've flown cross-country in a commercial jet, you've traveled in Class A airspace.

Class B Airspace

The "B" in Class B can be remembered as "big airports." These include the major airports at major cities: New York, Chicago, Atlanta, Denver, Salt Lake City, San Francisco, etc. You're not even going to want to fly in to these airports for a while, so it's a good thing that the sport-pilot certificate doesn't allow it until you've received additional training and an endorsement.

When we begin reading charts later in the chapter, you'll see that you can actually fly under, over, and near airspace around these big airports. Around many Class B airports are smaller airports that you might be able to land at *if* you obey the rules.

Class B airspace, if seen from the side, looks like an upside-down multilayer cake. The controlled airspace expands as it goes up so that IFR aircraft can descend at an angle toward the airport. You can refer to the *Aeronautical Information Manual* and sectional charts for more specifics on Class B airspace.

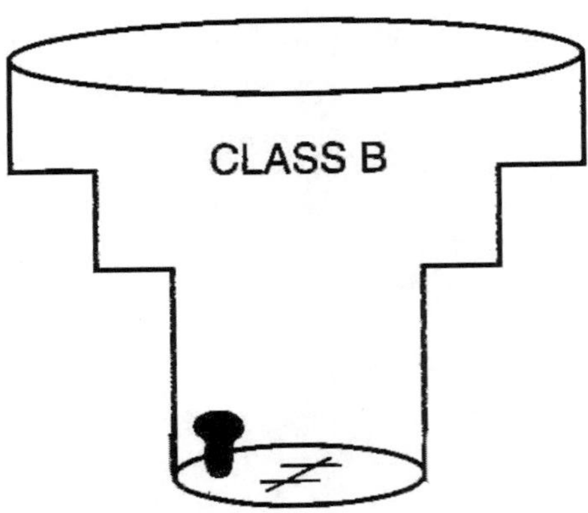

Outline of Class B airspace.

Class C Airspace

Class C airspace is "crowded," meaning there are many aircraft trying to take off or land and requiring assistance, but not as much as at Class B airports. Class C airports include Sacramento, California; Boise, Idaho; Portland, Oregon; and others.

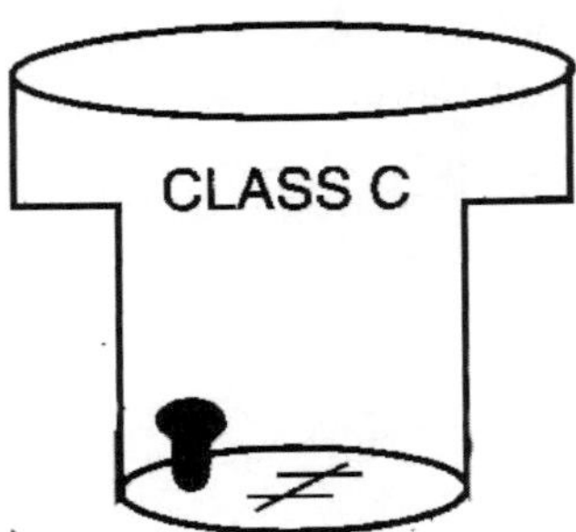

Outline of Class C airspace.

Class C airspace looks like an upside-down *two*-layered cake. Most Class C airports have a 5-mile radius around the airport that goes from ground level to 4,000 feet AGL, then a larger 10-mile radius above it going from 1,200 to 4,000 feet AGL. If there is another airport nearby, the two airspaces can take nibbles out of each other so they both look like partially eaten cakes. You'll learn how to determine the size and shape of controlled airspace as you learn to read sectional maps later in this chapter.

Class D Airspace

Class D airspace typically extends from the ground to 2,500 feet AGL above other airports with a control tower. Even if you have an endorsement for entering this airspace, you're not supposed to do so unless you get permission by calling on your communication radio. You start a dialog with the controllers.

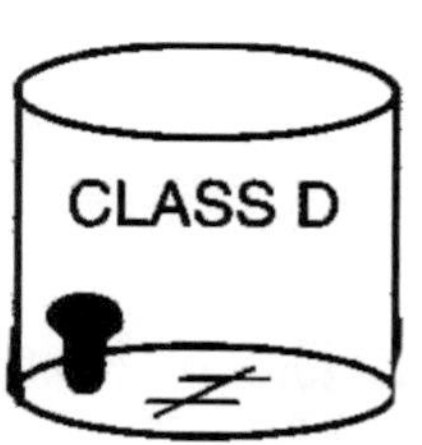

Outline of Class D airspace.

As you can imagine, there are many more Class D airports than there are B or C airports. In fact, you'll find many of them underneath Class B or C airspace. It can get confusing. Fortunately, the communication frequencies for these airports are widely published and you must know them as you plan your flight—once you get your controlled airspace endorsement.

Class E Airspace

If it's a controlled airspace, but it isn't Class A, B, C, or D around airports, it's considered Class E. Class E airspace is often referred to as the controlled airspace between airports although sometimes it surrounds an airport and starts at the surface. It can also start at 700 feet AGL, 1,200 feet AGL, or 14,500 feet MSL. Class E airspace tops out at 18,000 feet MSL. For all you trivia nuts, Class E starts again at 60,000 feet MSL (Flight Level or FL 600) and goes to the end of the atmosphere. Of course, sport pilots are limited to an altitude of 10,000 feet MSL!

Class G Airspace

As a sport pilot you might be doing much of your flying in Class G (uncontrolled) airspace—or some Class E (controlled) airspace. The good news is that most low-altitude airspace is Classes E and G. In Classes E and G airspace no radio is required, so you're on your own. That simply means if you have a radio, you will monitor common communication channels for traffic and announce your intentions if you are flying into an uncontrolled airport. (Although a radio is not *required*, it's still a good idea to have one.)

> CAUTION
>
> **Stall Warning!**
>
> Even though Class G airspace carries the moniker (uncontrolled), remember that VFR minimums apply. If you can't see, you can't fly.

Other Airspace

There are other airspace designations that you should be aware of. Refer to the FARs for specifics, but here is an overview:

- **Prohibited areas:** ones in which you cannot fly
- **Restricted areas:** ones in which you cannot fly without permission or following published rules
- **Warning areas:** include strong cautions when flying over large bodies of water
- **Military operation areas (MOAs)**: might limit your movement in them or simply tell you what to watch for and where.
- **Alert areas:** tell you of special traffic notices such as an abundance of student pilots
- **Controlled firing areas:** *Don't go there!*
- **National security areas:** protect the national and state capital buildings as well as where the president or vice president might be working or vacationing

Reading Charts

So how do you know what airspace class or area you're going to be flying in? Read the chart! The FAA publishes detailed charts of the airspace over the United States. The most popular is the sectional aeronautical chart. There are 37 of them, each named for a primary city on the map: San Francisco, Albuquerque, Charlotte, Chicago, Miami, Billings, and so forth.

Another popular chart is the world aeronautical chart (WAC) that covers about twice as much area as a sectional, but with less detail. Most sport and private pilots prefer the sectional charts. Sectionals are official for six months, then are replaced by a new sectional with changes. You cannot rely on an out-of-date sectional chart to guide you in flying.

Reading sectional and WAC charts is relatively easy because they have legends that tell you what all the symbols mean. There's a lot of information on a chart, so you first need to spend some time trying to figure out the legend. Read on for some tips.

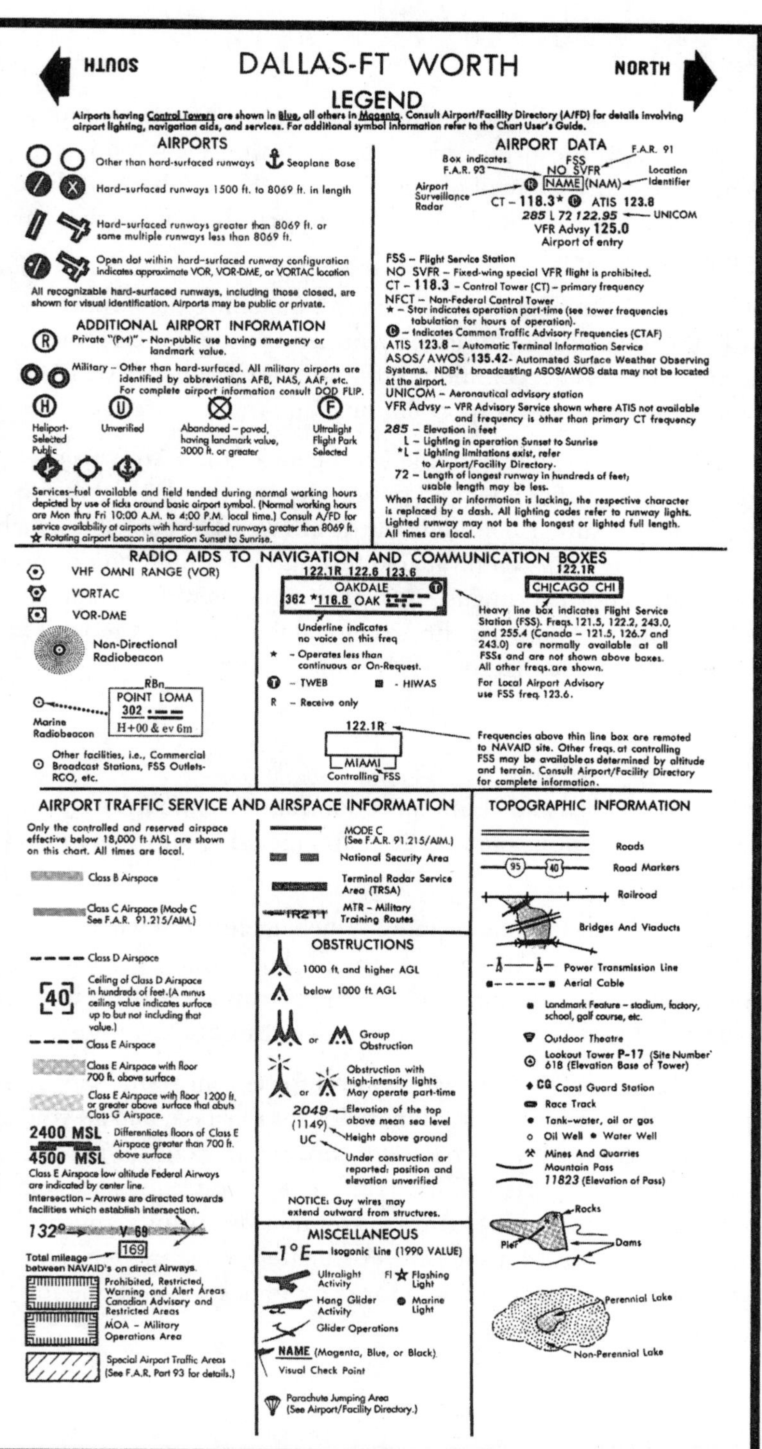

Sectional aeronautical chart legend.

Airport Data

Sectional and other charts, obviously, tell you where airports are. They do so with a small symbol in blue or magenta. If the airport has a control tower, the symbol is in blue; if not, it's in magenta. Most airport symbols also indicate the number and direction of runways. If aviation fuel (avgas) is available at the airport, the symbol will have four ticks or bumps around the symbol perimeter.

Near the airport symbol will be additional data you'll need, including the airport name (for example, "Little River") and FAA location identifier or code (for example, O48). You'll also see the airport's altitude, common traffic advisory frequency (CTAF), and other information about radar services, airport lighting, and traffic patterns.

The sectional chart should be supplemented with the latest copy of the FAA *Airport/Facility Directory* that gives more specifics about all public airports (available through www.faa.gov). Alternately, you can subscribe to one of the aftermarket publishers such as *Flight Guide Airport and Frequency Manual* (available through www.flightguide.com) that includes up-to-date airport information and some area maps, as well as data on nearby hotels, food, and recreation. There are three regional volumes for the United States, and the binders are easier to use than the FAA publication.

Navigation

Chapter 4 goes deeper into navigation and communication radios, sometimes called nav-com. For now, be aware that sectional and other charts include radio aids to navigation and communication.

Aircraft navigation can require following one or more radio signals from where you are to where you want to be, though not always in a straight line. Your chart will tell you what those navigation radio station frequencies are so you can enter them in your plane's nav radio. The chart will also show you the location of those transmitters.

Aircraft communication means talking by radio with control towers, air traffic services, and other pilots. Your plane will have communication radios for this task, and all you'll need is the frequencies. Your charts and *Airport/Facility Directory* (AFD) will tell you what those frequencies are. Larger airports will have different radio frequencies for automatic terminal information service (ATIS), tower, ground (for taxiing), approach clearance (APC), and other communication stations. Fortunately, most modern aircraft have at least one radio with two channels: one for communication and one for standby to make switching to the second channel easier.

You'll be flying in Classes E and G airspace for a while so you might not need all this information, but it is there on your chart and the AFD. Many airports without control towers use a common frequency, published on the chart, for any pilots in the area to communicate their intention with other pilots: "Ukiah traffic, experimental 6-8-1-7-Juliette, on final approach for runway 1-5 Ukiah."

Wing Tips

Experienced instructors suggest that you spend as much time planning and reviewing your initial flights as you do flying them. You have many things to learn, and most of them are much easier to learn on the ground than in the air.

Air Traffic Service

Any airspace that is controlled or reserved is marked on the charts to tell you what and where. Fortunately, the chart legend will help you figure it out. Here are some tips:

- Wide blue lines encircle Class B airspace; remember, there are *multi* layers or circles, solid and shaded.
- Wide magenta lines encircle Class C airspace; there are *two* layers or circles, solid and shaded.
- A dashed blue line encircles Class D airspace.
- A dashed magenta line encircles Class E airspace at an airport, starting at the surface and continuing up to 18,000 feet MSL.
- Prohibited, restricted, or other areas are indicated on aeronautical charts with their own symbols.
- Airways (think of them as highways) are shown on charts. VFR pilots, including sport pilots, may use them but are not required to do so. All airways below 18,000 feet are called "victor" airways and they are assigned numbers for identification.

Topography

In addition, aeronautical charts include topographical information such as the terrain and mountain heights. It's always good to know how tall a mountain in your path is!

Knowledge Test

When reading chart coordinates, remember that latitude is listed first, then longitude. Forget which is which? Remember that *long*itude is the *long* line on the chart. The other is latitude.

Longitude and latitude on a world map.

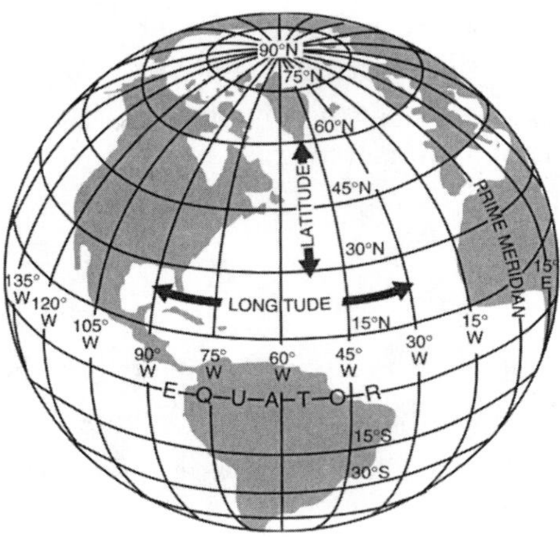

It's also important to know where landmarks are: roads, railroad tracks, lakes, rivers, radio towers, and other large objects. You'll be flying by what you see—under visual flight rules (or VFR)—so a chart is vital to figuring out where you are. I talk more about this aspect of flying in the next chapter.

Of course, it will take you many hours before you can easily read aeronautical charts. So get a chart for your area, available for under $10 including shipping from the FAA or at larger airports, and start practicing. You'll soon see how useful they are for helping you enjoy flying.

The Least You Need to Know

- Federal Aviation Regulations (FARs) cover what you can and cannot do as a pilot.
- Sport pilots fly under visual flight rules (VFR) rather than instrument flight rules (IFR).
- Airspace is segmented to make flying safer and more efficient.
- Aeronautical charts tell you what you need to know about airspace, airports, navigation, and communications.

Chapter 4

Ground School

In This Chapter

- Pilotage: navigating by looking out the window
- Dead reckoning: navigating by calculations
- VOR: navigating by ground-based radio signals
- GPS: navigating by satellite
- Keeping up your end of the flight conversation
- How to read the weather for a safe and fun flight

If you're like many folks, you're eager to get flying. Maybe you've already been up a time or two. Or maybe you're returning to flying via the new sport-pilot regulations. In any case, keep reading!

Before you take off into the wild blue yonder, you need to know some additional things about sport flying. You need to study the basics before you can hope to apply them in the air. That's where ground school comes in—it's where you study the ABCs of flying. If you're already taking flight instruction, this chapter helps clarify what you're learning. If you've not yet selected a flight school or instructor, it introduces you to what you're going to learn. If you're still undecided whether you want to fly, this chapter gives you more ammunition for talking yourself into it.

Navigating by Sight

You probably want to fly for two reasons:

- You want to see things from above.
- You want to go somewhere.

Pilotage offers you both. It means simply navigating by looking out the window and figuring out where you are by reading your aeronautical chart. It's much like driving in a new town; you look for landmarks and road signs, comparing them with your map. "Okay, turn left at the courthouse, follow the road west for four blocks, and turn right at the city park."

Flying Words

Pilotage is navigation from point to point by comparing accurate aeronautical charts to large landmarks on the ground.

Pilotage is similar. "Follow the main highway north until it jogs west near the big lake, then look for a smaller highway heading east." Your sectional aeronautical map has these and many other landmarks clearly indicated on it.

So the trick to pilotage is learning how to compare what you've read on the sectional chart with what you see out the window. Chapter 3 explains sectional and world aeronautical charts (SACs and WACs). As you use charts you'll learn how to find numerous ground references that can guide you in pilotage. They include …

- Roads (freeways, highways, and local).
- Railroad tracks.
- Power transmission lines.
- Lakes.
- Rivers.
- Bridges.
- Large buildings and complexes.
- Race tracks.
- Water towers.
- Transmission towers and other large obstructions.
- Mountain peaks (with altitude MSL).
- Mountain passes.

That's the great thing about flying under visual flight rules (VFRs): You can actually see where you're going. IFR pilots can, if necessary, go from point A to point B hardly looking out the window. But all *you* really need is a chart.

For many of your sport-pilot flights you won't be going from point A to B. You'll just meander around the skies on a pretty day. Or you'll fly toward point B, but won't mind if you or a passenger wants to reroute to point C or even return to point A. It's more about the flying than the destination. If you get a little disoriented, you simply look for landmarks to find your way. You might even wind up following a major highway home.

No matter how far you take your aviation, learning pilotage navigation will serve you well. Even if someday you're an ATP (airline transport pilot) flying cross-country commercial jets, you'll have days when you will look out the cockpit window for landmarks and think back on the days you started as a sport pilot.

Navigating by Calculator

Wouldn't it be great if you could drive between two points by simply making your own direct highway? You can (with some limitations) in the sky. You can fly between points using a navigation system called *dead reckoning.*

It's an unfortunate term, dead reckoning. The "dead" part probably came from the word "deduced," because dead reckoning means navigating an airplane based on calculations. If you fly in a straight line at 100 knots for 2 hours you have traveled 200 nautical miles. You then turn to a compass heading of, say, 180 degrees (south), and fly another hour. By planning your path in advance (called a flight plan) and sketching it out on your sectional chart, you know which direction you'll fly and for how long to get to your intended destination.

Flying Words

Dead reckoning is navigation using computations based on airspeed, course, heading, wind direction, wind speed, ground speed, and elapsed time.

Of course, flying isn't quite that easy. In your car you know that if your odometer says you've driven 100 miles, you have. The wheels, in contact with the ground, have rolled 100 miles. As you've learned, there are other factors that add or subtract from the total distance traveled in an aircraft. For example, a tailwind (one from behind the aircraft) of 10 knots increases your speed over the ground. If the plane is flying at an airspeed of 100 knots, your ground speed is 110 knots (100 + 10). Likewise, a headwind (one coming toward you from directly in front of the aircraft) subtracts from your airspeed of 100 knots and gives you a ground speed of 90 knots (100 – 10). As the ground speed changes, so does your time and fuel needed to get to your destination.

To make things more confusing, most winds don't come at the plane directly from in front or the rear. There is what is called a crosswind component. The crosswind affects your ground speed and it also affects the direction you must point the plane to get from point A to point B. Part of your training will include learning to use an E6B or other computer to figure the crosswind components on a flight. (The E6B really isn't an electronic computer, but a type of slide ruler, although electronic calculator versions are available.)

Dead reckoning is a navigation system that calculates your flight path based on …

- Course (the path you've marked on the chart).
- Heading (the direction you fly on your compass).
- Track (the actual path you fly over the ground; you hope it matches your planned course).
- Wind direction (how the wind will affect your course).
- Indicated airspeed (what the airspeed indicator reports).

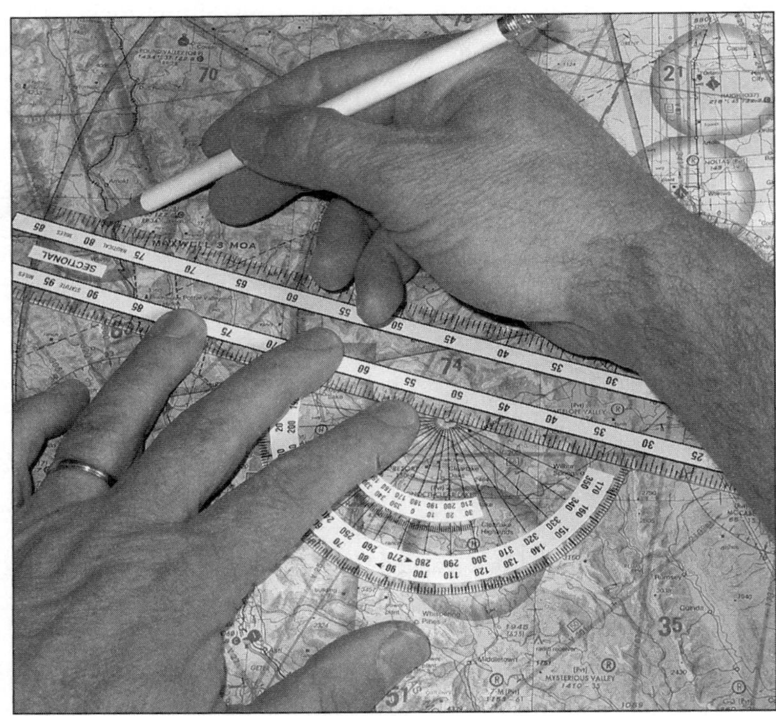

Plotting your course on a sectional chart.

Estimating your heading.

- True airspeed (the indicated airspeed adjusted for altitude and temperature corrections).
- Elapsed time (how long it has been since you started or since you encountered a specific checkpoint).

The challenge of dead-reckoning navigation is that there are so many corrections required to get an accurate answer. To name a few:

- The crosswind component changes your groundspeed and your track.
- The compass heading might be challenging to maintain in a plane that is encountering turbulence.
- Drifting off your heading can result in a change in your track and you will not maintain your planned course.

Fortunately, the E6B computer and its calculator cousins make recalculating heading and true airspeed (TAS) relatively easy—once you understand how to use these tools.

Knowledge Test

You will be asked questions on the FAA sport-pilot knowledge and practical tests about dead-reckoning navigation, so be ready. Buy an E6B computer (under $15) or E6B or flight calculator (under $80) and read the instructions to know how to use it.

Using the E6B flight computer to estimate true airspeed and other flight calculations.

Navigating by Ground-Based Radio

Another popular method of aviation navigation is by ground-based radio signals. For many years aircraft have been fitted with radio receivers to pick up signals that indicate the position of the aircraft relative to the radio transmitter. The most popular for small aircraft is the VHF omnidirectional range (*VOR*). As you will discover later in this chapter, there are two types of radios on many aircraft: navigation and communication. As a sport pilot, you aren't required to have either one onboard—but you still should know how they work and why you *should* have them.

The VOR system uses a frequency that is just above the FM radio band. To use it, you select a specific radial (such as 320 degrees) signal and fly either *to* or *from* the station. The VOR has 360 radials radiating from the station that allow you to fly in any direction on the compass. There are a few variations to the VOR system. You'll hear them referred to as VORTAC, meaning VHF omnirange/tactical air navigation system, a mouthful that means it's a VOR that the military uses, too. And you'll see references to VOR-DME or NDB-DME, which means the signal can be read by aircraft with distance-measuring equipment (the DME part) to also tell you how far you are from the VOR. There will be knowledge test questions on these systems and how to use them, so refer to your FAA publications for the official mantra.

> **Flying Words**
>
> **VOR** is a ground-based electronic navigation aid transmitting very high frequency (VHF) radio signals in all directions. Receiving equipment in an aircraft can identify the location, relative position, and (if equipped) distance to or from the VOR transmitter.

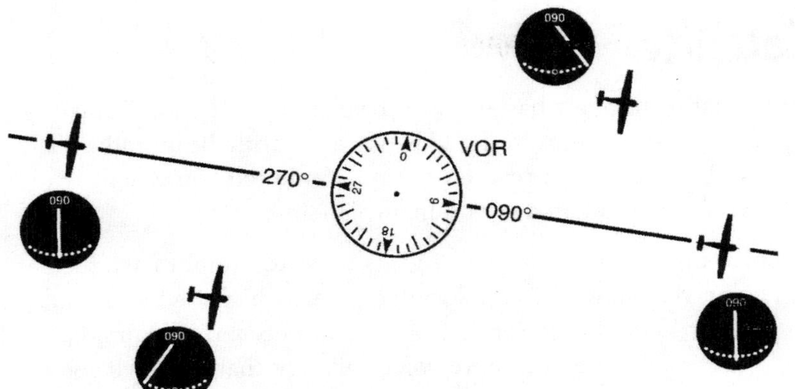

Tracking a VOR signal.

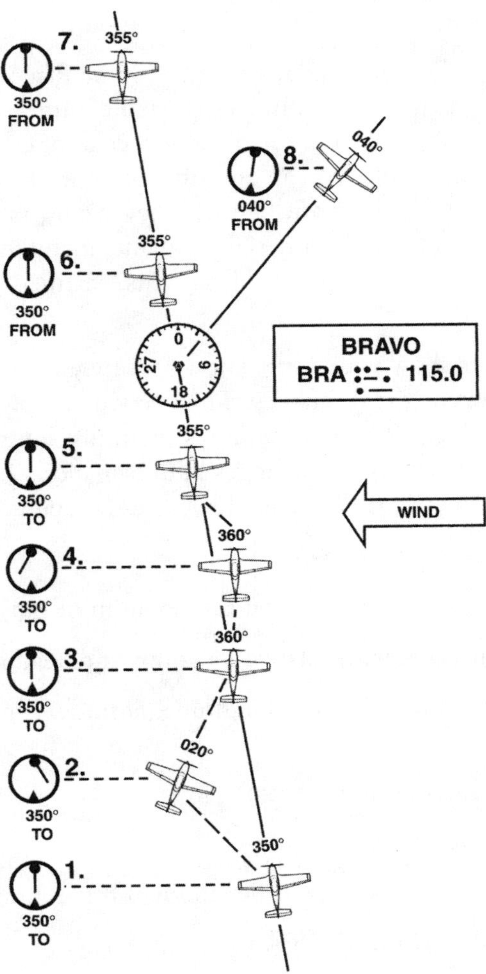

Tracking VOR radials in a crosswind.

Navigating by Satellite

One of the greatest gifts that technology has given to travelers is the *Global Positioning System (GPS)*. Twenty-four fixed satellites in the U.S. sky constantly beam radio signals toward Earth. Any GPS decoder can read those signals and tell you exactly where you are—even if you're moving in a car or an airplane!

GPS systems have been an option in cars for a few years now. You might have seen their screens, often in color, that show the car's location, nearby highways and roads, and even services such as motels and restaurants. Some even have voice software that will give you directions to where you want to go: "Turn left. No, your *other* left! Hey, watch out for that car. Uh-oh, it's a police car! Goodbye."

> **Flying Words**
>
> The **Global Positioning System (GPS)** is a space-based radio navigation system. Receivers in an aircraft, car, truck, train, ship, or on the ground use signals from satellites in the system to identify the receiver's position, velocity, and time. Software in the receiver interprets this information for the viewer.

Today's aircraft can be fitted with GPS systems, too. In fact, portable units are available for planes at a relatively low cost ($500 to $2,000) that give you an amazing amount of information in your aircraft. Because they are portable, you can use them in any type of plane, including the new light-sport aircraft, ultralights, certified craft, or whatever you're flying.

What do GPS decoders show you? First, know that they include updatable software with information on airports and services. The decoder simply reads the signal from at least 5 of the 24 satellites. The good thing is that most units have a method of updating the data periodically to reflect changes in information. To answer the question, here's what you'll see on your GPS navigation system (depending on the model):

- Your plane's location over a map
- The location of nearby airports (you can zoom in or out)
- A list of nearby airports with relative locations and headings from you
- Information about those airports (longitude, latitude, runway numbers, length, services, etc.)
- The track you are flying (in degrees)
- Flight planning information
- Terrain (in color or shades of gray, depending on the model)
- Land-based navigation aids (VORs, for example)

- Outlines of controlled airspace (Classes B, C, D, E)
- Other landmarks you might find on an aeronautical chart

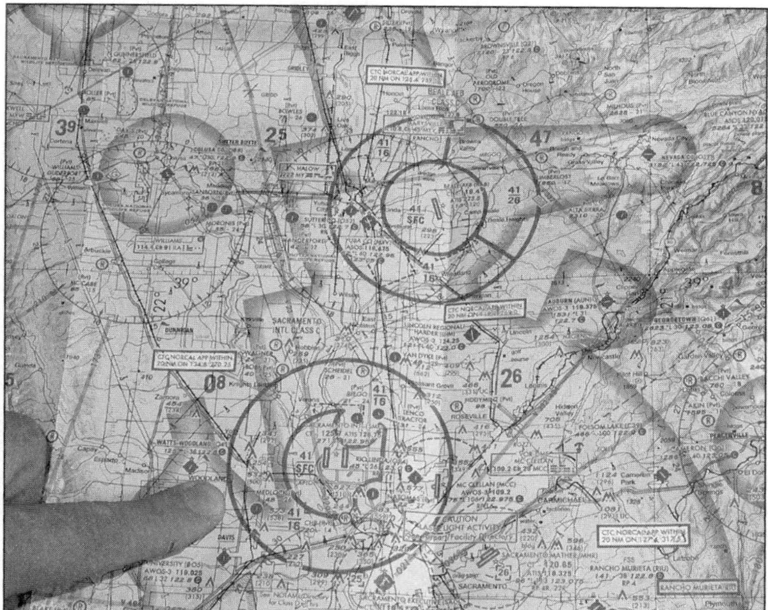

Your sectional aeronautical chart will show you the location and perimeters of controlled airspace.

Amazing! In addition, the latest (read: more expensive) models include a logbook for recording your flights, turn-by-turn directions for your flight plan, steering guidance (images of what your flight instruments should look like at any given time), various clocks and stopwatches, and much more.

Some models include or can be retrofitted with databases that offer data more specific to automobile drivers or even boaters. They can be used anywhere!

You also can buy installed GPS systems, but they're more expensive. Some new systems now combine the traditional flight instruments onto a precision display panel for ultimate flying.

> **Knowledge Test**
>
> The sport-pilot knowledge test will ask few if any questions about GPS, but might ask many on other navigation systems. Make sure you've read your *Aeronautical Information Manual (AIM)* and other FAA publications.

Communicating with Pilots and Air Traffic Controllers

I've talked about the basics of aeronautical navigation for sport pilots. The other job that aviation radios do is communications or talking with air traffic control (ATC) and other pilots. It's not like being on a citizens band (CB) radio: "Ten-four, good buddy. Smokey at twelve o'clock." Rather, it's communicating to make flying safer for everyone. Communication radios aren't a legal requirement of sport planes, but you will soon see the advantages to having them.

What's so important about communication? Here's what you can do with your plane's communication system:

- Get up-to-date weather information during your flight
- Ask ATC to watch over you (called a flight watch) while you're flying through its area
- Open, change, or close an existing flight plan
- Talk with other pilots in the area
- Ask for help or declare an emergency

> **Wing Tips**
>
> Contrary to popular opinion, VFR pilots are *not* required to file a flight plan with the FAA. Only IFR pilots must do so. However, you may if you wish, and it makes good sense if you expect to fly someplace where getting lost can be a problem. Many instructors suggest that you always file a flight plan until you have at least 100 hours of flight time.

As I've mentioned, sport pilots don't have to use communication radios, but most soon discover the benefits of knowing and being known. To communicate with other aircraft and the area ATC, you'll need equipment and information. Many aircraft have comm (short for "communication") radios installed. If not, you can buy hand-held comm radios (technically, they are called transceivers) for $200 to $500. The better ones actually are nav-com transceivers that allow you to use VOR navigation aids as well as communicate with ATC and pilots. You can buy them through your local flight school, Sporty's Pilot Shop, King Schools, or other sources (see Appendix B for specifics).

If you haven't been flying yet or much, you might not be aware of how loud an aircraft engine can be, especially when a smaller aircraft is climbing. For this reason, many pilots invest in a headset. It's similar to a headset used to listen to music except that it also includes a microphone and a "talk-no talk" button. Better models can be used to talk with passengers through their headsets, and with a flick of a switch, to ATC or other pilots. Cost is $200 to $800 per set. Tell Santa! He's a pilot!

How will you communicate with ATC and other pilots? It's just like talking on the telephone (remembering that it's a party line). "Bob, this is Dan. I'm about five miles from your house and want to stop by for a soda." However, your flying conversation will go more like this: "Covington Airport, Zodiac four two seven bravo charlie downwind for landing runway two-six Covington." The common communication elements are …

- Who you are calling (Covington Airport).
- Who you are (Zodiac 427BC).
- Where you are (downwind for landing).
- What you want to do (land on runway 2-6).

If you're talking with ATC, they will acknowledge your call (as soon as they have time) and confirm, deny, or give further directions. If you're in uncontrolled airspace and you're simply announcing your intentions to any other pilots monitoring that frequency, they typically won't respond. Nor will they snicker, so don't be afraid to communicate.

Must you communicate with ATC? Only if you're going into radio-controlled airspace. If you're in Class E or uncontrolled (Class G) airspace, you don't have to talk with anyone—though it's a good idea to let everyone in the area know that you're there.

Another important radio you might have in your plane is actually a transmitter only, called a transponder. It helps radar controllers "see" your plane on the radar. ATC radar can pick up airplanes without a transponder but with one, they get a positive identification from your plane. It sends out a signal that identifies you on their radar screen. If you ask for radar service, the controller will say something like "squawk four two one one," which means dial in 4221 (or any number they assign to you) on your transponder. The info will then appear on the ATC radar screen and traffic control can watch over you. If you have a transponder but are not using radar services, the standard "squawk" is 1200. This code means you are flying VFR and don't require radar separation, just an angel on your shoulder.

CAUTION

Stall Warning!

Other squawk codes include 7700 (emergency), 7600 (you've lost other communication radios), and 7500 (you're being hijacked!). Don't let anyone play with the transponder or you might find that you suddenly have a jet fighter escort!

Summary of Recommended Communication Procedures

Facility at Airport	Frequency Use	Outbound	Inbound	Practice Instrument Approach
1. UNICOM (no Tower or FSS)	Communicate with UNICOM station on published CTAF frequency (122.7; 122.8; 122.725; 122.975; or 123.0). If unable to contact UNICOM station, use self-announce procedures on CTAF.	Before taxiing and before taxiing on the runway for departure.	10 miles out. Entering downwind, base, and final. Leaving the runway.	
2. No Tower, FSS, or final UNICOM	Self-announce on MULTICOM frequency 122.9.	Before taxiing and before taxiing on the runway for departure.	10 miles out. Entering downwind, base, and final. Leaving the runway.	Departing approach fix (name) or on final approach segment inbound.
3. No Tower in operation, FSS open	Communicate with FSS on CTAF frequency.	Before taxiing and before taxiing on the runway for departure.	10 miles out. Entering downwind, base, and final. Leaving the runway.	Approach completed/ terminated.
4. FSS closed (no Tower)	Self-announce on CTAF.	Before taxiing and before taxiing on the runway for departure.	10 miles out. Entering downwind, base, and final. Leaving the runway.	

Facility at Airport	Frequency Use	Outbound	Inbound	Practice Instrument Approach
5. Tower or FSS not in operation	Self-announce on CTAF.	Before taxiing and before taxiing on the runway for departure.	10 miles out. Entering downwind, base, and final. Leaving the runway.	

If you eventually earn an endorsement to communicate with ATC, you'll need to learn the phonic alphabet, used because some letters and numbers sound similar over a radio. The *Aeronautical Information Manual (AIM)* includes more information on the phonic alphabet.

CHARACTER	MORSE CODE	TELEPHONY	PHONIC (PRONUNCIATION)
A	•-	Alfa	(AL-FAH)
B	-•••	Bravo	(BRAH-VOH)
C	-•-•	Charlie	(CHAR-LEE) OR (SHAR-LEE)
D	-••	Delta	(DELL-TAH)
E	•	Echo	(ECK-OH)
F	••-•	Foxtrot	(FOKS-TROT)
G	--•	Golf	(GOLF)
H	••••	Hotel	(HOH-TEL)
I	••	India	(IN-DEE-AH)
J	•---	Juliett	(JEW-LEE-ETT)
K	-•-	Kilo	(KEY-LOH)
L	•-••	Lima	(LEE-MAH)
M	--	Mike	(MIKE)
N	-•	November	(NO-VEM-BER)
O	---	Oscar	(OSS-CAH)
P	•--•	Papa	(PAH-PAH)
Q	--•-	Quebec	(KEH-BECK)
R	•-•	Romeo	(ROW-ME-OH)
S	•••	Sierra	(SEE-AIR-RAH)
T	-	Tango	(TANG-GO)
U	••-	Uniform	(YOU-NEE-FORM) OR (OO-NEE-FORM)
V	•••-	Victor	(VIK-TAH)
W	•--	Whiskey	(WISS-KEY)
X	-••-	Xray	(ECKS-RAY)
Y	-•--	Yankee	(YANG-KEY)
Z	--••	Zulu	(ZOO-LOO)
1	•----	One	(WUN)
2	••---	Two	(TOO)
3	•••--	Three	(TREE)
4	••••-	Four	(FOW-ER)
5	•••••	Five	(FIFE)
6	-••••	Six	(SIX)
7	--•••	Seven	(SEV-EN)
8	---••	Eight	(AIT)
9	----•	Nine	(NIN-ER)
0	-----	Zero	(ZEE-RO)

Phonic alphabet used by pilots and air traffic controllers.

Understanding Weather

Many books have been written about weather, especially aeronautical weather. That's because weather impacts flyers. If there's a thunderstorm brewing and you need to get to work, you'd probably drive there. As a VFR pilot, you'd *never* think of flying near a thunderstorm.

The FAA's *Pilot's Handbook of Aeronautical Knowledge* includes information about weather to help you pass your knowledge and practical tests as well as teach you how weather affects flying. Because sport pilots are VFR daylight-only fliers following specific weather minimums, you don't need to become a meteorologist. However, you do want to know how weather works for you and against you when flying.

FAR 91 outlines basic VFR weather minimums, telling you the minimum conditions in which you can fly as a sport pilot. Smart pilots (that includes you!) have personal minimums that are higher, especially when first learning to fly. Chapter 3 tells you what the FAA minimums are for sport pilots. Sport pilots should have personal weather minimums that are greater than those required by FAR 91.

In addition, you should be able to read weather maps and understand meteorological reports that the FAA and National Weather Service (NWS) provide to pilots. Fortunately, most of the maps and reports include a legend to help you decipher them. Some practice will help, so refer to the *Pilot's Handbook of Aeronautical Knowledge* and similar publications for more specifics.

Unfortunately, the knowledge test will ask you questions about teletype weather codes that aren't frequently used anymore. Even so, you have to learn them to pass the test. To help, I recommend aftermarket training material such as are offered by King Schools, Sporty's, Jeppeson, and other educational aids written specifically to help you pass the knowledge and practical tests. Pay special attention to Direct User Access Terminal Service (DUATS) reports and how to get weather briefings from FAA flight service stations (FSS) because you will use them more than the old teletype services.

You also can call up an FAA automated flight service station (AFSS) for a personal weather briefing, or you can listen to the Pilot's Automatic Telephone Weather Answering System (PATWAS). (Don't you just *love* all these acronyms? If you're having trouble keeping them all straight, see the handy list of acronyms and abbreviations in Appendix D.) It's PATWAS that gives you a recorded weather briefing for the area within 50 miles of the FSS. The telephone number for any AFSS is 1-800-WXBRIEF.

Another useful type of weather report is called the PIREP, short for pilot weather report. These are observations from real pilots flying in specific locations and speaking to the needs of other pilots. Of course, a PIREP from a Northwest Airlines pilot at 35,000 feet isn't much use to you at 3,500 feet in your sport aircraft. Fortunately, the reports indicate who is reporting, when, what the pilot is flying, and what the pilot saw.

Here's a summary of how weather impacts flying. First, air moves because it gets heated up by the sun's rays. The heat exchange makes air move from a high-pressure system (marked H on weather maps) to low-pressure systems (marked L). As the atmosphere moves across the surface of the earth it can whirl, eddy, or even stop depending on the terrain over which it travels. That's the surface wind. Winds at higher altitudes could be coming from a different direction or at a dissimilar speed.

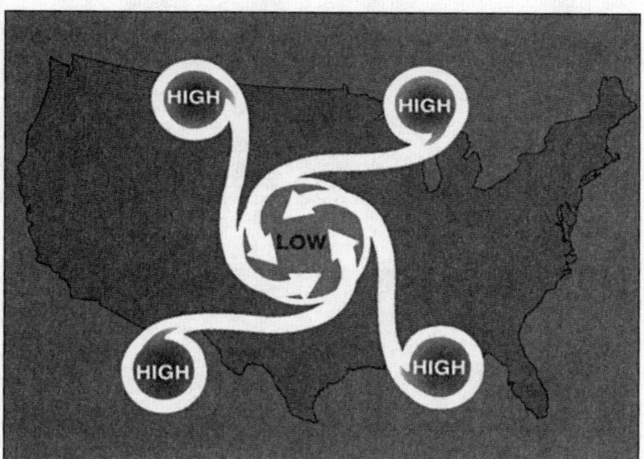

Low-pressure system.

Clouds are simply pockets of moisture in the air. If the moisture becomes saturated, it will turn into liquid and fall to the ground as rain, snow, sleet, or hail, depending on air temperature. The point at which moisture turns into a liquid is called the dew point.

Clouds are named for their shape. Stratus (layered) clouds are flat. Cumulus (accumulated) clouds are chubby. If the clouds are raining, the term "nimbus" is added: "nimbostratus" or "cumulonimbus." High clouds are identified by the prefix "alto," as in altostratus. Broken clouds are called "fracto," as in fractocumulus.

So let's discuss cloud cover, also known as sky condition. Clear (abbreviated SKC) means there are no clouds in the sky (except maybe a tiny wisp of a cloud on the horizon). Scattered (SCT) means that ⅛ to ½ of the sky has cloud coverage. Broken (BKN) means that ⅝ to ⅞ of the sky is covered with clouds; also known as "mostly cloudy." Overcast (OVC) means what it says: the entire sky is covered with clouds (except maybe a tiny blue spot on the horizon). These terms are important because VFR pilots must abide by ceiling limits. A ceiling is the *lowest* broken (more than ⅝ coverage) or greater layer of clouds.

Low-, intermediate-, and high-level cumulus clouds.

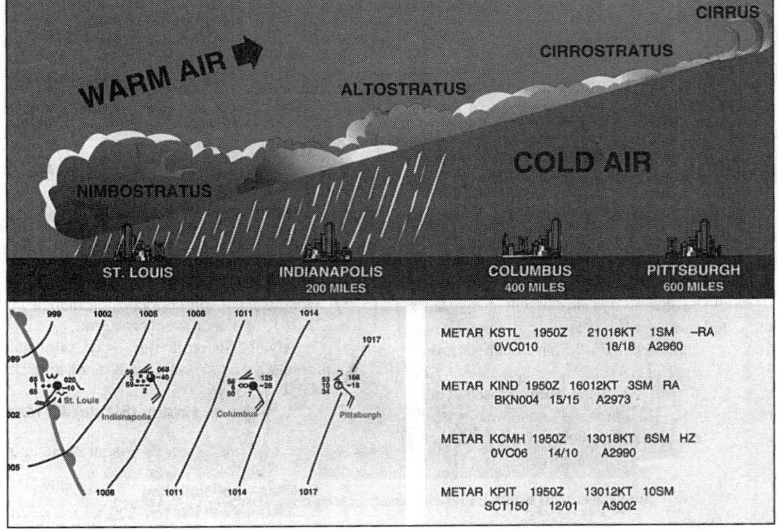

Interpreting weather patterns (upper) from a weather map (lower left) and an aviation weather report (lower right).

You'll learn more—much more—about clouds and weather as you advance in your flying toward the private-pilot and advanced certificates. For right now you are a sport pilot, meaning that you're supposed to stay away from clouds. In fact, the next chapter moves your flying inside, where the weather is always what you make it.

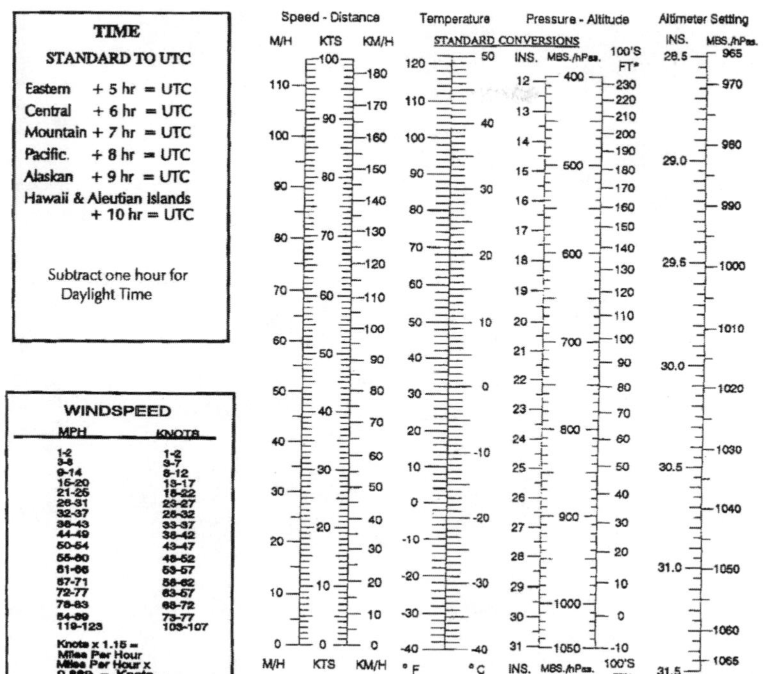

TIME

STANDARD TO UTC

Eastern	+ 5 hr	= UTC
Central	+ 6 hr	= UTC
Mountain	+ 7 hr	= UTC
Pacific	+ 8 hr	= UTC
Alaskan	+ 9 hr	= UTC
Hawaii & Aleutian Islands	+ 10 hr	= UTC

Subtract one hour for Daylight Time

WINDSPEED

MPH	KNOTS
1-2	1-2
3-8	3-7
9-14	8-12
15-20	13-17
21-25	18-22
26-31	23-27
32-37	28-32
38-43	33-37
44-49	38-42
50-54	43-47
55-60	48-52
61-66	53-57
67-71	58-62
72-77	63-67
78-83	68-72
84-89	73-77
119-123	103-107

Knots x 1.15 = Miles Per Hour
Miles Per Hour x 0.869 = Knots

Table of weather element conversions.

The Least You Need to Know

- Pilotage is flying by referencing landmarks on the ground.
- Dead-reckoning navigation uses calculations to get you from here to there.
- Ground-based radio navigation is slowly being replaced by global positioning satellite systems.
- The best way to avoid problems—and report problems—is to learn how to communicate with controllers and other pilots.
- Sport pilots are safer pilots as they learn to interpret the weather.

Chapter 5

Flying at Home

In This Chapter

- Setting up your "home airplane"
- Flight simulation programs that help you practice your flying skills
- Prepping for knowledge and practical tests using your PC
- Have fun flying at home!

Flying—even sport flying—can get expensive. And it's frustrating to try to learn the intricacies of flight at two dollars a minute! That's why modern students and even certified pilots save money by flying at home!

This chapter introduces you to the world of home aviation: learning, practicing, relaxing, and enjoying your flying time from the comfort of a spare bedroom or home office. You can even take your flying on the road with a laptop computer. Let's go flying!

Learning to Be a Desk Pilot

When I first began writing about private aviation more than 20 years ago, personal computers (PCs) hadn't really hit the consumer market. Within 10 years there was not only a proliferation of PCs, but also many software programs to help you pretend to fly. They helped you hone your skills—especially if you bought a joystick or yoke controller to go with it—but ground terrain was simulated by dots to give you some perception of height. Okay, but not realistic.

Today, computers and graphics are dramatically more powerful. So are control systems. For an investment of about $300 (in addition to a PC) you can be flying a variety of aircraft with such reality that you might want to keep an airbag nearby! Let me illustrate …

You start up one of the popular flight simulation programs on your computer, select an aircraft, and select a departure airport. You can pick an airport near your home or you can fly your craft out of Baghdad International; it's your choice. Apply the throttle, move the rudder pedals under the desk with your feet to keep the craft near the centerline, and when the plane reaches climb speed, it will either fly off the runway by itself or with a little encouragement from you pulling back on the joystick or yoke. All the instruments that you'd see in a real aircraft are in front of you and telling you things.

Flight simulation programs can be very realistic.

Depending on the program you've selected and the add-ons purchased, you will see a realistic representation of conditions you will face flying out of your selected airport. At the least, mountains will look approximately like mountains, and cities will look like cities. Add-on scenery products can show you, for instance, what flying over Manhattan and the Statue of Liberty looks like. You'll even see ferry boats on the Hudson!

This book's Appendix B gives you sources for some of these tools, but let me tell you about the most popular systems. I'm assuming you have a computer—or access to a computer—with one of the later Microsoft Windows operating systems such as NT, 2000, or XP, a good-quality monitor with a better-quality graphics card, and a flight simulation program.

View from inside your virtual sport plane. Yes, all the instruments work!

The most widely used flight simulation program by far is *Microsoft Flight Simulator* (www.microsoft.com). You can buy it for less than $100 just about anyplace that sells game software. Just make sure your computer at least meets the minimum system requirements listed on the package. The leading manufacturer of flight simulation hardware is CH Products (www.chproducts.com).

Stall Warning!

Always read the fine print before buying flight software for your computer. Though some programs are cross-platform and run on two or more operating systems (Windows, Macintosh, Linux, for example), some require newer computer chips, especially for graphics. Read the box or contact the manufacturer to make sure that the system you buy is fully compatible with your computer. Once you break the box seal, many retailers won't give you credit for returned software.

Another popular flight simulation program is called *On Top*, available through Aviation Supplies & Academics (ASA) (www.asa2fly.com). However, it's intended more for instrument pilots and is more expensive. If your ultimate goal is to fly commercial aircraft, consider this program for learning how to fly as a sport pilot and beyond.

Another popular online source for multimedia flyers is PC Aviator (www.pcaviator.com). Besides publishing *Computer Pilot* magazine, PC Aviator offers a wide variety of software and hardware toys for flight simulation. A truly international company, PC Aviator is based in Australia with offices in the United States as well.

Computer Pilot *magazine includes articles and programs for home aviators.*

You really don't need a flight simulation yoke or rudder pedals. You can fly using your PC's keyboard. For example, you'll start the aircraft engine by pressing the Ctrl and E keys at the same time, increase the throttle with the F2 key, decrease throttle with the F3 key, and so on. You'll also be able to use your computer's mouse to select options and perform flight actions.

Wing Tips

Want to have more fun flying at home? Take a look at a monthly publication titled *Computer Pilot* (www.computerpilot.com). It includes articles, product reviews, and tips on flying all types of aircraft using flight-simulation software. The accompanying CD has freeware and demo software to keep you in the virtual skies.

However, if you're serious about flying at home, I recommend you invest in at least a joystick (under $100) or control yoke (about $150). Rudder/brake pedals are about $100, but the software can be set up for "automatic rudder control" so you don't need them. Of course, that means you can't practice rudder control unless you use the keyboard. The cost will be quickly covered by your savings in expensive flight time. Frankly, you will "go flying" as recreation as well as training, spending hours planning and flying a virtual trip from your favorite local airport to, say, Orlando or some other fun destination. As you get into this growing hobby, you might even find yourself competing with other pilots over the Internet!

I'll tell you more ways you can take advantage of your "desk plane" later in this chapter. For now, be thinking of the ways you can learn and have loads of fun flying at home—safely!

Preparing for the Knowledge Test

You'll soon have the knowledge of aviation to take your first pilot test—the sport-pilot knowledge test. In fact, chances are excellent that you will take the test on a computer. So learning and practicing on a computer makes sense. Where do you start?

The first place to start is by going online (if your PC is equipped with a modem and Internet browser software) to take a look at what the FAA is all about. Go to www.faa.gov, and you will discover that the FAA really is set up to help people learn to fly. The site could seem intimidating at first because it serves not only new sport pilots, but also private and commercial pilots, plus all those consumers who fly and travel on commercial airplanes. Spend some time poking around onsite and you'll see that it has lots of useful information for you.

Next, I recommend that you visit online sites set up by various flying organizations. Your first stop should be www.sportpilot.org, operated by the Experimental Aircraft Association (EAA) (www.eaa.org), a major player in getting the new SP/LSA rules developed and implemented. The site offers a wide variety of resources for new and even experienced pilots who are new to sport flying. Membership in EEA is inexpensive and highly recommended.

Another leading organization for pilots is the Aircraft Owners and Pilots Association (AOPA; www.aopa.org). It, too, offers extensive resources for new and experienced pilots. Consider joining, especially if your long-term goal is to get a private-pilot or higher certificate.

If you get a chance, stop by my website at www.SportFlyingGuide.com. I'll use it to update information in this book and help you get started in sport flying.

Now, back to the knowledge test and how you can prepare for it using your computer. The knowledge test for sport pilots is comprised of 30 multiple-choice questions on regulations, aerodynamics, airspace, navigation, weather, aeromedical, and related topics. We've already covered some of these topics in this book and will cover the others before the end.

Passing score for the knowledge test is 70 percent. That means you have to get only 21 multiple-choice questions right to pass the test. However, the *real* test is actually flying, when you need to remember and apply what you've learned. So don't do the minimum—do the maximum. Study, restudy, review, take sample tests, and make sure

Knowledge Test

You can actually take a lifelike knowledge test online. Sporty's Pilot Shop (www.sportys.com) and others offer sample tests as a free service. In addition, Sporty's offers videos, CDs, and DVDs that teach the information needed for many pilot-knowledge tests as well as other aspects of flying.

you're absolutely ready for the knowledge test, the oral test, and the reality test—flying. Computers can help you do this.

King Schools (www.kingschools.com), the largest aviation school in the United States, offers a course of instruction specifically developed for the new sport-pilot certificate. It's available on interactive DVD, CD, or video, and includes printed material for supplementation and review. It goes beyond what you need to know for the test, covering things you should know to fly. John and Martha King have been training pilots for decades.

The interactive courses work like this: You watch a video presentation, then answer questions very similar to the ones that will appear on your knowledge test. You're immediately graded on your answer and are told why the answer is correct or incorrect. Finally, you can take one or more practice tests just before you go for the FAA knowledge test. Those who use this training method often get passing scores of 90 percent or more, and some get 100 percent!

Most test schools also offer a computerized course or component specifically on taking the practical test (the checkride), which is the test you take when you're finished training and your instructor has signed you off. A typical course coaches you on what to expect and how to take the test. During the actual test, an FAA-designated pilot examiner (DPE) will ask you to plan a flight, will discuss the flight to verify your knowledge, and then take you flying. During the checkride you will be tested on your skills as a pilot. I cover the knowledge and practical tests in greater detail in Chapter 11.

As you can see, your computer can do more than help you practice your flying. It also can help you pass the required tests with "flying" colors!

Practicing Your Flying

As you can see, there are many cost-effective resources available to sport-pilot students who have access to a computer. And you don't have to be a computer wizard to use them. Installation of the flight-control hardware is easier than it used to be, especially if it uses USB ports and your PC has them. It's really "plug and play." Soon you'll be ready to take your home plane up and practice flying.

What can you practice? You name it. You can use flight simulation software and hardware to practice ...

- Standard takeoffs and landings.
- Short-field takeoffs and landings.
- Soft-field takeoffs and landings.
- Coordinated turns.
- Straight-and-level flight.
- Shallow and medium turns.
- S-turns.
- Stalls.

These are the maneuvers you'll be tested on during your FAA practical test, so you might as well begin practicing them now at home. If you have yoke/joystick and rudder controls, you'll get some practice on the process and its steps without having to rent an aircraft. Of course, flying at home and flying a real aircraft are going to be different, but you will gain some skills that are easy to adjust once you get to fly a real aircraft.

Let me suggest that, as much as possible, you practice at home on an aircraft that has the approximate characteristics of the one in which you really practice, your trainer aircraft. Flight-simulator programs typically give you a choice of aircraft so you *can* fly in a Boeing 727 commercial jet, a Ford Tri-Motor of the 1930s, or even the first airplane of 100 years ago, the Wright Flyer. Don't train on these aircraft. Instead, select a simple tri-gear or taildragger aircraft that approximates your real-world trainer aircraft. If you can't find one that's relatively close, do an online search for plane configuration files that are similar.

For example, you can virtually fly a Zenair Zodiac XL, a two-place kit light-sport aircraft, by downloading and installing files from www.zenithair.com. If you're flying a taildragger trainer, consider the Piper J3 Cub that comes with Microsoft Flight Simulator. As light-sport aircraft become increasingly popular you'll see additional models available for virtual flying. I'll try to keep an up-to-date list on my website at www.SportFlyingGuide.com. Also make sure that if your trainer has a stick rather than a yoke for control that your flight-sim hardware includes a joystick.

Wing Tips

Utilize *all* of your flight simulation program. Some programs offer additional flying resources including flight lessons. Microsoft Flight Simulator, for example, contains a flying school taught by Rod Machado for student, private, instrument, commercial, and airline transport pilots. That's more than you need to know, but it will give you a taste of what it takes to upgrade your certificate—and you'll have fun. What you will learn in these courses will not contradict what your instructor is teaching, but supplement it. In fact, it might help you think of good questions to ask your instructor during the next lesson—and good questions make good pilots.

Enhancing Your Flying Skills

Flying is really about learning. First, others teach you some basics, then you begin teaching yourself. Others help, but you're the *real* teacher as well as the student. It's the continual learning that keeps people fascinated with flying for decades.

One of the major advantages of flying at home is that you can make real-time mistakes and walk away from them. If stuck in a flight predicament, for example, you can press the "pause" button, think over or research what you should do, then unpause and apply what you've learned. You also can save and replay flights to continue learning from good ones and bad ones. Remember, we usually learn more (hopefully) from our mistakes than our successes.

Yes, you will crash your home plane. Maybe you gave your taildragger too much right rudder on the takeoff roll and it spun out (called a ground loop). Simply start over and learn from the error. You can change the software settings to make it crash-proof (the plane will bounce, for example, instead of crash on a bad landing), but I advise that you don't let it. To learn from mistakes you must make them.

In addition, most flight simulation programs allow you to view your aircraft from various angles. Microsoft Flight Simulator, for example, lets you see the full control panel, part of the control panel, watch your plane fly from about 20 feet away (in front of, behind, or from the side), or watch from a spotter plane nearby. The learning event here is that you can move various controls and see what actually happens to the aircraft. A left movement of the yoke or joystick, for example, moves the left aileron up and the right one down.

One of the many benefits of flight simulation software is you develop the skills to make coordinated turns, climbs, and descents, all without risk of personal injury. You're coordinating numerous controllers rather than one, and you can visually verify how those skills are being developed. Sure, it won't be exactly the same as you actually fly your trainer plane, but it will give you an approximation. It's much easier to learn to fly your second airplane (your trainer) after you've practiced on your first one (your home plane).

Another feature of newer flight-sim packages is the inclusion of virtual GPS systems. (You learned about GPS in Chapter 4.) You can see how they work and actually use one in your virtual flying in packages such as Microsoft Flight Simulator.

Remember, virtual flying can save you time and money on reality flying. It can't replace the real thing, but it can make the real thing much easier to understand and do. When going for a private-pilot license, for example, one pilot calculated that he saved 10 to 15 hours of flying time by using flight simulation software. Even at solo prices, that's about $1,000 in savings. And it's a blast!

What's next? The next chapter covers where to learn to fly: getting good instruction. But don't forget that you can always increase your learning experience and reduce training costs by flying at home!

The Least You Need to Know

- Flight simulation programs can dramatically cut the cost and increase the fun of flying.
- You can prepare for your knowledge and practical tests with computer-based instruction.
- Flight simulators give you a chance to make mistakes and learn from them without having to involve an insurance company.
- Even as your training moves to real aircraft, depend on flight-simulation software and hardware to help you learn more about flying.

Part 2

Into the Wild Blue Yonder

Hey, if you think *that* was fun, wait until we actually go flying!

This second part gets you up into the air—safely! It shows you how and where to get quality instruction, how to make sure your plane is ready to fly, how to get it up in the air and back again, and how to fly to other places.

Most important, it tells you what you need to know to pass your sport-pilot certificate test. You'll find out what's required to earn your wings. You'll even watch as a "typical" student pilot—hey, that's *you*—passes the practical test with flying colors!

Excited? You should be. You're about to join the millions of folks who enjoy flying into the wild blue yonder!

Chapter 6

Flight Instruction

In This Chapter

- Finding appropriate flight training
- What you'll typically learn lesson by lesson
- Selecting a flight instructor who matches your needs
- Going up for the first time
- What to know before and after you solo
- Preparing for the test

"The Wright brothers didn't have a flight instructor and they did okay!"

Yes, but that was before the FAA and before thousands of other aircraft crossed the skies. Besides, I believe that Wilbur and Orville would have preferred learning from an instructor instead of repeatedly crashing their newborn aircraft.

The fact is, you'll need flight instruction. All new pilots do. It's the law. And it's for your own good, because many of the things you'll learn from an instructor you might not appreciate until the day you try to make your airplane climb too fast or you have to make an emergency landing or handle an equipment failure at 4,000 feet.

"*Help!!!!!!!!*"

So be glad that someone is willing to take you flying and show you how it's done. This chapter guides you toward finding the best flight instructor for your money and your future in flying.

Your Instructional Options

In life, you have lots of options. Flying is no different. You have many options for how and where you will learn, how much it will cost, what you will get out of it, and what you can do with it.

What is *not* optional is the FAA requirements for flight instruction. As you learned in Chapter 1, sport pilots are required to …

- Train a minimum of 20 hours flight time, including 15 hours with a flight instructor who is qualified to teach sport pilots and 5 hours solo-flying time.
- Train 2 hours of cross-country flying (more than 75 nautical miles).
- Pass the FAA knowledge test (30 questions requiring a 70 percent or better score).
- Train 3 hours in preparation for the FAA practical test (checkride).
- Pass the FAA practical test.
- Present a valid automobile driver's license or a third-class medical certificate as proof of medical health.

You'll probably spend more than 20 hours in preparation for your sport-pilot certificate, but that's okay. In fact, many pilots quickly earn their student sport-pilot certificate, then take their time getting ready for the final checkride. Once you have your student-pilot certificate, you can fly around by yourself—as long as you adhere to your limits, such as no cross-country flying until you have a cross-country endorsement in your logbook.

Why Are You Flying?

Some of your learning options include flight schools, independent flight instruction, and colleges. I'll cover them in greater detail in a moment. First, consider where you want flying to take you. If you've already made up your mind that you want to be a commercial pilot and sport flying is just your first step, consider one of the colleges or larger flight schools designed to train professional aviators. Why? Not only will you learn more about commercial aviation, your diploma will be more acceptable to a major airline than if you take training from an independent flight instructor at

Podunk Field. In addition, scholarships are available for many of the formal training institutions, some of them paid by commercial airlines that would like you to come to work for them after graduation.

The majority of new pilots—especially those who already have careers—opt to take less formal instruction, in which case Podunk Field is just fine. In fact, they will be flying in and out of Podunk Field for the foreseeable future, so why not start there? It's handy to home and work. Or if there's a well-known flight school within driving distance, new pilots might enroll there to take advantage of the opportunity to fly more frequently.

Also, as sport flying catches on, there will be more facilities that specialize in SP/LSA, but maybe there's not one near you right now. You might need to check into an accelerated sport-pilot training course somewhere. See Appendix B for some websites; also visit www.SportFlyingGuide.com for the latest training opportunities.

The point here is that the type of training you select depends on what your long-term flying goals are. If you really don't have any, a local flight school or independent flight instructor is as good a place as any to start.

Wing Tips

Ground school is classroom training in preparation for flight. The flight instruction method you select will often dictate the ground school you use. For example, Cessna Flight Schools use their own training package and the ground-school materials come with it. Independent flight instructors often have a ground-school package of their own, have a preference for which ground school you use, or are willing to make some recommendations and leave the final decision up to you.

Flight Schools

A flight school is like any school, offering you an organized program that has successfully trained good pilots. How can you select the best one for you?

Do your homework! What flight schools are available within driving distance? Do they offer a sport-pilot program? Can they provide a list of satisfied students to whom you can talk? How many students are typically in a ground-school class? How often can you fly? What will you be flying?

So, once you've found a few flight schools to consider, how can you select the best one? Here are some questions to ask:

- What airplanes are used for instruction? (Remember, the trainer plane must be sport pilot-eligible.)

- How many flight hours have the aircraft logged? (Like car mileage, the lower the better.)
- May I inspect the maintenance logs for these aircraft? (If not, why not?)
- Are copies of the aircraft's operating handbook available for purchase and study? (Better schools will provide them so you know what you are flying.)
- How many flight instructors does the school employ? (Fewer instructors means fewer hours of instruction are available.)
- What are the credentials of the instructors? (I'll cover this in a moment.)
- What ground-school training system does the school use and why? (The "why" is more important than the "what.")
- What is the curriculum for new sport pilots? (Get a printed copy if possible, to compare between schools.)
- May I talk with some of your current students and recent graduates? (How easy they make it tells you more about how they conduct business.)
- What are the costs of flight instruction at this school? (Get a breakdown so you can compare it with other schools.)

Also refer to *A Guide to Choosing a Flight School* published and available through the Aircraft Owners and Pilots Association (AOPA) (www.aopa.org) and Sporty's Pilot Shop (www.sportys.com). Free copies are available at many flight schools and online.

Independent Flight Instructors

FAR 61, Subpart H, spells out the requirements for flight instructors. To earn a sport-pilot or other pilot certificate you need to be taught by an FAA flight instructor who has training and experience in the type of aircraft being used for instruction. That makes sense.

An independent flight instructor is one who is available for hire outside of a flight school. The instructor might also work under contract to a school, work as a commercial pilot as well, or have some other type of job. The point is that the flight instructor can be hired by anyone who wants to learn to fly.

Who are instructors? Many are aviation "undergraduates." They are working toward their own commercial or airline transport-pilot (ATP) certificates and need more flying time for their pilot log. Just as some college undergraduates teach college courses, undergraduate flight instructors teach flying in order to learn more about it. Don't worry, they are well-qualified and certified. However, not all are as focused on training top pilots as are most who make a career of flight instruction.

You can find independent flight instructors through pilot friends, fixed-base operators (FBOs) who run airports and sell service, or on airport bulletin boards. Why choose an independent flight instructor? Because there are no local flight schools, there are no other training opportunities for sport pilots, or because your flying schedule requires someone who is independent from a formal school.

Can't find a nearby sport-pilot instructor? Find a pilot willing to become a well-qualified instructor and offer to be her or his first sport-pilot student. The pilot must first get qualified to teach in sport pilot-eligible aircraft (relatively easy), then teach you. Just make sure you can train in a sport pilot-eligible airplane to make it all legal.

If available, look for Gold Seal flight instructors. A Gold Seal instructor is one who has recommended at least 10 students for practical tests within the last 24 months and at least 80 percent of them have passed their practical test the first time. There are other requirements, too, all telling you that the instructor is serious about teaching flying.

One more point about independent flight instruction: It can be your best option if you have unique circumstances. For example, if you don't have an aircraft of your own, you sometimes can train in the instructor's aircraft. There are even gypsy flight instructors who will fly to your location for intensive training in their craft. An independent instructor might be practical if you don't live near a flight school or you are looking for nonstandard training, such as mountain flying or floatplane flying. In addition, independent instructors are typically less expensive than hiring a flight school. How much will the instructor charge for flight instruction? Less than a plumber.

Colleges and Universities

Want to get serious about flying? As sport flying grows, you will see it as an option at colleges and universities that already have aeronautical programs. In fact, many will offer one-semester or quarter-semester courses that will earn the student a sport-pilot certificate. Their motivation will be to bring private aviation—and aviation careers—into the realm of reality for more students. Just as some students take golf courses to help them in business, others will be offered courses to develop sport pilots who will eventually fly as part of their business.

To find out more about colleges and universities that have aviation programs, contact the University Aviation Association (uaa.auburn.edu).

What You'll Learn

The goal of flight instruction is to help you gain the knowledge and skills to make flying safe and fun. That's especially the aim of the new sport-pilot rules recently enacted. The exact flight path to this destination will vary depending on the flight instructor, school, your time, and your current skills—especially the skill of learning.

Your sport-pilot training will go something like this:

- **Lesson 1.** Become familiar with your airplane, including the theory of flight and the preflight check
- **Lesson 2.** Ground operations, normal takeoffs and landings
- **Lesson 3.** Basic flight maneuvers: climbs, descents, straight-and-level flight, coordinated turns
- **Lesson 4.** Additional flying maneuvers: slow flight maneuvers, power-on and power-off stalls, and emergency procedures
- **Lesson 5.** Ground reference maneuvers: rectangular course, S-turns, turns around a point, some more takeoffs and landings
- **Lesson 6.** Airport operations: airport signs and data, flying the pattern, cross-wind correction for takeoff and landing
- **Lesson 7.** Review of procedures learned thus far, endorsement for solo flight, then your first solo (typically, three takeoffs and landings at your home airport)
- **Lesson 8.** Advanced takeoffs and landings: short-field takeoffs and landings, soft-field takeoffs and landings
- **Lesson 9.** Navigation techniques and cross-country trip preparation
- **Lesson 10.** Solo cross-country trip
- **Lesson 11.** Review of all flight maneuvers and additional training as needed (could require additional lessons as well as solo practice time)
- **Lesson 12.** Final preparation for the sport-pilot oral and practice test

Once your instructor feels you are ready, he or she will endorse your logbook confirming that you are ready for the practice test, and help you set an appointment with an FAA examiner. Before this point, hopefully very early in your instruction, you will have studied for and passed the sport-pilot knowledge test by enrolling in a ground school or taking a multimedia ground school you can study at home.

Your First Flight

To develop your comfort level with flying, I strongly suggest that you try out a flight simulation program (see Chapter 5) or a simulator at your flight school. It will help prepare you for the dozens of new things that will be thrown at your brain during your first flight. If flight simulation isn't available, get an instrument panel wall poster from one of the pilot shops or manufacturers so you can visualize yourself inside the aircraft. Another option is to ask your flight instructor if you can sit in your trainer aircraft for a half hour and make notes *if you promise not to touch anything*. You want to be as comfortable as possible with your new environs.

Before you get to go flying, your instructor will explain how your aircraft stays up in the air (shown here, a Vega).

The aircraft instrument panel and cockpit might seem daunting as you first sit in your trainer, but it will soon make sense. Review Chapter 2 to understand what each instrument does. Know that each of the many controls, instruments, and gauges are important, but they don't all have equal weight in your learning process. Some, like the control yoke or stick, are most important and will be used all the time, but the nav-com radio (if equipped) won't be used as often during initial training.

Your first flight will probably be the easiest. Most instructors want to share their love of flying without making you afraid to ever go up again. Your first flight—and every subsequent flight—will start with a preflight inspection to make sure the aircraft is airworthy. Then you'll learn to start the engine, let it warm up, and taxi to the runway (the instructor will handle communications with the control tower or other aircraft), and take off. In fact, some instructors will have *you* do the first takeoff! It's that easy. Of course, the instructor will be inconspicuously poised to take over if there's any problem. I cover typical preflight operations in the next chapter.

Your first flight will continue with a climb, turn, and either leaving the *traffic pattern* or staying in the pattern for a landing made by the instructor. As you continue climbing, you'll notice new sensations and a new respect for pilots. Your instructor's goal for this first flight is to give *you* a goal: to do whatever it takes to learn how to fly on your own. That means there won't be any steep turns, fast descents, or other abrupt maneuvers to shake your confidence. In fact, the most unusual thing you will probably do is turns, banking the aircraft with the ailerons and adding some rudder to make a coordinated turn toward the left or right. Following directions, you might do much of the flying on your first flight!

Flying Words

The **traffic pattern** is an imaginary rectangular flight pattern around the landing runway at an airport.

Of course, each instructor presents a little different lesson plan for the first flight. However, all instructors' goals are approximately the same: to help you begin the transition from ground-bound to airborne. They know that you have much to learn and the good instructors will be patient with you—unless you make excuses. Remember: *Millions* of people have taken their first flight and the survival rate is excellent.

From your first flight you will sit in the left-hand seat and be the "pilot in command" (shown here, a Sky Boy).

Before You Solo

"When's my instructor ever going to let me solo?" It's a common question, asked by many student pilots after only a few hours of flight instruction. The predictable answer is: When *you* are ready.

First, there are some things you need to learn about flying—more specifically, about flying out of a problem. Common flying problems include running out of fuel, stalling the aircraft (nosing the aircraft up until it quits flying), and becoming disoriented due to fear or visibility. So, before your instructor ever climbs out of the aircraft and tells you to "take it around," you can bet that the instructor will need to be comfortable that you can handle these problems without him or her onboard.

Of course, you're not going to be able to "talk" your instructor into letting you solo. Instead, you will listen to instruction, respond, ask questions, learn from mistakes, and illustrate that you can fly the airport pattern without endangering yourself and the free world. Instructors recognize that a student's learning often levels off early in training. That's the first plateau and, if you're ready, you might be endorsed for solo flight (discussed in Chapter 9).

After You've Soloed

Once you've soloed, you can start limited flying on your own. However, the wiser decision is to get back in the aircraft with your instructor and move to phase two of learning to fly, honing your skills toward precision flying. No, you won't be doing acrobatics; you'll be maintaining a specific heading, climbing and descending smoothly, making numerous and varied takeoffs and landings, and maintaining an altitude within 100 feet plus or minus of the given altitude.

You'll also learn more about wind and how it impacts your flight path. You'll practice takeoffs and landings with a crosswind. You'll fly patterns in the sky, making adjustments to compensate for the direction and speed of the wind as you go. You'll also learn what a stall really is, how to avoid it, and how to fly out of it.

Once your instructor believes you are ready, he or she will endorse your pilot log for a solo cross-country trip. Before that you'll need to plan the trip, with the help of your instructor, using current weather forecasts, sectional charts, a flight computer, and the aircraft owner's manual. If you're like most student pilots, your first solo cross-country flight will be one of the most exhilarating and intimidating times of your life. On the one hand, you're free. On the other hand, it's all up to you.

Wing Tips

If you can, fly your first solo cross-country trip using a flight simulator program before you fly the real thing. Develop your flight plan, use the simulator to communicate with air traffic control (ATC) or other pilots if you wish, and get a sense of what it will be like. It will not only prepare you mentally, it will help you get over that first-solo fear. Chapter 10 shows you how to plan your first and subsequent cross-country flights.

Your Practical Test

Finally, it all comes down to a few hours on a wondrous day when you have an appointment with the FAA's designated pilot examiner (DPE) to take your flying practical test. I tell you more about what's involved and how to prepare for it in Chapter 11.

For now, know that everyone—including your instructor and your examiner—want you to pass the test. The paperwork is much easier for them if you pass. Your instructor thought enough of your developed skills to recommend you for testing, and the results reflects on the instructor's record. What could stop you from passing your test is nervousness, being fearful, and not doing your best. If you're really not quite comfortable, ask your instructor for additional training, or at least use some solo-flying hours to get more comfortable. Then go for it!

The Least You Need to Know

- You have many instructional options for learning to fly based on your own goals, needs, and limitations.
- The coursework for earning a sport-pilot certificate is simple and can be completed in 12 to 15 lessons plus a solo cross-country trip.
- Your instructor will not let you solo or go for your practical test until you've learned what you need to know to fly safely.
- Everyone is working to help you pass your practical test, and rooting for you to pass it the first time.

Chapter 7

Preflight Operations

In This Chapter

- Preflight inspections: a necessity for safe flying
- Preparing your airplane for flight
- Planning your flight
- Taxiing and prepping for takeoff

"Oops! I'm low on fuel. Think I'll land on that cloud over there and fuel up."

It won't happen! The ground is your last chance to take care of fuel, oil, maintenance, and other requirements. No matter what you've seen on the Wings cable channel, in-flight refueling is *not* an option!

As you fly more and more you'll discover the importance—the *necessity*—of making sure everything is ready for uneventful flight *before* you go flying. For now, take my word and the word of your instructor that preflight operations are the most important thing you'll do toward safe flying.

This chapter covers the basics of preflight operations for the "typical" sport pilot-eligible aircraft. Because there are various models and configurations, your preflight checklist will probably be slightly different. The checklist will be in the plane's operating manual that came with the aircraft. It's worthwhile reading.

Inspecting Your Aircraft

It's said there are old pilots and bold pilots, but no old, bold pilots. This is especially true when it comes to preflight inspections. Pilots who are in a hurry to get flying and don't bother to do the preflight, run a much greater chance of in-flight problems than those who take the time to do the job right.

What is the *right* way to inspect your aircraft before flying it? There are a variety of methods and your instructor will show you what he or she prefers. However, most are built around the same procedure—starting inside the cockpit, and then working around the aircraft in a counter-clockwise direction until you're back to the pilot's door and ready to start the engine.

Checking the Cockpit

Your first step in a preflight inspection is to make sure your aircraft is legal. What's required to be legal? Your aircraft must have paperwork onboard that indicates it is airworthy and registered. In addition, it should have the operating handbook with weight and balance information and a list of installed equipment.

If you're renting a craft, or even if you own it, don't assume that all the paperwork is onboard. Make sure it is. Typically, the critical paperwork is in a see-through pouch on the pilot's door or in a glove compartment along with the operating handbook. Get into the habit of verifying that it's there, because the FAA examiner will want to see you verify it during your checkride.

Wing Tips

The preflight inspection list might seem long, but, with practice, it will take you less than 10 minutes and will save you many hours of worry.

Also make sure you have *your* paperwork: your student or sport-pilot certificate, your valid driver's license or third-class FAA medical certificate, and your flight log.

While you're inside the cockpit, do the following:

1. Remove any leftover trash and stow anything that's loose, as appropriate.
2. Make sure the parking brake is set. You don't want the plane rolling away while you're inspecting it.
3. Remove any locks on the control yoke or stick (installed to keep the plane from lifting off the ground in a strong wind).
4. Make sure the ignition switch is off.
5. Make sure the mixture control (if equipped) is off (typically, pulled out).

6. Turn on the master switch, if needed, to check instruments.
7. Check the fuel meter for quantity. Some airplanes might have sight gauges that don't need the master switch turned on.
8. Turn on the aircraft lights and inspect them for operation, then turn them off. Sport pilots can't fly at night, but you might want to turn on aircraft lights to make your plane more visible.
9. Turn off the master switch, if appropriate.
10. Make sure the fuel tank selector is in the correct position, depending on the number and location of fuel tanks.

Take a final look around and then leave the cockpit to continue the inspection. Get rid of any trash you found inside the cockpit.

Examining the Fuselage and Tail

Moving counter-clockwise around the plane, inspect your craft for overall condition as well as the condition and operation of control surfaces such as ailerons, elevators, and rudder. Why? Things can happen. Even if you flew yesterday and parked your craft overnight, you should perform a full preflight inspection. Someone might have accidentally run into and bent a control surface, for example. It's easier to find it now than to write it on an accident report.

Here's a generic preflight–inspection list for the fuselage and tail of your sport aircraft:

1. Inspect the fuselage from behind the pilot's door to the tail section, looking for condition and damage. Remember to squat down and look at the underside of the fuselage as well.
2. If the elevators or rudder have control surface locks (to protect them from moving in wind gusts), remove them.
3. If equipped with a tail wheel, inspect the wheel, attached spring, and steering mechanism.
4. Disconnect the tail tie-down (the chain or rope attaching the tail to the ground), if any.
5. Carefully check the elevators for smooth movement, and inspect the cable and hinges that control them.

Wing Tips

These preflight inspection steps assume that your craft is parked outside with tie-downs. Of course, if it's parked in a hangar—lucky it!—removing tie-downs isn't necessary.

6. Carefully check the rudder for smooth movement, and inspect the cable and hinges that control it.
7. Inspect the trim tab (if any) on the trailing edge of the elevators and rudder.
8. Inspect the fuselage from the tail section to the right wing.

Examining the Right Wing

You're nearly half done with your preflight inspection. Continue it by inspecting the right wing, its control surfaces, and fuel tanks. Here's how it's done:

1. Inspect the flap surface, control rod, and hinges for condition if the plane is equipped with them. Some sport aircraft combine flaps with ailerons, called flaperons, and other craft don't have flaps.
2. Carefully check the right aileron for smooth movement, and inspect the cable and hinges that control it.
3. Inspect the right wingtip for condition, especially if it has been a rental plane or has been parked near other planes.
4. Inspect the wing-tip light lens for damage if lights are installed.
5. Check the condition of the right wing's leading edge, looking for damage, excessive bugs, or ice that can reduce the plane's ability to lift.
6. Disconnect the tie-down from the right wing.
7. Inspect the right tire for proper inflation and make sure there are no grease leaks from the wheel bearings or hydraulic leaks from the brakes.
8. Inspect the top and underside of the right wing for obvious damage.
9. Use the quick drain and vial to draw and inspect fuel from the right-wing tank, if equipped. Each plane is different, so make sure you read the operating handbook to find out the right way of doing this. You are verifying the octane color (noted in the operating handbook) of the fuel, as well as looking for sediments or water in the fuel.
10. Check the level of fuel in the right-wing tank. This is relatively easy in low-wing aircraft, but might require a ladder for high-wing planes.

CAUTION

Stall Warning!

Make sure the gas cap vent hole is clear of debris and make sure you replace the cap securely. You don't want fuel spilling out in a bank or being siphoned off by the wind!

Inspecting the Engine

The engine of your sport aircraft could be easy to inspect or difficult, depending on the design of the cowling (cover). Some slower craft don't have cowling, so the engine is hanging out there in the breeze. Other planes have cowling that is difficult to remove, so your inspection will be limited to opening an inspection door to check oil and look around. Here's the typical process:

1. Find and remove the oil level stick following the manufacturer's recommendations. Make sure you know what the "full" level and what the "add" point are; they're not always written on the stick. As needed, add to the oil, but never above the "full" mark.

Wing Tips

Some airplanes have oil tanks with a sight gauge rather than a dipstick. It's also possible you might fly a plane powered with a two-cycle engine that mixes the oil with the fuel.

2. Inspect the engine for signs of fuel or oil leaks.
3. Look around for nesting critters, debris, or other problematic stowaways.
4. Inspect the engine mounts, wires, and any other connections that could come loose in flight to spoil your day.
5. Check the propeller and spinner (cover) for nicks and damage.
6. Check the air filter for debris, and clean or replace as needed.
7. Make sure the cowling and any inspection doors are securely in place.
8. Inspect the nose-wheel tire for proper inflation and the nose-wheel shock-absorbing system condition.
9. Remove the nose-gear chocks (the wedges that block the movement of the wheel), and move them out of the path the plane will take to taxi out.
10. Inspect the static source hole for blockage, typically located on the fuselage.
11. Inspect the windshield and clean as needed.

Examining the Left Wing

You're almost back to the pilot's door. Just one more wing to go. It has some extras that the right wing didn't, so let's take a look:

1. Inspect the top and underside of the left wing for obvious damage.
2. Check the level of fuel in the left wing tank, if equipped, making sure the gas cap is securely in place and the cap vent is clear.
3. Check the condition of the left wing's leading edge, looking for damage, excessive bugs, or ice.
4. Check the stall warning indicator (if installed) on the leading edge of the wing, following instructions in the craft's operating handbook.
5. Inspect the pitot tube below the wing's leading edge, making sure that the orifice isn't blocked with debris. Some pitot tubes have protective covers that must be removed before flying; others must be pulled out for operation.
6. Disconnect the tie-down from the left wing.
7. Inspect the left wingtip and light lens for condition.
8. Carefully check the left aileron for smooth movement, and inspect the cable and hinges that control it.
9. Inspect the flap surface, control rod, and hinges for condition, if the plane is equipped with them.
10. Inspect the left tire for proper inflation and leaks.

Congratulations on completing your preflight inspection! It's a vital part of safe flying and as you get more proficient, you can reduce the time needed to finish, but *never* take shortcuts. This is your last chance to do anything about problems that could ruin an otherwise fine day of flying.

Starting and Taxiing Your Aircraft

How to start and taxi your sport plane depends somewhat on the model. However, most general aircraft have similar starting procedures that we cover here. Your plane's operating handbook and your instructor will offer variations, but the following should get you started.

Start Your Engine

Starting an aircraft, especially a simple aircraft, is easy. It's a little more complex than starting a car, but not by much. You'll soon have the process down and do it smoothly in a matter of seconds. Here's a typical list:

1. Adjust seat, and latch your seatbelts.
2. Test the brakes and press them down. If your craft has a parking brake, move it to the "off" position.
3. Make sure all circuit breakers are in place and electrical equipment is off.
4. Move the fuel tank selector valve(s) to the correct position for takeoff.
5. If your engine is equipped with a manual primer, prime the engine per the operating handbook (typically two to five pushes on the primer for cold engines), then lock the primer. Some airplanes use an electric primer and some do not use a primer at all.
6. Push the carburetor heater, if your airplane has one, all the way in (cold).
7. Place the throttle to the specified starting position.
8. If a mixture control is installed, set it to the correct position for starting. After starting, the mixture control might have to be adjusted for *density altitude.*
9. Turn the master switch to "on."
10. Turn the ignition switch to "start" and release once the engine starts (just like on a car). If your craft doesn't have a starter, you'll need someone to turn the prop for you; make sure it's someone who knows how to do it safely.
11. Check the oil pressure to make sure it's within the green range within 30 seconds; if not, shut down the engine and investigate. Remember, two-cycle engines do not have an oil-pressure gauge.
12. Check the ammeter for proper operation if your airplane has a generating system.
13. Turn on the anticollision light and radio if your airplane has this equipment.
14. Verify that flaps, if equipped, are up.

Flying Words

Pressure altitude is what the altimeter reads when the pressure is set to 29.92 inches of mercury. **Density altitude** is the pressure altitude corrected for nonstandard conditions such as high or low temperature. Density altitude is also known as performance altitude, or the altitude at which the plane thinks it is flying at. For example, a high-density altitude can make an aircraft think it is taking off from a high-altitude airport and require a longer runway. Your plane's operating handbook will give you more specifics.

Taxiing

Taxiing an aircraft is different from driving a car, primarily because power isn't in the wheels but in the propeller. The prop has to pull (or push) your plane along, and it takes a nudge to get it moving, especially if your plane is parked on grass.

Here's the typical process for taxiing at an uncontrolled airport:

1. Push the throttle in enough to get the plane moving forward, then reduce power so it is moving at the pace of a fast walk.
2. Reduce the power to idle and gently test the brakes for smooth, even grip, then apply enough power to continue taxiing.
3. Use the rudder pedals to direct the aircraft nose, stepping on the pedal on the side you want to go. Make sure you don't inadvertently hit the brake pedal.
4. As needed, apply the brakes to make a tight turn on a taxiway. Don't press hard and continuously on the brakes.
5. Watch the heading and turn indicators (if equipped) to make sure they're responding to your movements of the aircraft controls.
6. Continue taxiing toward the appropriate runway (which depends on the wind direction) and stop short of the runway for the run-up (your final check before takeoff).

CAUTION

Stall Warning!

Make sure you know how much crosswind your plane can fly in. It's in the operating handbook. Some older planes do not list a crosswind limit, so ask your instructor.

As you taxi you could be facing a head-, cross-, or tailwind that, if excessive, can push your little plane around. To counteract this, use your control yoke or stick to deflect the wind's power on your wings. For headwinds and frontal crosswinds, turn the yoke or stick fully *toward* the wind and keep the elevator neutral. For tailwinds and rear crosswinds, turn the yoke or stick fully *away* from the wind with the elevators down (controller away from you).

The Run-Up

Somewhere just short of the runway you will perform a final check (called the run-up) of all systems by following your craft's before-takeoff checklist. It's your last chance to make sure everything is working smoothly before heading off into the wild blue yonder—where there are no service station clouds. Here's a typical before-takeoff checklist:

1. Make sure all cabin doors are closed and locked, and that all seat belts or shoulder harnesses are fully secured.
2. Because you will add power to the propeller, look behind your craft to make sure that doing so won't spray loose gravel or other hard objects onto people or other planes.
3. Set the parking brake, if equipped with one.
4. Push in the throttle to the manufacturer's recommended run-up RPM, typically about 50 percent of full power.
5. Watch the engine tachometer as you check each magneto for a couple seconds each. Your operating handbook specifies how much power you could lose when the engine is run with one magneto turned off. When done, make sure the engine is running on both magnetos.
6. If your engine has carburetor heat, watch the engine tachometer as you pull it on and verify that the RPM drop is what the manufacturer recommends.
7. Check each engine instrument to make sure it's running in the green (okay) range.
8. Pull the throttle back to the idle speed, referring to the tachometer and the operating handbook.
9. If equipped, set the navigation and communications radios.
10. Check the fuel quantity against what you discovered during your preflight inspection of the fuel tanks.
11. Check each of the flight instruments to make sure they are operating correctly.
12. If a heading indicator is installed, set it to match the magnetic compass reading.
13. Move the flight controls to make sure they move freely and appropriately, looking back to see how the ailerons and, if you can see them, elevators and rudder respond.
14. Set the mixture control depending on the density altitude (see above).
15. If a carburetor heat is installed, place it in the full-cold position.
16. Make sure the fuel selector(s) is set to the correct position for takeoff.
17. Set the flaps (if equipped) and the elevator trim to the takeoff positions.
18. Get mentally ready to move forward and take off.

That wasn't so hard. You'll soon discover that it takes much more time to read these steps than to actually do them. Your craft's operating handbook will have specific checklists for the preflight inspection, starting, taxiing, and pretakeoff processes. Practice them. Memorize them. But don't depend on your memory. Use your checklists to help ensure that you and your future passengers all have enjoyable and safe flights.

In the next chapter you actually take off and fly your plane. You'll also learn about flying airport patterns and other important steps to becoming a sport pilot.

The Least You Need to Know

- Preflight operations are vital to your having a safe and enjoyable flight, so make sure you do them every time.
- Most of the preflight inspection is checking to make sure that things are as they are supposed to be; if you don't know what they should be, ask or read up.
- Taxiing an aircraft is a relatively easy task, but it isn't like driving a car, so new skills need to be developed.
- The run-up is your final chance to make sure everything is ready to fly before heading into the sky.

Chapter 8

Pattern Flying

In This Chapter

- Taking off from the airport
- Flying straight and level
- Making moderate turns
- The key to landing your airplane safely

Excited? I hope so. You've completed a preflight inspection, started your plane, and taxied it to the runway. You're ready to fly!

The most important component of flying is takeoff and landing at an airport. Your instructor will go over airport-pattern flying with you in the specific plane you've selected as your trainer. This chapter introduces you to the flight process (if you haven't yet flown) and serves as a lesson refresher (once you've flown). If available, also use a flight-simulation program (see Chapter 5) to help you practice until you can take off and land in your sleep. It's like driving a car—soon you'll be doing it smoothly and easily.

Normal Takeoff and Climb

Flying off an airport runway is relatively easy. In fact, once you reach take-off speed, your aircraft will want to lift off without any help from you.

You're still the boss, but airplanes are inherently aerodynamic, which should make you feel more comfortable flying them.

I'll cover "normal" takeoff and climb here, meaning without crosswinds and not on a short or soft airstrip. You'll learn those later. For now all you need to know is how to "fly the pattern"—that is, how to take off and land at an airport according to its takeoff and landing pattern, which varies slightly between airports.

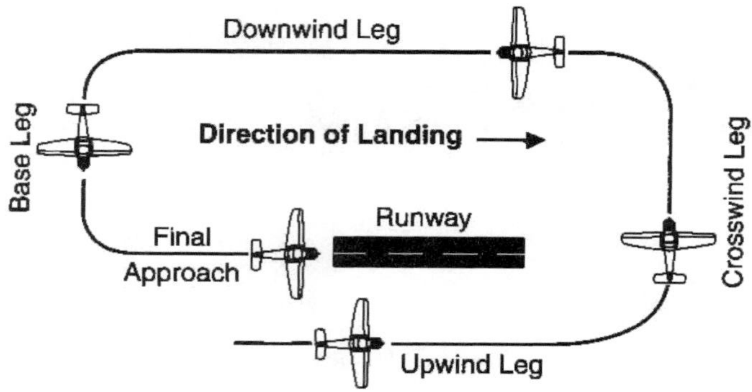

Simple sketch of a traffic pattern.

The Pattern

An airport pattern is the invisible rectangular space over an airport. Most smaller airport patterns are approximately the same, so flying the pattern typically looks like this:

1. Fly off the runway and continue climbing the upwind leg.
2. At about 700 ft. above ground level (AGL), turn the aircraft 90 degrees to the crosswind leg (usually a left turn).
3. At about 1,000 ft. AGL and ½ mile from the runway, turn another 90 degrees to the downwind leg.
4. Fly straight and level until you're about ½ mile past the start of the runway, then start descending.
5. At about 700 AGL, turn 90 degrees to the base leg and begin a descent to lose altitude.
6. Once your plane is lined up with the runway, make a 90-degree descending turn on the final leg.
7. Make control adjustments needed to keep aligned with the runway and pointed at the landing location.
8. Just above the landing point, gently pull the aircraft nose up to make it stall inches above the runway.

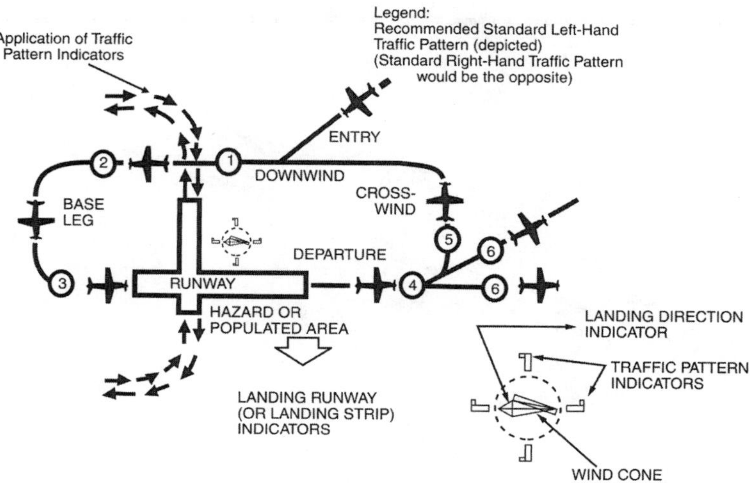

Standard airport pattern including legs and entry points.

As you'll learn, that's a very simplified look at taking off and landing an airplane. Most airports use a left-hand pattern (all turns are to the left) and others have a right-hand pattern. A few have left-hand patterns on some runways and right-hand patterns on others to make sure planes don't bump into each other. Your instructor will tell you what pattern is used at your airport if you haven't figured it out already. And your airport facility directory (AFD) will make it official.

As you can see, the skills you will need to take off and land your aircraft at an airport, called pattern flying, are takeoff, climb, straight-and-level flying, moderate turns, descent, and landing. That's what you'll be introduced to in this chapter.

Taking Off

So your aircraft is ready to taxi on to the runway and take off. First, take a look around the airport pattern to see if any other aircraft are trying to land. If they are, wait. If your plane has a communications radio, you can use it to tell other pilots what you're doing (at an uncontrolled airport): "Evergreen traffic, Kitfox two niner sierra ready for takeoff runway one five Evergreen."

After a final look around the pattern, especially on the base leg, you taxi your aircraft to the centerline of the runway, apply full power to the engine with the throttle, and use the rudder controls to keep the craft lined up with the center of the runway. Once the aircraft reaches the runway liftoff speed (identified in the aircraft's operating handbook) the plane will want to fly itself off the runway.

Normal takeoff and climb.

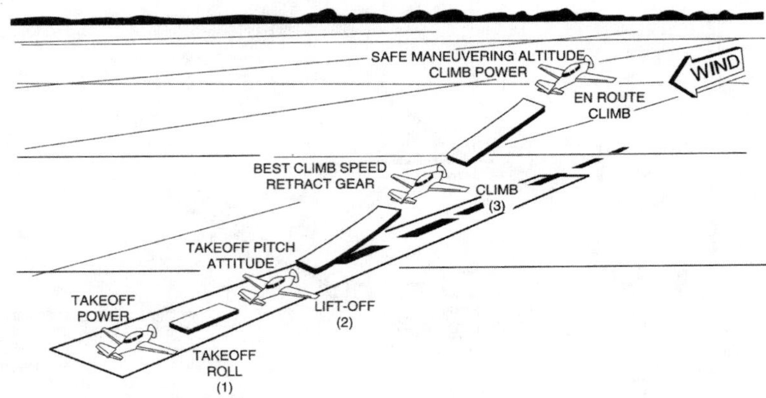

Once the plane is ready to fly you will put it in the takeoff attitude or angle.

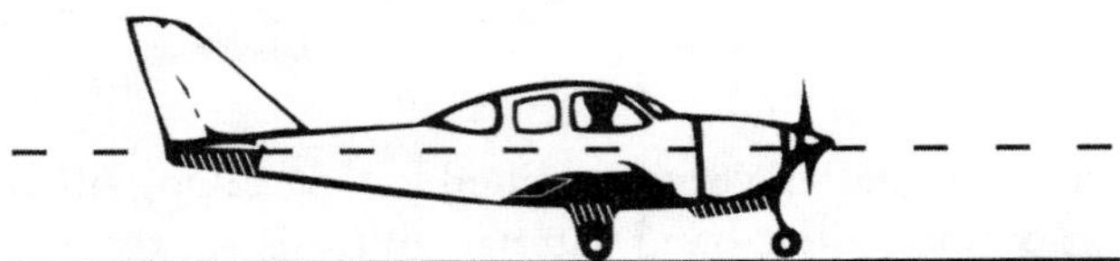
A. Initial roll

B. Takeoff attitude

Stall Warning!

CAUTION

The reason you practice stalls is to know how to recognize and handle one when it happens. Stalls really aren't dangerous—unless they occur at an altitude lower than required for recovery from a stall. So practice, practice, practice those stalls.

If you're flying a tailwheel aircraft, the tail will lift off first as the wind over the wings and elevators start to make the aircraft want to fly. Don't try to force the plane off the ground until it is fully ready. Meanwhile, keep your hand on the throttle in case you have to pull it back to abort the flight.

You probably can't fly along just above the ground forever, so you'll next want to climb. Just make sure the airspeed indicator says you have enough speed to safely do so.

Climbing

As you learned in Chapter 2, the attitude indicator (if your plane is equipped with one) shows you the plane's attitude (angle) in relationship to an artificial horizon. This attitude corresponds to the angle your plane is flying relative to the real horizon. One of the skills you'll be developing is learning the relationship between what the attitude indicator is telling you and what your eyes looking out over the plane's nose and out the windows tell you.

Without an attitude indicator, you'll use the nose attitude angle by looking at the outside horizon. You can also look left and right at the wingtips to determine a pitch angle. This is what instructors call "flying by the seat of your pants" and it's fun!

Instruments during a climb.

For now, know that there is a specific speed and attitude for various types of climbs. If your engine is running at a specific speed and the plane is at a specified angle or attitude, the aircraft is designed to climb (or descend) at a specified rate. So it's very important that you know what this speed and attitude are so you can make your plane climb efficiently—and safely.

Wing Tips

If your aircraft has elevator trim, you can use it to remove some of the pressure required to hold the control yoke or stick back as you climb.

The normal climb speed and attitude for your aircraft is indicated in the aircraft's operating handbook. Once you're flying it's too late to go look it up, so make sure you know what it is. The normal climb speed is called the V_Y or best-rate-of-climb speed. There's another speed for climbing when there is an obstacle (such as big trees or a building) at the end of the runway, called the V_X or best-angle-of-climb speed; it's covered in Chapter 9.

Maintain the normal climb speed until the plane reaches about 500 ft. AGL, or whatever number your instructor tells you. The altitude depends on what the traffic-pattern altitude is and what buildings and obstructions are near the runway.

Turning to Crosswind

The next phase of flying the pattern is making a moderate turn from the takeoff leg to the crosswind leg. It's a gentle turn using coordinated controls, moving the control yoke or stick to bank the aircraft and simultaneously applying rudder pressure as needed (left rudder on a left turn). You can make sure the turn is coordinated by watching the turn coordinator instrument (if you have one) or looking out the window to compare the plane's attitude against the horizon.

Instruments during a turn.

When should you turn from the takeoff (upwind) leg to the crosswind leg? Most pilots suggest that you do so once you can see the nearest end of the runway about halfway between the wing and tail as you look back. This technique also works for determining when to turn from the downwind leg to the base leg later.

Remember that your aircraft is still climbing at the normal climb or best-rate-of-climb speed and attitude. You must maintain this speed and attitude during the turn. For most folks, the climbing turn is a bit challenging, so don't get discouraged if it takes practice to get it right. And it's where you can get into trouble if it's not done smoothly, so your instructor will have you practicing this combination maneuver until you can do it easily.

Wing Tips

If you have a flight-simulation program or a flight simulator available to you, practice flying the pattern—especially climbing and descending turns—until you can do them well. You will not only gain flight confidence but also speed your learning process. Refer to Chapter 5 for more information on flight simulation.

Straight and Level Flying

You've reached pattern altitude, typically 800 to 1,200 AGL and are about ½ mile from the airport. It's time to turn to the downwind leg of the traffic pattern. Remember that it's a coordinated turn. Also remember that your altitude indicator measures in feet above mean sea level (MSL), so add the airport altitude to the AGL-pattern altitude to determine what the altitude indicator should read as you traverse the airport pattern. For example, over an airport at 600 ft. MSL, you should fly a 1,000 ft. AGL pattern at 1,600 ft. MSL.

Straight-and-level flying simply means cutting back on the engine speed to what's called the cruise speed. It is the airspeed at which all four forces (lift, weight, thrust, drag) are equal and your plane flies straight ahead with wings level. Much of your flying and certainly the easiest flying you'll do is straight and level.

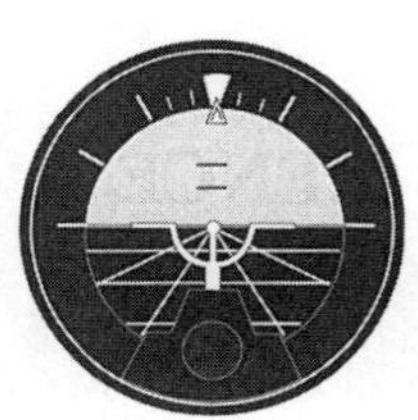

Instruments during straight-and-level flight.

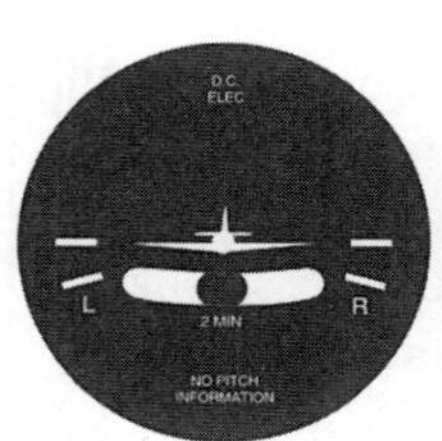

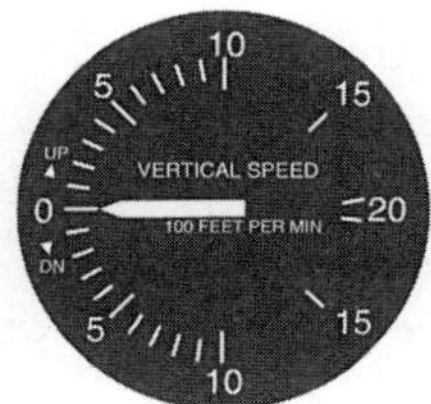

The straight part means flying so that the aircraft is flying in a straight line forward. Make sure you are maintaining a constant course (not left or right) on the magnetic compass or heading indicator.

The level part means keeping the wings equidistant above (high-wing aircraft) or below (low-wing aircraft) the horizon. Your plane's attitude indicator (if your plane has one) will help, but it's better to simply look out the side windows and make appropriate control adjustments:

- If the left wing is low, apply *light* right-aileron and coordinated right-rudder pressure.
- If the right wing is low, apply *light* left-aileron and coordinated left-rudder pressure.

One of the skills you must develop for the FAA practice test, as well as for your own flying, is holding a heading during straight-and-level flight. First, make sure your heading indicator is adjusted to match the heading on the magnetic compass. In fact, you shouldn't even attempt to set the heading indicator until you're in straight-and-level flight and the compass (bouncing around in a liquid) has settled down for an accurate reading. If you don't have a heading indicator, you maintain your heading by using the magnetic compass.

A magnetic compass can wobble around a bit but remember, magnetic compasses have been successfully used to guide airplanes from shortly after the Wright brothers first flew. The best way to hold a heading with a mag compass is to pick a distant object on the ground and fly toward it. Check the mag compass often and if a correction in your heading is needed, adjust to a new target object on the ground.

Knowledge Test

For the practical test you will need to maintain a heading within 10 degrees (plus or minus) of the assigned heading. That is, if the assigned heading is 180 degrees, you'd better not drift beyond a heading of 170 or 190 degrees. In addition, you'll need to maintain an altitude within 100 feet of the assigned altitude. If the assigned altitude is 3,500 ft. MSL, you must stay in the range of 3,400 to 3,600 ft. MSL. In fact, your instructor won't let you take the practice test until you have proven you can do this consistently.

One more point about the downwind leg of the traffic pattern: If you're flying in to another airport, standard operating procedure is to join the downwind leg at a 45-degree angle at about the midpoint of the downwind leg. At 45 degrees you can see and be seen by other aircraft more easily. If you're flying into a controlled airport, you must ask permission to land from air traffic control (ATC). If you're flying into an uncontrolled airport, you must announce your intention to pilots in the area this way: "Evergreen traffic, Kitfox two niner sierra entering downwind for full landing runway one five Evergreen."

Remember, sport pilots cannot fly into controlled airspace nor land at controlled airports until they have had appropriate training and their logbook is endorsed for controlled-airspace flying by a flight instructor.

Descent

What goes up must come down, including your plane. That's good—as long as you do it safely! As you've probably figured out already, the trick to descent is reducing your airspeed to normal descent speed, which varies between aircraft. Here's the typical process:

1. Abeam (90 degrees from) the end of the runway, begin the plane's descent by reducing power to the recommended descent speed (V_{SO}).
2. As needed or instructed, apply carburetor heat if the airplane is equipped with one.
3. Once airspeed is within the white (flap operating range) range of the airspeed indicator, apply flaps (if equipped) as recommended in the plane's operating handbook to slow the aircraft down.
4. Make a coordinated turn to the base leg while continuing the descent.
5. Apply additional flaps, as recommended, to further reduce airspeed as suggested by the manufacturer and your instructor.

Instruments during descent.

6. Make a coordinated turn to the final leg while continuing the descent.
7. Coordinate the throttle and elevators to control the plane's approach speed and rate of descent.

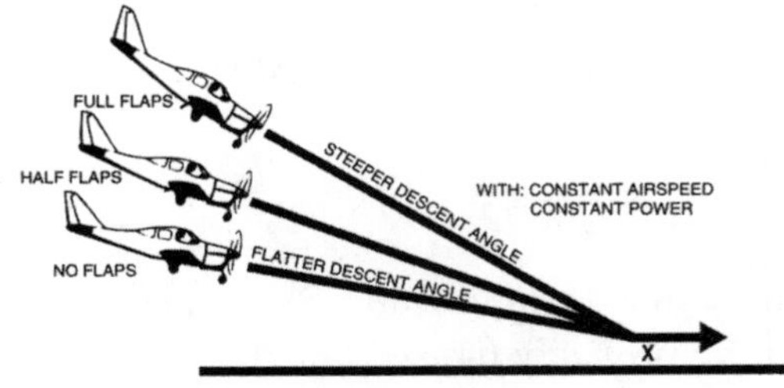

Flaps reduce your landing airspeed.

You're ready to land your plane. You're almost home!

Landing Your Plane

It's said that landing an aircraft is the most challenging part of flying. It can be. It's also the one you will practice the most. You'll have dozens of landings under your belt before you ever go for the practice test. And many of the maneuvers you'll be taught as you learn to fly will simulate good landings and teach you how to avoid bad ones.

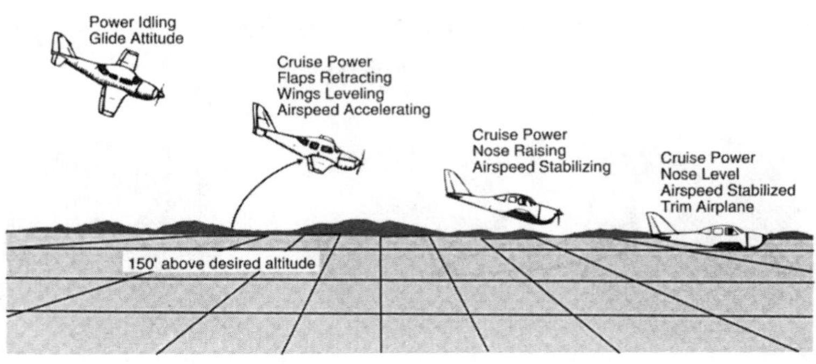

The key to landing is doing it at the attitude and speed for which the plane is designed to land.

The key to landing is doing it by the numbers. That is, your aircraft has a specific approach speed and attitude (angle) that works best. Make sure you know what these conditions are before you ever try to land your aircraft. The most common cause of bad landings is incorrect airspeed—either too fast or too slow. Because you are descending, the tendency is to come in too fast.

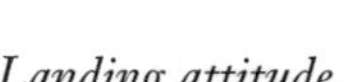

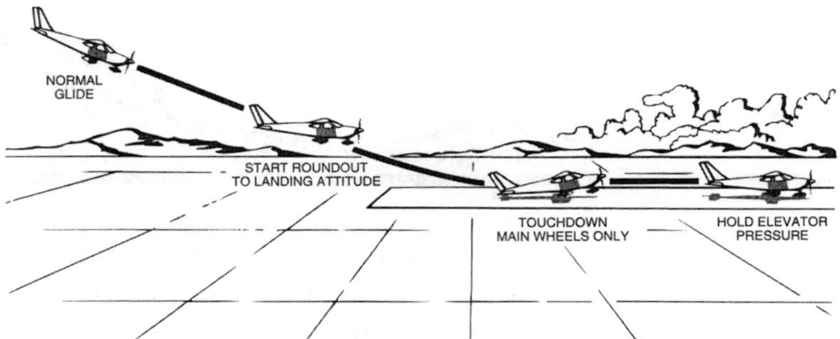

Landing attitude.

Another key to good landings is knowing what a good landing should look like from the cockpit. That takes practice and is why your instructor is sitting there talking you through it. Here's what he or she might be telling you:

First, know that the outline of the runway should be long and straight ahead of you, not tipped to one side or the other in your vision.

Second, a good landing means aiming for "the numbers," the runway identifier numbers at the beginning of the runway. You must fly directly to them (until the last few seconds), which means that they should appear to stay in the same place on your plane's windshield. If they seem to move up you're coming in too low. If they're moving down on the windshield you're coming in too high. Many airports have visual slope indicators (VSIs), lights that help you determine if you're coming in too high or too low. Refer to the FAA's *Pilot's Handbook of Aeronautical Knowledge* or your ground-school course for specifics on how to use them.

Knowledge Test

Make sure you know how to read all the markings and signs found on airport runways. If you're coming in on final approach, you won't have time to look up something in your *Aeronautical Informa-tion Manual*. That's why studying for your FAA knowledge test is so important.

Third, as soon as you pass the runway threshold (beginning), the throttle should be positioned as described in the plane's operating handbook (usually at idle or with a small amount of power). You then change the flight angle of your aircraft to slow and control your descent to the runway. Your instructor will help you see what this looks like.

Fourth, once you get within about 10 feet above the ground, you will run into ground effect, a layer of air that tries to keep you from landing. Think of it as an air pillow. As you near the runway, you will slowly level out by pulling back on the control yoke or stick until your craft begins to "stall" or quits flying and turns into a land vehicle. Your goal is to make this happen inches above the runway surface.

Ground effect can keep your plane from landing smoothly, called a "bounce."

If you're flying a tailwheel, you instructor will probably start by teaching you three-point landings. In a three-point landing, the tail wheel and the main gear touch down at the same time. If you're flying a tri-gear aircraft, you will touch down on the two main wheels, then the nose wheel. The nose and tail wheels aren't intended to take much abuse, so make sure you're on the ground and rolling slowly before allowing these wheels to touch the ground. At that point, your control yoke or stick will be fully pulled back toward you.

Congratulations! You've made your first landing. They'll get much easier as you practice controlling the aircraft. Again, consider using a flight simulator to practice landings ad nauseam.

In coming chapters you learn how to handle takeoffs and landings at short and soft (grass or dirt) fields. You'll also learn how to fly the pattern when the winds are not coming straight down the runway toward you (which rarely happens). You'll also learn how to handle emergencies that can occur on takeoff, landing, during climbs or descents, in turns, and even during straight-and-level flight. Meantime, pat yourself on the back for learning how to fly the pattern.

The Least You Need to Know

- Flying the pattern means taking off, climbing, turning, flying straight and level, descending, and landing your plane.
- Make sure you read your plane's operating handbook to get the optimum speeds for flight attitudes *before* going flying.
- To fly the pattern smoothly, practice making coordinated turns while climbing and descending.
- Much of your future flying will be straight and level as you go from here to there.
- The key to good landings is controlling airspeed and descent to smoothly transition from flying to rolling.

Chapter 9

Solo Flying

In This Chapter

- The thrill of your first solo flight
- Practicing ground-reference maneuvers
- Advanced takeoffs: crosswind, short-field, and soft-field
- Advanced landings: crosswind, short-field, and soft-field

One of the greatest thrills of flying is about to happen. You're going to solo your sport aircraft—you're going to take off, fly, and land with no one sitting beside you to say, "Pitch, power!"

Scary, huh?!

It shouldn't be. In fact, what you're probably feeling is excitement rather than fear. The difference between the two is that excitement occurs when the butterflies in your stomach fly in formation without crashing into each other. And it is knowledge that controls them.

This chapter starts after your first takeoff (discussed in Chapter 8) and moves you toward your first cross-country trip (discussed in Chapter 10). In this period you will learn many new flying skills. Most important, you will learn confidence in your aircraft and in yourself.

Let's go flying!

Your First Solo

Chapter 6 introduced you to what you'll be doing as you learn to fly, including a typical lesson plan for sport pilots. The step that gets most folks' attention is the solo flight. It's usually just a few takeoffs and landings at your home airport, but it's significant in that it's the first time you fly by yourself. Once your instructor endorses your logbook and your student certificate for solo flight, you can legally fly by yourself—as long as you don't do anything you're not endorsed for, such as fly into controlled airspace or fly a cross-country trip (more than 75 miles).

For your instructor, your solo flight also has significance because it's your first payoff for the effort you both have been putting in to your learning to fly. Your instructor now has your heightened attention and you're ready to learn at a new level. To get to the point of soloing, most instructors give you training in additional flight maneuvers, ground-reference maneuvers, and airport operations. Some give you rudimentary training in these skills, let you solo, and then bring you back down for additional dual (with instructor) training. Others teach as many of these skills as you're willing to learn before turning you loose with your first solo. Let's take a look at what you'll probably be learning before you get to solo.

Wing Tips

Your airplane could *sound* different to you on your first solo flight. What you hear is the silence of *not* hearing your instructor "nagging" at you. It's a wonderful silence, so enjoy it while you can!

Intentionally Stalling Your Plane

A stall occurs when the wings can no longer support the aircraft in flight. Weight is greater than lift. What happens? The plane enters a high rate of descent that cannot be allowed to continue to the ground.

Here's a secret: Your plane is designed to *not* stall. In fact, some aircraft are difficult to make stall. You'll have to do something dumb like keep pulling back on the yoke or stick to keep it in a stall. If you let go of the control the nose will dip in a stall, airspeed will build up and it will—without your interference—recover itself from a stall. The only time this isn't true is when the altitude required for recovery is less than your altitude off the ground. That's why you'll be learning to force a stall at altitude so you can learn how to quickly recover. Many sport aircraft can recover from a stall in just 100 to 200 ft. of altitude.

So you'll be practicing stalls with your instructor, typically at 2,000 ft. above ground level (AGL) or above. You'll practice both power-on and power-off stalls. A power-on stall can occur during takeoff and a power-off stall can occur when you're attempting to land. Remember, you *want* a power-off stall to occur a few inches above the runway when you land. Any higher and you're going to bounce or crash.

When will you know that your aircraft is at or near a stall? Your plane will tell you. Many aircraft have a stall-warning device mounted on a wing, a noisemaker that is activated when the wing's angle of attack is too high for the relative wind over the wings. On some aircraft it sounds like a dysfunctional duck call. In addition, as a plane approaches a stall, the controls will become less responsive or "mushy" and you'll need more effort to control the craft than at higher speeds.

Stall Warning!

Never attempt a practice maneuver in which the lowest altitude you reach is less than 1,500 ft. AGL. It just doesn't give you enough room to recover before planting your plane.

Some aircraft have very pronounced stalls, but most newer models simply dip their noses to build up airspeed and fly themselves out of the stall. Your response to a stall should be …

1. Apply moderate forward pressure on the yoke or stick to increase airspeed.
2. Simultaneously add throttle to recover lost altitude.

One of the reasons you'll be practicing is to show you how much forward pressure is needed on the yoke or stick. If you don't put the nose down enough or you pull the nose back up too quickly, your plane could stall again—called a secondary stall.

Remember, stalls are not something you do in everyday flight. You are learning them for three reasons:

1. To recognize the onset of a stall so you can prevent one from occurring
2. To recover from a stall with a minimum loss of altitude if one does occur
3. To demonstrate a stall during the practical test

Flying Slowly

As you've learned, the slowest flying you will do is when landing your airplane. Slow flight is a challenge for new pilots. There seems to be so much to remember and so little time to remember it. That's why you'll learn—and repeatedly practice—the fine art of flying slowly.

Slow flight means keeping control of your aircraft at a speed just above the speed at which it stalls. Check your plane's operating handbook for the specific airspeed suggested for slow flight maneuvers. Your instructor will know the numbers, too. For many planes it's 1.2 times the stall speed. For a craft with a stall speed of 39 knots, the slow flight speed is 47 knots (39 × 1.2).

The purpose of slow flight maneuvers is to illustrate what the controls feel like as the plane approaches its stall speed. Because the craft is flying at a slower speed—meaning less relative wind is flowing over the wings and tail—the controls don't respond in the same way they do when lots of relative wind goes by. So, naturally, the flight controls require more movement to get the same effect they have when the plane is flown faster.

Here are the typical steps to maneuvering your aircraft in slow flight:

1. Apply flaps (if equipped) to reduce the stall speed.
2. Pull carburetor heat on (if equipped with it and recommended by the manufacturer).
3. Reduce power.
4. Reduce airspeed and maintain altitude by applying back pressure on the control yoke or stick.
5. Apply rudder pressure as needed to maintain flight coordination.
6. As airspeed approaches stall speed, add power to maintain altitude.
7. Adjust pitch attitude to control airspeed.
8. Apply trim as needed to maintain slow flight with the least back pressure on the yoke or stick.

From this point of slow flight you can practice—gently—various flight maneuvers such as climbs, descents, and turns. Your instructor also will show you how to maintain slow flight with incrementally more flaps (if your plane is equipped with flaps).

Practicing slow flight makes sense. You're not only learning how controls respond at low speeds, you're also getting to practice a simulated landing at a safe altitude. If you goof, you have a 1,500-plus–foot margin for error.

Knowledge Test

When performing any practice maneuvers, make clearing turns before you start. That means turning your aircraft left for a 90-degree turn, then right for 90 degrees, checking around you to see what other traffic is nearby. The clearing maneuver also tells other aircraft in the area that you're going to practice maneuvers and that they should stay clear. During your FAA practical test, your flight examiner is apt to flunk you if you don't remember your clearing turns!

Practicing Emergencies

It's the rare pilot who has actually had to make an emergency landing with an aircraft. However, all good pilots are constantly thinking about "what if …?" Your flight instructor will help you develop this mindset. In fact, once you're comfortable with flying, your instructor might reach over, pull the throttle back and say something like: "You just lost your engine. Where are you going to land?"

The first time it happens you might not have a good answer. The second time it happens you'd better have one. Pilots who fly older aircraft know that a plane that's seen hundreds of thousands of air miles can quit flying. Unfortunately, even new aircraft can—for different reasons.

The most common reason why aircraft quit flying is the same reason cars block rush-hour traffic: They run out of gas! And, just as there are no gas stations in the middle of the freeway, there are none in the clouds, either. So the best way to prepare for an emergency is to make sure you've done everything to prevent it. Chapter 7 covers preflight inspection, the most important step in minimizing flight emergencies. The second step is: be prepared.

Remember that your instructor isn't there just to ask tough questions. He or she is there to teach you to fly safely. That means you can ask the instructor the same question: "I just lost my engine. Where am I going to land—and why?" Your instructor will probably tell you, above all, "No matter what happens, keep flying the aircraft." You'll quickly learn about maintaining control, analyzing wind direction and speed, setting up a glide, attempting to resolve the emergency, and other important factors. In fact, your plane's operating handbook might even have a checklist for logically handling in-flight emergencies.

Ground-Reference Maneuvers

Flying isn't a contest, so why should your instructor ask you to fly a rectangular course, perform coordinated S-turns, or make even turns around a point? Because these are skills you will use when flying, especially when flying airport patterns with a wind.

Wind can help you get to your destination or make it more difficult. In most cases, it simply wants to blow you off course. You want to go straight ahead toward your destination and it wants to push you to one side. What's the solution?

Learning to deal with the unseen wind might seem like a lose-lose situation, but it isn't. Once you actually "see" the wind and visualize how it will impact your flight, you can make adjustments to diffuse much of its power. In fact, a tailwind (one from behind your aircraft) can increase your speed over the ground.

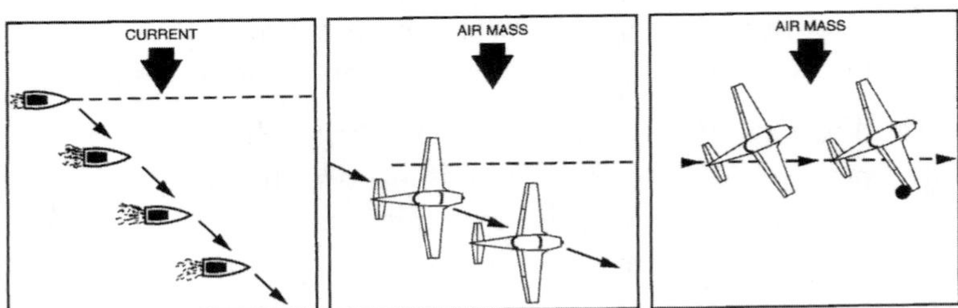

Ground-reference maneuvers help you learn how to compensate for winds.

How can you see the unseen wind? By looking for telltale signs. It's relatively easy at airports, because you'll see windsocks and other devices that show you the wind's direction at ground level. You want to take advantage of the wind there and fly into the wind, if possible, so that it will let you set down at a lower ground speed. But even up in the air you can quickly learn how to read the wind by looking at factory smoke, large trees, or the wind across the water. In addition, weather forecasts (what will happen soon) and weather reports (what's happening now) will give you a good idea of what the wind is probably doing.

The easiest way to compensate for wind is to pick a point on the horizon or at least 10 miles away and fly toward it, compensating for crosswinds by pointing the nose of the plane a little off to one side of the target. You might not be pointed at the target but if your angle is correct, you will be traveling toward it. This maneuver is called crabbing, and the correction angle you are holding is called the crab angle. There are other ways, including using an E6B computer to set a course heading that compensates for wind direction. However, winds change and by the time you use the computer, you might be off course, so first learn how to visually adjust for wind.

During your practical test you must show the examiner that you can perform various *ground-reference maneuvers* while maintaining an altitude within 100 ft. of the starting altitude and airspeed within 10 knots.

Flying Words

Ground-reference maneuvers are practice maneuvers that require you to control the aircraft over a pattern on the ground. Their purpose is to help you develop control skills, especially in relation to winds from various directions.

Rectangular Course

Flying a rectangular course is practice for flying an airport pattern. On each of the legs (upwind, crosswind, downwind, base, final) you will need to compensate for some element of wind, unless it's a rare still-wind day. You need to determine the wind direction and fly a course that tracks you directly over straight lines on the ground (often roads or fence lines).

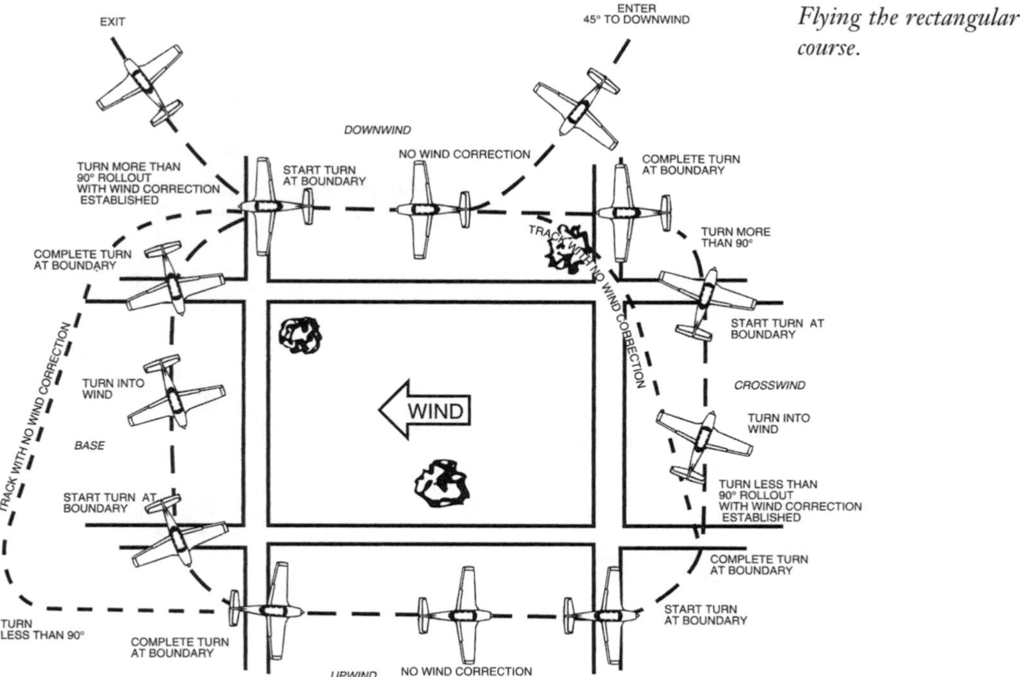

Flying the rectangular course.

Depending on what type of aircraft you're flying (high- or low-wing), you will learn to develop visual cues to convert what you see (your plane drifting to the left due to wind) with what you automatically do (applying a crab angle). The skill is the same, it's the visual cues—estimating drift based on the visual relationship between the wings and ground objects—that you will teach yourself by practice.

Remember to use the turn coordinator (if your plane has one) on all turns to make sure they are smooth. Also, keep a constant distance from the perimeter of the rectangular course. The best method of doing this is to line up visual elements (roads and fences, for example) approximately the same distance below the wing of a high-wing aircraft or above the wing of a low-wing aircraft.

S-Turns

S-turns are ground-reference maneuvers designed to improve your flying skills when confronted with wind, which is most of the time. If there were no wind for this maneuver, you would simply fly half a circle on one side of a road or other marker, then level out, turn, and fly the other half of the circle. The trick is compensating for the wind.

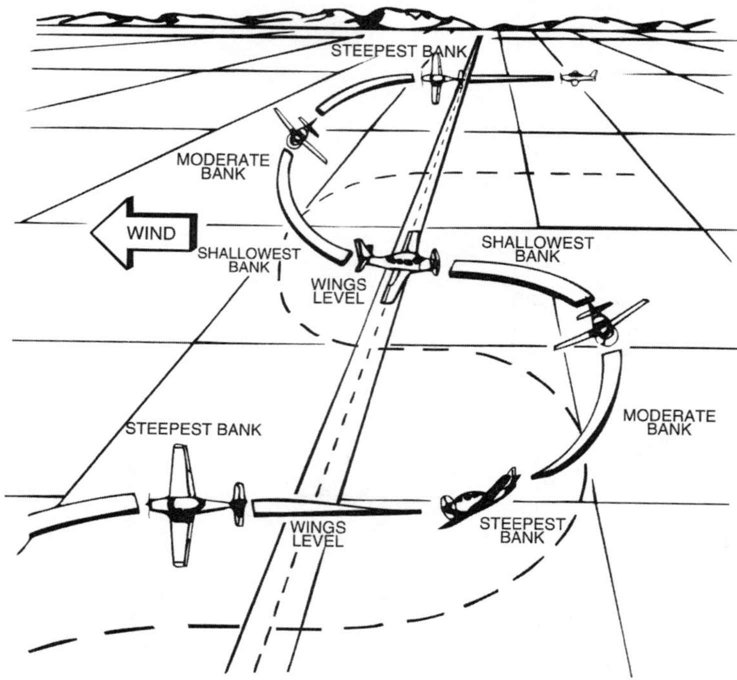

Flying S-turns.

As with other ground-reference maneuvers, the key is compensating for the direction and strength of the wind. To compensate for direction, remember to crab or turn the nose slightly toward the wind. To compensate for wind strength, remember that the wind will increase your ground speed when flying away from it and slow you down as you fly toward the wind.

Turns Around a Point

The purpose of practicing turns around a point is to teach you to make smooth, coordinated turns. For example, if you experience poor visibility and must quickly make a 180-degree turn and go back where you came from, it's good to know how to do it without losing altitude or airspeed.

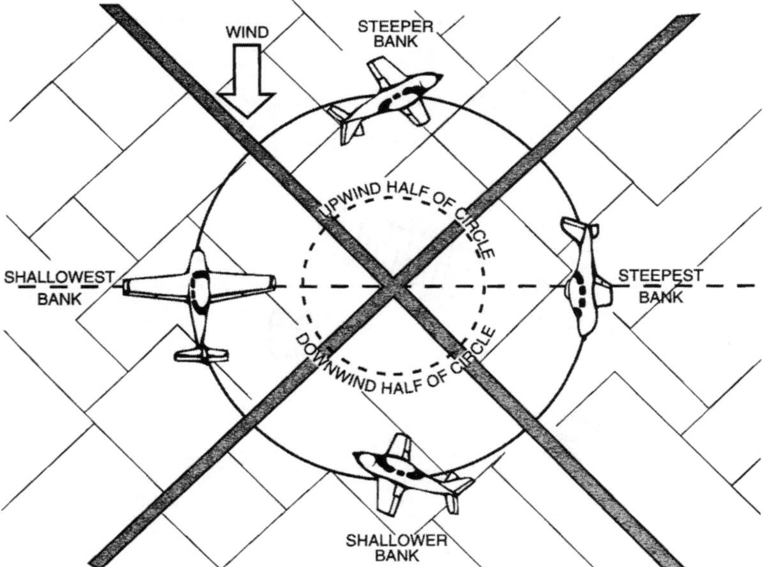

Flying turns around a point.

Your practical test will require two or more complete circles around a ground reference without losing altitude or airspeed. The ground point selected typically is a major road intersection or some other visual target like a large tree. You will adjust the bank angle depending on where the wind is coming from, with the shallowest bank made as the wind becomes a crosswind.

The tricky part of this maneuver for most pilots is the constant adjustments that need to be made, especially of the plane's bank. You'll be looking inside the cockpit to various instruments, then outside to verify that you're making a smooth circle around the object, and then back inside to the controls, and back outside … until the circle is complete.

Advanced Takeoffs

It would be great if all your takeoffs were into the wind, because the wind speed lowers the amount of airspeed your plane needs to begin flying. It also would be nice if all runways were at least 5,000 ft. long and weren't surrounded by obstacles you need to avoid. In the real world, 1,800-ft. grass runways always seem to have trees at both ends and wind that's trying to push you sideways.

That's why you need to practice advanced takeoffs: crosswind takeoffs, short-field takeoffs, and soft-field takeoffs. They are all relatively easy to master and your instructor will help you get the practice and the skill to make them part of the fun of flying. Meantime, expect lots of "do it again!" from your instructor. To help you, here are some tips:

- Always check the windsock or other indicators and make sure you know the direction of the wind at that moment.
- Select a visual reference point directly ahead of the runway centerline and maintain a straight path by applying the rudder as needed.

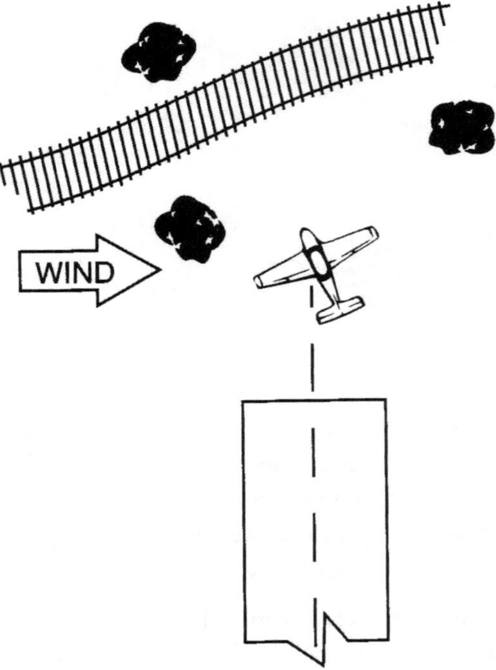

Takeoffs with a side wind require turning slightly into the wind so the plane is not pushed off course.

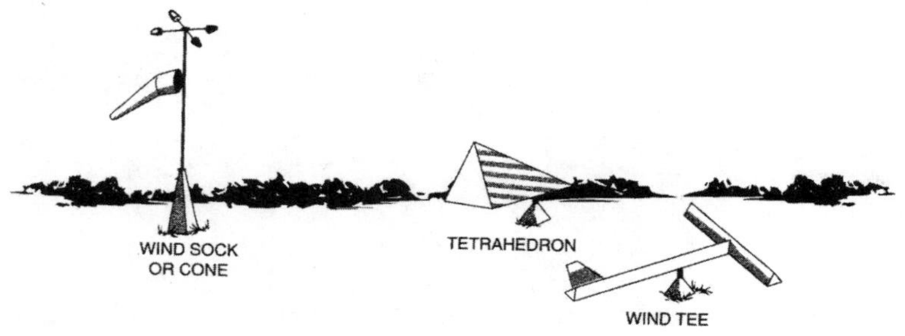

Wind direction indicators.

- Keep your hand on the throttle, ready to cut it if you need to abort the takeoff.
- The purpose of a crosswind takeoff is to compensate for the wind effect on the side of your aircraft. Hold full aileron into the wind, reducing it as your ground speed increases.

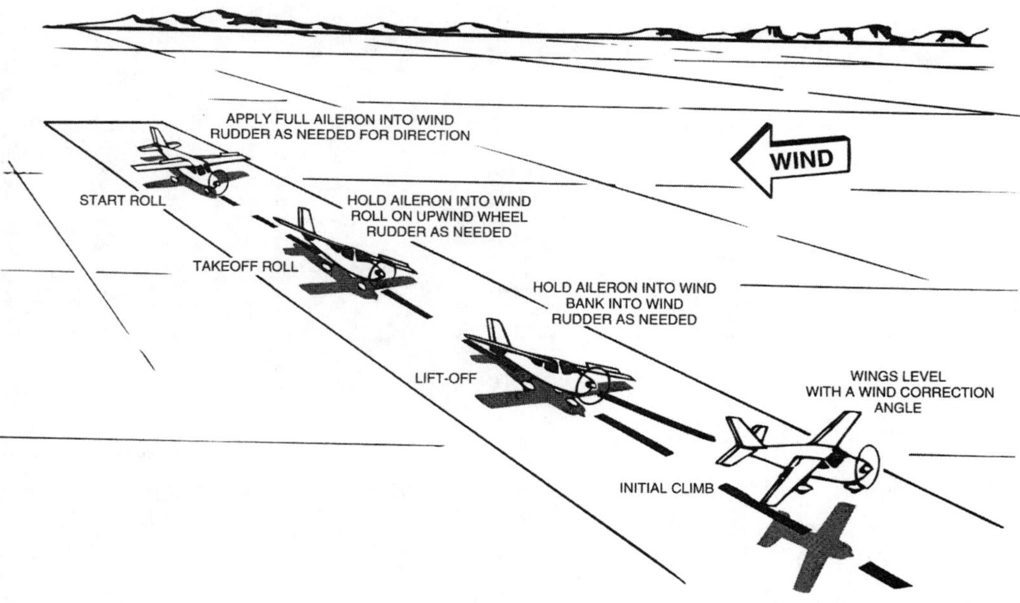

Crosswind takeoff.

- The purpose of a soft-field takeoff is to get the nose wheel off the ground as soon as possible to minimize damage. On a tailwheel airplane, you try to keep the tail wheel low and make a three-wheel liftoff. Apply wing flaps (if equipped) as recommended by the manufacturer to increase lift.

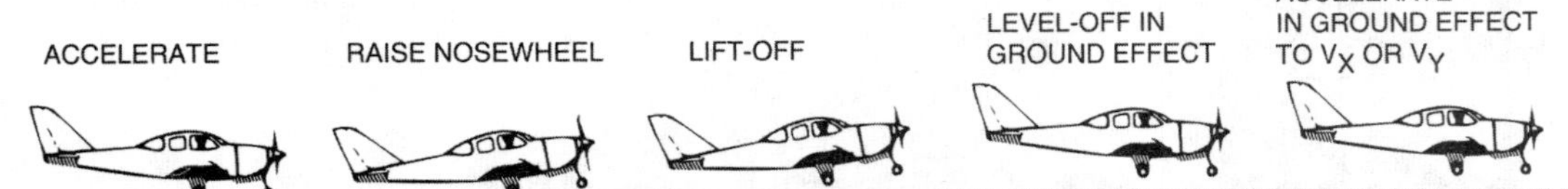

Soft-field takeoff.

- The purpose of a short-field takeoff is to get off the ground at the best angle of climb (V_X) to clear an obstacle. Make sure you know and use the best angle of climb airspeed and attitude as recommended by the manufacturer.
- The most practical way to perform a short-field takeoff is to set the brakes, run the engine up to nearly full throttle, then release the brakes to minimize ground roll.

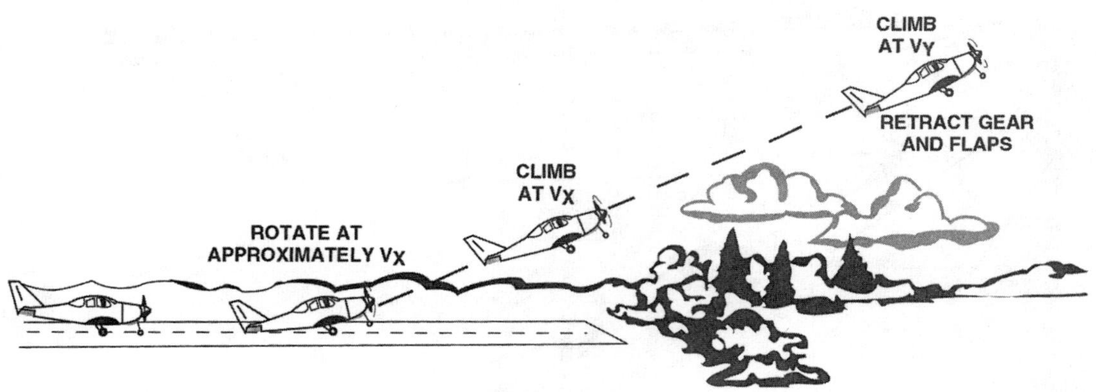

Short-field takeoff.

Your instructor will have you practice these procedures many times before releasing you for the practical test (checkride). That's good. If you ever face an emergency where you have to take off on a short, soft field with crosswinds you'll be glad you practiced, practiced, and practiced some more!

Advanced Landings

Landings are never boring. They require your undivided attention as you transition your vehicle from an air- to a land-craft. Fortunately, they also can be fun because you face a variety of challenges to your skills. They can—and should—be relaxed, but they won't be boring.

Advanced landing maneuvers are similar to those for advanced takeoffs. You'll practice landing with a crosswind, on short airfields, soft airfields, and a combination of these. In fact, your solo practice sessions could include many such advanced landings to help you develop your skills. Remember, the most critical part of flying is landing.

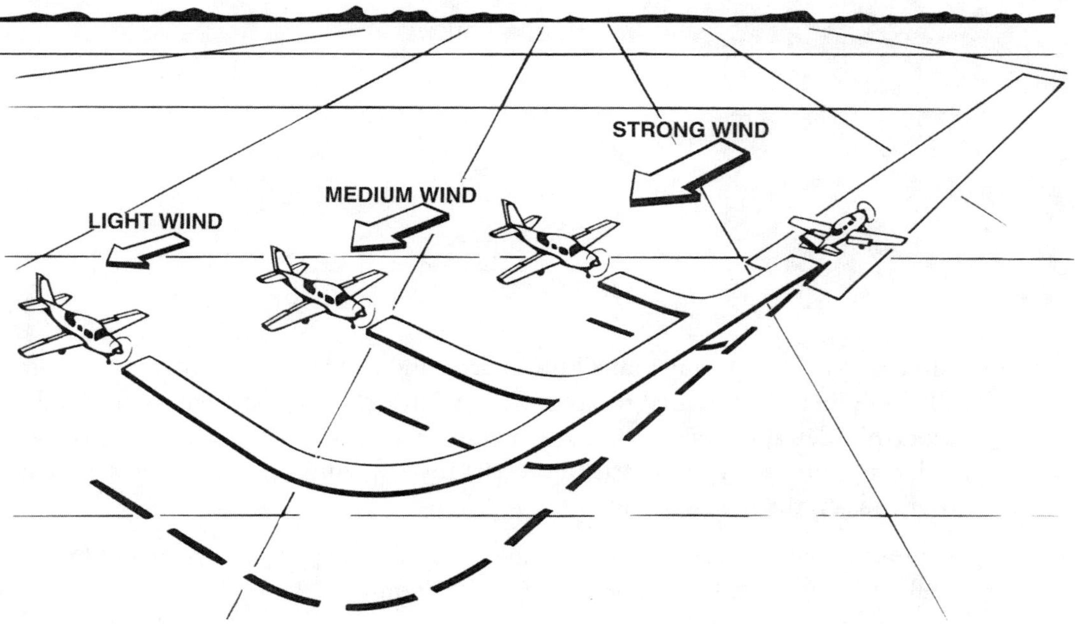

The location where you turn for final approach depends on the direction and strength of the wind.

Your instructor will help you learn how to perform these maneuvers in your specific sport aircraft. Here are some proven tips for making the task easier:

- The crosswind landing will start by holding a crab into the wind on final approach. You will be traveling straight down the runway, but the nose will be off to one side. This is a good way to start but, of course, you can't land like this.
- As the airplane approaches the beginning of the runway you will transition into a "sideslip." This aligns the nose with the runway centerline and actually slides the airplane sideways into the crosswind.

Adjusting for crosswind effect.

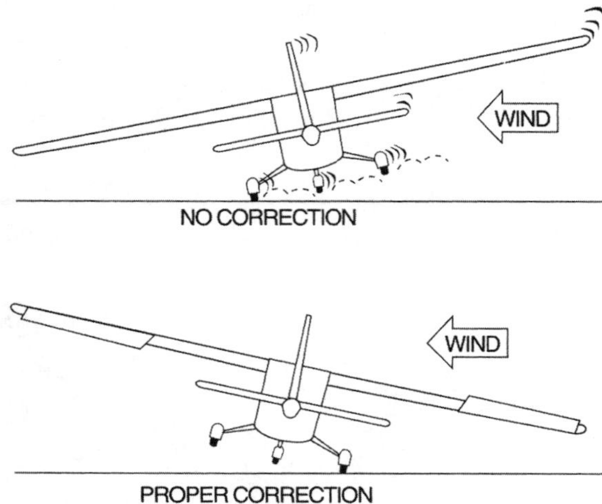

- To enter a sideslip, you control the aileron and rudder differently than in normal flight. The rudder is used to keep the nose straight and the ailerons are used to control sideways movement. For example, in a left crosswind you move the left aileron (using the yoke or stick) to offset the left wind, and move the right rudder to keep the nose straight.
- Always know and use the manufacturer's suggested approach speed and procedures for crosswind, soft-, and short-field landings.

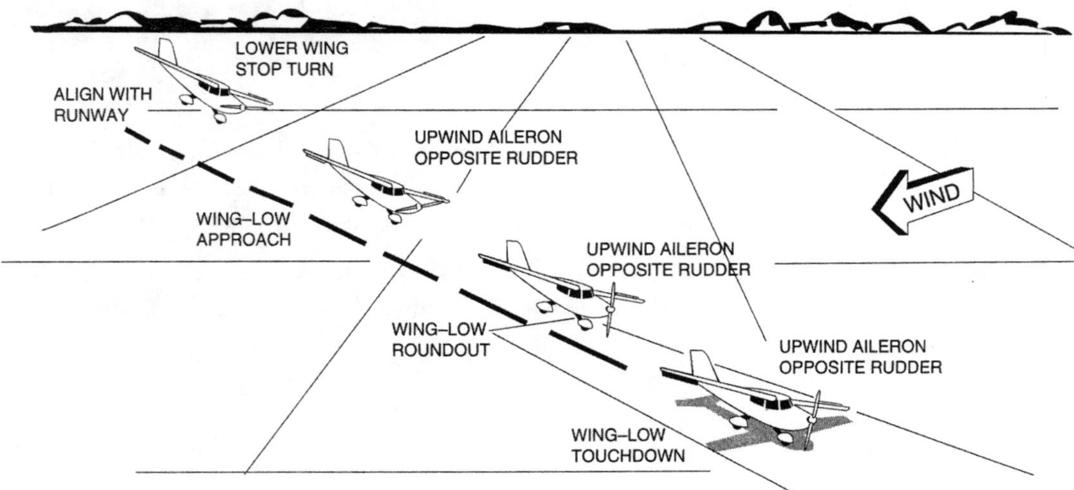

In a crosswind landing, you must sideslip the plane.

- As you cross over the runway threshold (beginning of the runway) power should be at idle or what is recommended in the plane's operating handbook, but your hand should be on the throttle in case you need to abort the landing and perform a *go-around.*
- Short-field landings with an obstacle at the threshold require that you use the plane's best rate-of-descent speed and procedures once you're past the obstacle.
- Soft-field landings require that you land on the main landing gears and keep the nose wheel from touching the ground until speed is reduced to minimize possible damage to the more fragile nose wheel components. On a tailwheel airplane, the touchdown should be made with the tail on the ground or as low as possible.

Flying Words

A **go-around** is a rejected landing that becomes a takeoff so you can go around the traffic pattern again for another landing. Go-arounds are wise to employ when you're coming in too fast or too slow, or there's an object on the runway. If the object is an airplane taking off (oops!), fly to the right side of the craft and get away from it as soon as possible.

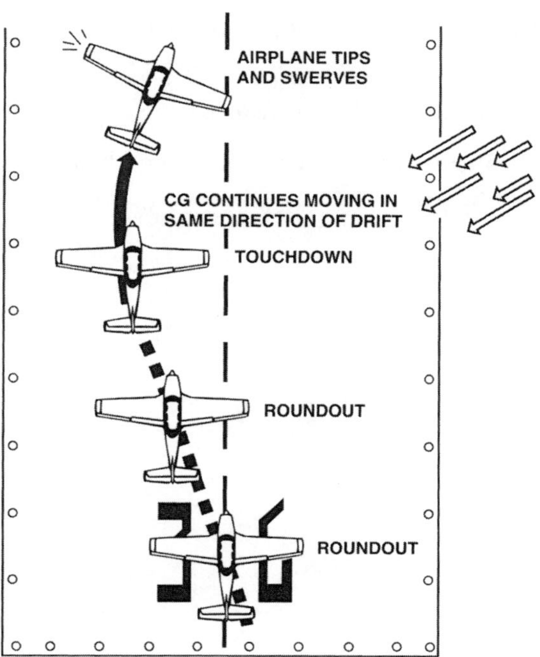

Not compensating for a crosswind on landing can put you at the beginning of a ground loop.

Wing Tips

One of my most exciting moments of flying was performing a short-field takeoff from a 1,300-ft. runway with obstacles (trees) at the end, and realizing at the halfway point that I hadn't retracted the flaps after the prior landing. Fortunately, I buzzed a couple of the shorter trees without contact. Most important, I learned a very valuable lesson about pretakeoff checklists!

Once you and your instructor have practiced and practiced these standard and advanced maneuvers, your instructor will feel more confident that you can fly your airplane solo. You'll then be able to practice what you've learned on your own. Soon you'll be anxious to move to the next step—and next chapter—cross-country flying.

The Least You Need to Know

- Your first solo flight will be one of the most memorable experiences of your life.
- A stall is simply the loss of lift; your aircraft is designed to recover from a stall without your help.
- Slow flight maneuvers help you develop skills that can make flying safer and more enjoyable for you.
- Ground-reference maneuvers help you visualize the effects of wind on your flying.
- Make sure you're proficient at advanced takeoff and landing maneuvers so you will be ready and confident.

Chapter 10

Cross-Country Flying

In This Chapter

- Planning your solo cross-country flight
- How to use the flight computer
- Guidelines for calculating your plane's weight and balance
- Getting weather reports and forecasts
- Your cross-country flight plan
- Putting your world in perspective from 3,000 feet

For many folks, cross-country trips are what flying is all about. Instead of simply flying around their own airport and town, they would prefer to fly somewhere for the weekend—or a week—without having to follow winding roads in the family car. They want to travel "as the crow flies"—except faster.

Even if you never want to leave your home base, there's much you can learn about flying by preparing for your first solo cross-country flight. You'll learn about using a flight computer, maintaining a heading, calculating your ground speed, and many other vital skills. Besides, a solo cross-country trip is required to get your sport-pilot certificate. Who knows? Someday you might decide to take your new sport airplane on vacation to WallyWorld!

Going from Here to There

If you were driving on vacation to a new resort, you wouldn't just pack the car and start driving in the general direction of the resort. Instead, you would take a good look at the map, determine the best path, select some stopping points for food and fuel, and probably estimate the length of the trip in miles and time. That's exactly what you're going to do to plan your first solo cross-country trip.

Unlike driving, flying means you won't find fuel stations at every other corner. In fact, not all airports sell fuel. You need to plan a little more carefully so you don't run out of fuel along the way. Also unlike driving, flying *does* mean you can go from here to there in a relatively straight line. You don't have roads to follow; you can create your own path. And, for sport pilots who don't fly in congested airspace, you don't have to worry about traffic jams, either. They're all below you.

Where Are You Going?

Good question! Until you move up to your private-pilot license, or at least get a logbook endorsement for flying in tower-controlled airspace, your cross-country trips are limited. Your instructor will help you select a trip on which you can learn new elements of flying without getting frustrated.

Fortunately, you have a "road map," a sectional aeronautical chart for the area in which you live and fly. Reading and interpreting sectional charts is covered in Chapter 3. You can simply lay out the chart on a flat surface and draw a straight line between where you are and where you want to be. That's your course.

How Will You Get There?

As you mark your course on the sectional chart you might see reasons to avoid specific areas. For example, your course might cross a restricted area or other temporary flight activity that could be dangerous. Or you might decide to avoid a mountainous area until you're more comfortable with flying.

Wing Tips

My first solo cross-country had me crossing directly over an airport that was relatively inactive—except on the day I wanted to fly over. That was the day the airport held their annual air show with stunt fliers and all types of traffic a student pilot shouldn't be in. Fortunately, the flight service station (FSS) notified me of the activity before I went flying and I simply charted a course around it. It was fun to watch—from a safe distance.

Along the course you select you will see numerous landmarks including airports. If you're flying by pilotage these will be your visual ground references. In fact, you should select the most prominent of these as your cross-country checkpoints, hopefully about 5 to 10 minutes apart. Depending on where you're flying, these landmarks can be lakes, mountain peaks, major road intersections, railroad train yards, towns, and even water towers (with the town name often written on them).

If you're flying by ground-based radio navigation, you will be depending on VOR (VHF omnidirectional range) radio stations to give you a signal. Depending on your navigation equipment, you could decide to fly from VOR station to VOR station because many of them are located near airports.

Remember, you can get additional information about your destination airport and others you'll pass along the way by referring to the FAA's *Airport/Facility Directory* (A/FD) or to one of the VFR (visual flight rules) facility directories such as *Flight Guide*. Listings in these resources include the airport name, location identifier, elevation, location relative to a nearby community, latitude and longitude, telephone numbers, operational information, and other things you should know, such as noise abatement regulations.

Each airport listing also offers airport frequencies including ATIS (automatic terminal information service), the tower frequency, CTAF (common traffic-advisory frequency), approach and departure control frequencies (if controlled), AWOS (Automated Weather Observing System), traffic-pattern information, and maybe even a runway diagram. The listing also tells you how long the field is, what surface (grass, gravel, paved), and other useful information for identifying and using the field. Most important, it tells you whether fuel is sold there, what kind, and when.

When Will You Get There?

Your ETA (estimated time of arrival) is important. Not only do you want to know approximately when you'll get there, but so does the FAA. If you file a flight plan (and you should), it will indicate your ETA. If you don't arrive within a couple of hours of your reported ETA, the FAA will start calling around to find out where you are. If they still can't find you, the FAA will send out the Civil Air Patrol (CAP) to look. Of course, at any time you can "close" a flight plan by contacting ATC (air traffic control) by radio or phone and asking them to do so for you.

> **Knowledge Test**
>
> Groundspeed is the true airspeed (TAS) plus or minus the effect of the wind speed.

To know when you'll get to your destination, you not only must know your airspeed, you also must know your groundspeed. The difference depends on winds and whether they are making you fly faster or slower than the indicated airspeed (IAS). You'll estimate your ETA using a flight computer. This is the dead-reckoning part of the flight preparation.

What If There's a Problem?

Sometimes nothing seems to go as planned. Even after you've spent time planning a flight, something like the weather or another factor can change your plans. That's okay. In fact, that can be part of the fun of flying: learning how to quickly and accurately change your plans and still enjoy flight.

Because you are a VFR pilot with a plotted course and a flight plan, you should know where you are at any given time. You might have just passed over a specific airport identified on your flight path and you can now see a large lake as it appears on your sectional chart. That means you know where nearby airports are, about how far away they are, and how the winds will affect your landing decision. Whether you're flying by dead reckoning, ground-based navigation radios, or GPS, you still should use pilotage navigation as a backup.

Wing Tips

Flying can be boring sometimes, especially on cross-country trips, so smart pilots use that time to play "what if …?" "What if my engine went out right now; where would I land?" "What if an aircraft crossed my path?" "What if I hit a large bird?" "What if I drank too much coffee before takeoff?" Knowing what to do before it happens will help you fly safer.

If the problem is minor, such as you're not sure of your exact position, you can call a flight service station or other communication resource and get your position. If your problem is mechanical (very unlikely because you did such a great preflight inspection!), you can use your emergency checklist and advanced-maneuvers training to get you down safely.

Using Your Flight Computer

The E6B computer has been used by aviators for many years. It's not an electronic computer, but a type of slide ruler, although electronic calculator versions are available, too. It's used to calculate true airspeed, density altitude, ETA, wind correction, and fuel consumption, and to convert temperatures. It originally was designed for the U.S. military, but is now available from pilot shops and other aviation retailers. The aluminum slide-ruler version is under \$30, the cardboard and plastic versions are under \$15, and the electronic calculator versions are under \$100. Regardless of which type you buy, they're all referred to as E6B "computers."

Density altitude is the altitude your plane *thinks* it's flying at, also known as performance altitude. It is the pressure altitude (set your altimeter to 29.92 to read your pressure altitude) adjusted for nonstandard conditions, such as a hot day. Your plane could be flying at 5,000 ft. MSL (mean sea level), for example, but perform like it's really at 7,000 ft. because of hotter, thinner air. Density altitude is important to know because it can mean you need more runway length on a low-density day than on a standard day. Your flight computer can help you calculate density altitude and the operating handbook will tell you how much runway the plane needs to take off and land.

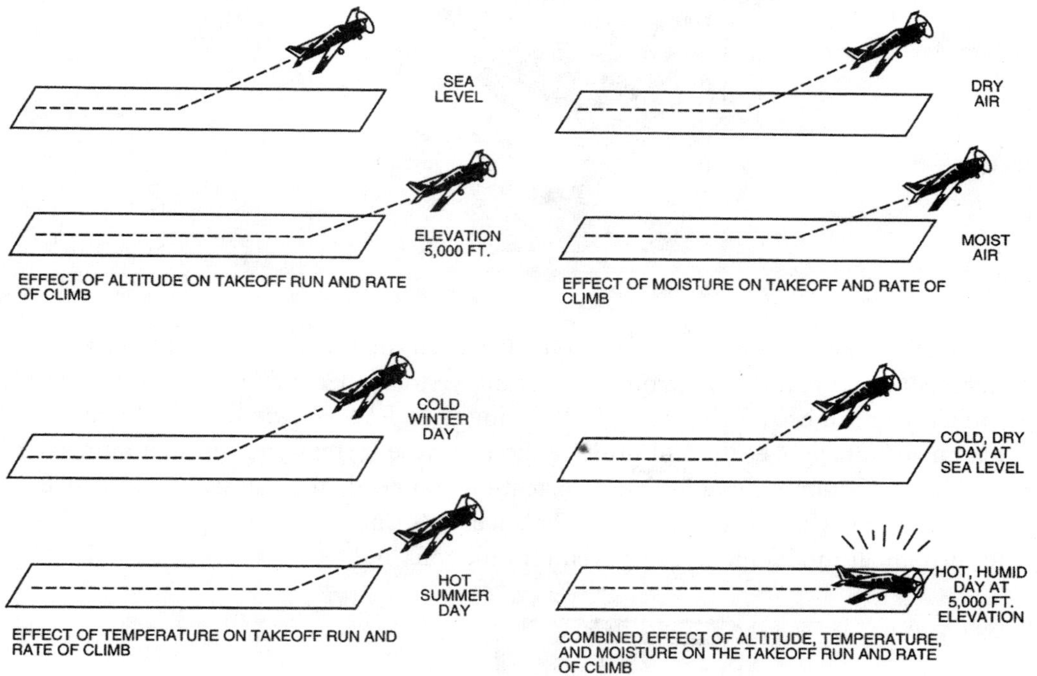

Density altitude is the performance altitude or the altitude (above MSL) that has similar response characteristics.

Rather than bore you with instructions on how to use your E6B computer during a cross-country trip, decide which type you want (slide-rule type or electronic calculator type), buy it, and read the instructions. It can easily help you solve many flight problems.

E6B flight computer (front and back).

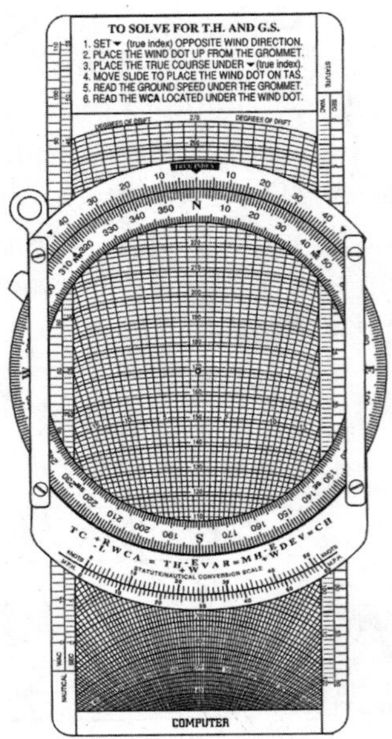

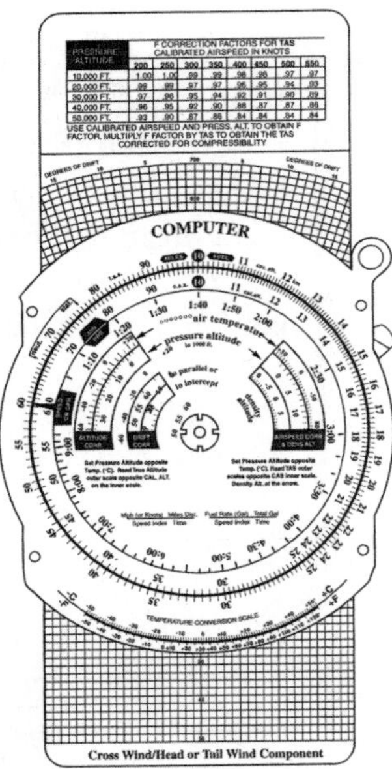

Though the aluminum slide-ruler model has been the mainstay of aviation for more than half a century, the electronic calculator version is becoming increasingly popular. In fact, you can use an electronic E6B during your FAA knowledge test if you wish. It has an advantage over the slide-rule version because it steps you through numerous problems, prompting you for the information you need. You can use it to calculate solutions to navigational, weight and balance, fuel, and conversion problems. The most popular model includes 19 aviation functions and 14 conversions at under $75.

E6B flight computer.

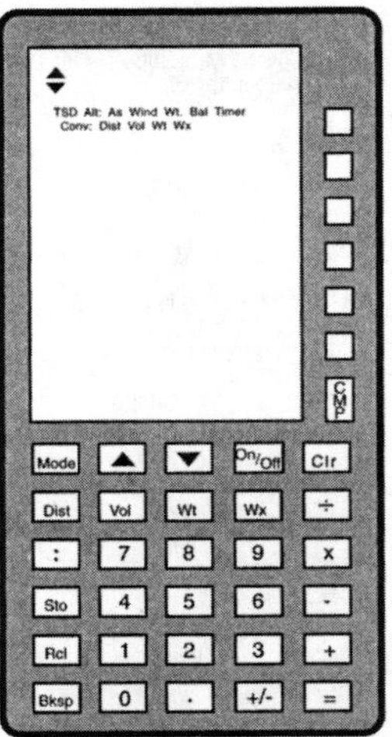

What kinds of calculations will you need to perform for your cross-country flight?

- Calculating the effects of wind and magnetic variation on your flight path
- Calculating estimated time en route in hours and minutes
- Calculating fuel consumption in gallons or time
- Calculating your estimated time of arrival
- Calculating the weight of fuel onboard
- Converting minutes into hours, temperatures from Celsius to Fahrenheit, and knots to mph

Remember that the course is the intended path of your aircraft to reach a specific destination, the heading is the direction in which you must point the aircraft nose, and the track is the plane's actual path over ground. The difference between the course and the heading is the wind-correction angle. This is also called the crab angle. The difference between the heading and the track is called the drift angle.

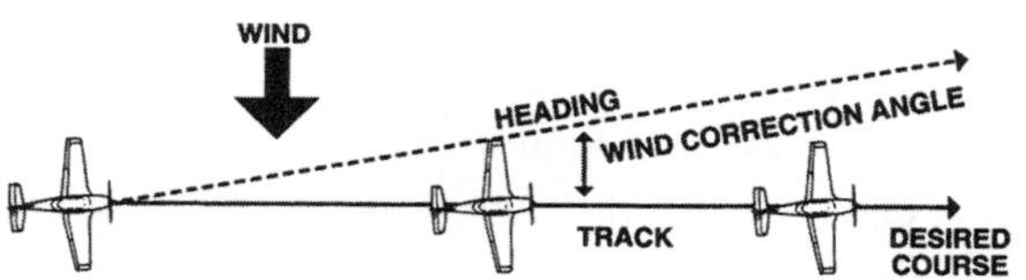

The difference between the track and heading is the wind correction angle.

Knowledge Test

The formulas you need for your FAA knowledge test (and future flying) are:

TH = TC [±] WCA

MH = TH [±] VAR

CH = MH [±] DEV

Where TH = true heading, TC = true course, WCA = wind correction angle, MH = magnetic heading, VAR = magnetic variation, CH = course heading, and DEV = deviation (compass error). Your E6B computer will help you solve these problems.

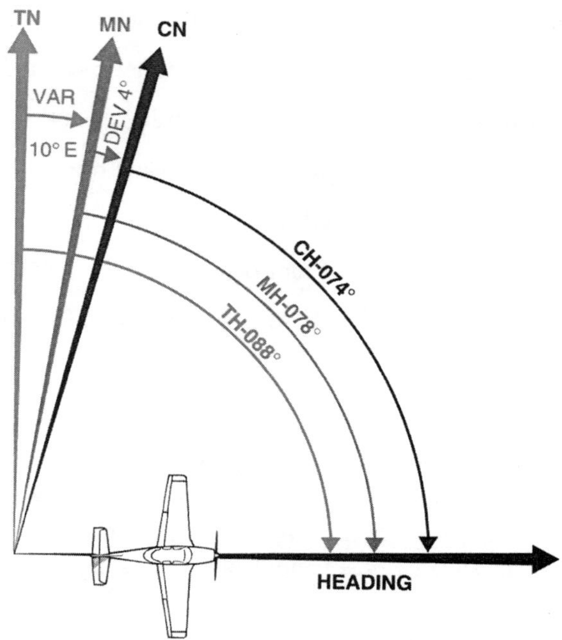

Relationship between true, magnetic, and compass headings.

The ground-school or knowledge-test preparation course you select will help you develop memory aids that can step you through various problems you will face as you plan your cross-country trip.

Another useful tool you'll need in planning your trip is a plotter. It's simply a ruler marked out in statute and nautical miles plus a protractor or half circle with degrees. You use it to mark a straight path on a sectional or WAC (world aeronautical chart), and then determine your course. You can buy a basic plotter for less than $15 for the fancier models, or half that for the simple ones. Better ones have rotating protractors and scales for both sectionals and WACs.

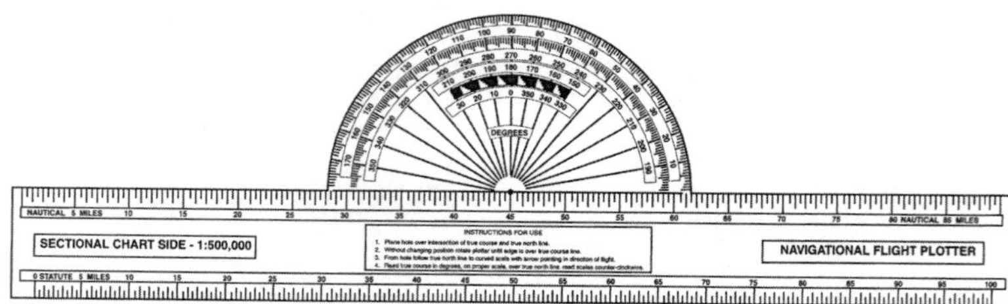

Plotter (ruler and protractor) for establishing flight paths on a chart.

Figuring Weight and Balance

With a car, you have to put massive rocks in the trunk before added weight appreciably affects how the car drives. With an airplane, you *must* follow weight and balance limitations when loading an aircraft for safe flight. Extra weight—especially weight in the wrong location—can make flight unsafe or even impossible. That's why your cross-country trips as well as your FAA knowledge and practical tests will require you to understand your craft's weight and balance requirements.

It's a good thing that the plane's operating handbook includes weight and balance information, as well as tips on how to calculate it. Sport planes, for example, are limited in gross weight to 1,232 lbs. and that's with *everything*, including the pilot, passenger, instruments, luggage, fuel, and oil. So use your craft's weight and balance tables along with your E6B computer to make sure your craft is not overweight and the weight is properly distributed before you go flying. Think of the center of gravity as the center point (fulcrum) on a teeter-totter.

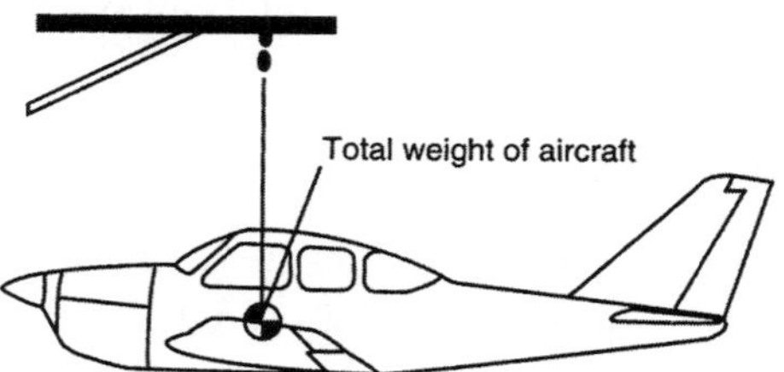

The center of gravity for your plane is its center of weight.

The operating handbook tells you the balance limits and how to load weight including passengers and luggage to stay within those limits. Here are some guidelines for calculating weight and balance in most small aircraft:

- The center of gravity or balance point is calculated based on the weight of the load and its distance from a specific point on the craft, called the datum line.
- The datum line for some aircraft is at the firewall behind the engine, while on other aircraft it's at the propeller; use whichever is suggested by the manufacturer.
- The arm is the distance from a specific point, called the datum line, to the weight.
- The moment is the arm multiplied by the weight.
- The location of the center of gravity is the total moments divided by the total weight.

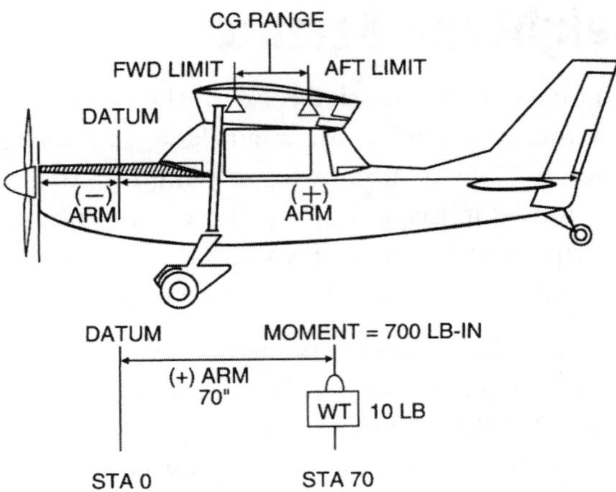

Calculating an aircraft's weight and balance.

Your E6B computer or calculator, along with the operating handbook, will guide you in establishing the craft's balance around its center of gravity. The handbook will show you if the balance, as loaded, is within the required limits.

Checking the Weather

For obvious reasons, you need to know what the weather will be like when and where you fly your cross-country trip. Fortunately, the FAA and the National Weather Service (NWS) have you covered.

There are FSSs (flight service stations) throughout the country that you can call to get the latest weather information for anywhere in the country. The flight service stations are supplemented with computerized weather and related flight services called DUATS (Direct User Access Terminal System).

The FAA's DUATS for pilots offers access to weather-briefing and flight-planning computers. You can sit at home and use this computer service online. If you have a computer with online access you can find DUAT services at www.duat.com (operated by Data Transformation Corp.) and www.duats.com (operated by Computer Sciences Corp.). Try them both and choose your favorite. You'll need to register for many of the services, but most are free. You will need your student-pilot license number to register.

What type of weather information do you need? Because you're a VFR (visual flight rules) pilot, you need to know if your flight will meet VFR visibility minimums. In fact, you should have personal flight minimums that are more conservative than regulations require, at least until you get more flying experience. As you gather weather information, remember that a weather report tells you what has happened or is happening, and a weather forecast tells you what (probably) will happen.

Winds are also important weather information. Note that the direction and velocity of winds could be different at ground elevation than at flight altitude, called winds aloft.

Your instructor won't sign you off for a solo cross-country trip until he or she is comfortable that you 1) are not flying into a weather problem, and 2) have the skills to handle probable weather changes. Remember, too, that the FSS or weather briefer will help you even more if you identify yourself as a student pilot planning your first cross-country solo. They're there to help you, not test you.

> **Knowledge Test**
>
> For your knowledge test you might need to know some weather codes, even though most reports and forecasts don't use these codes any more. Hopefully, future tests will change this. Meantime, your ground-school instructor or course will teach you what codes you'll need for the knowledge test.

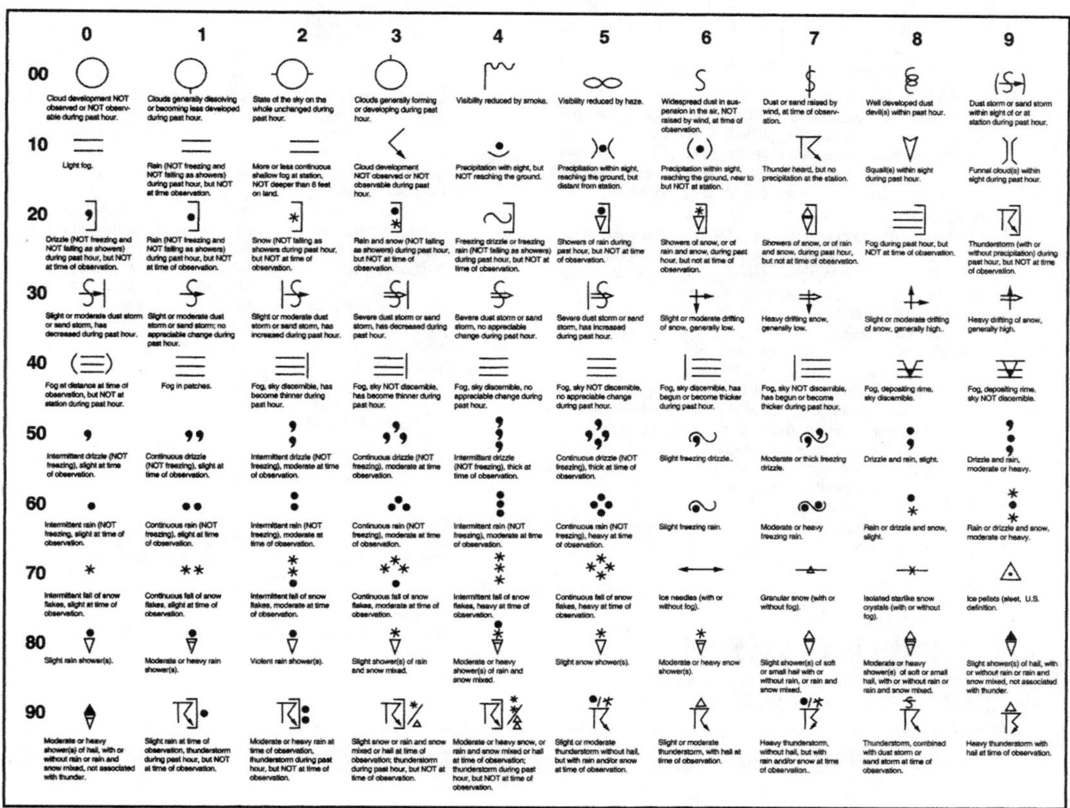

Key to interpreting weather chart symbols.

KEY TO METAR (NEW AVIATION ROUTINE WEATHER REPORT) OBSERVATIONS

TYPE OF REPORT:

There are two types of report—the METAR which is a routine observation report and SPECI which is a Special METAR weather observation. The type of report, METAR or SPECI, will always appear in the report header or lead element of the report.

STATION DESIGNATOR:

The METAR code uses ICAO 4-letter station identifiers. In the contiguous 48 states, the 3-letter domestic station identifier is prefixed with a "K." Elsewhere, the first two letters of the ICAO identifier indicate what region of the world and country (or state) the station is in. For Alaska, all station identifiers start with "PA;" for Hawaii, all station identifiers start with "PH."

TIME:

The time the observation is taken is transmitted as a four-digit time group appended with a Z to denote Coordinated Universal Time (UTC).

WIND:

The wind is reported as a five-digit group (six digits if speed is over 99 knots). The first three digits is the direction the wind is blowing from in ten's of degrees, or "VRB" if the direction is variable. The next two digits is the speed in knots, or if over 99 knots, the next three digits. If the wind is gusty, it is reported as a "G" after the speed followed by the highest gust reported.

VISIBILITY:

Visibility is reported in statute miles with "SM" appended to it. Runway Visual Range (RVR), when reported, is in the format: R(runway)/(visual range)FT. The "R" identifies the group followed by the runway heading, a "/", and the visual range in feet (meters in other countries).

WEATHER:

The weather as reported in the METAR code represents a significant change in the way weather is currently reported. In METAR, weather is reported in the format: Intensity, Proximity, Descriptor, Precipitation, Obstructions to visibility, or Other.

Intensity—applies only to the first type of precipitation reported. A "–" denotes light, no symbol denotes moderate, and a "+" denotes heavy.

Proximity—applies to and reported only for weather occurring in the vicinity of the airport (between 5 and 10 miles of the center of the airport runway complex). It is denoted by the letters "VC."

Descriptor—these seven descriptors apply to the following precipitation or obstructions to visibility:

TS – thunderstorm
SH – shower(s)
FZ – freezing
BC – patches
BL – blowing
DR – low drifting
MI – shallow

Precipitation—there are eight types of precipitation in the METAR code:

RA – rain
DZ – drizzle
SN – snow
SG – snow grains
GR – hail(>1/4 in.)
GS – small hail/snow pellets
PE – ice pellets
IC – ice crystals

Obstructions to visibility—there are eight types of obstructing phenomena in the METAR code:

BR – mist (vsby 5/8–6 mi)
SA – sand
FU – smoke
DU – dust
HZ – haze
VA – volcanic ash
FG – fog
PY – spray

Note: Fog (FG) is reported only when the visibility is less than five eighths of a mile otherwise mist (BR) is reported.

Other—there are five categories of other weather phenomena which are reported when they occur:

SQ-squall
DS-duststorm
FC-funnel cloud/tornado/waterspout
SS-sandstorm
PO-dust/sand whirls

SKY CONDITION:

The sky condition as reported in METAR represents a significant change from the way sky condition is currently reported. In METAR, sky condition is reported in the format:

Amount, Height, (Type), or Vertical Visibility

Amount—the amount of sky cover is reported in eighths of sky cover, using the contractions:

SKC-clear (no clouds)
SCT-scattered (1/8 to 4/8's of clouds)
BKN-broken (5/8's to 7/8's of clouds)
OVC-overcast (8/8's of clouds)

Note: A ceiling layer is not designated in the METAR code. For aviation purposes, the ceiling is the lowest broken or overcast layer, or vertical visibility into an obscuration. Also, there is no provision for reporting thin layers in the METAR code.

Height—cloud bases are reported with three digits in hundreds of feet.

(Type)—if towering cumulus clouds (TCU) or cumulonimbus clouds (CB) are present, they are reported after the height which represents their base.

Vertical Visibility—total obscurations are reported in the format "VVhhh" where VV denotes vertical visibility and "hhh" is the vertical visibility in hundreds of feet. There is no provision in the METAR code to report partial obscurations.

TEMPERATURE/DEWPOINT:

Temperature and dewpoint are reported in a two-digit form in degrees Celsius. Temperatures below zero are prefixed with an "M."

ALTIMETER:

Altimeter settings are reported in a four-digit format in inches of mercury prefixed with an "A" to denote the units of pressure.

REMARKS:

Remarks are limited to reporting significant weather, the beginning and ending times of certain weather phenomena, and low-level wind shear of significance to aircraft landing and taking off. The contraction "RMK" precedes remarks. Wind shear information is denoted by "WS" followed by "TKO" for takeoff or "LDG" for landing, and the runway "RW" affected.

Key to interpreting aviation routine weather reports (METARs).

Filing Your Flight Plan

Flight plans are not a legal requirement for VFR pilots. They are for IFR (instrument flight rules) pilots. However, smart VFR pilots file a flight plan with the FAA, especially when required to do so by your instructor or the designated pilot examiner (DPE).

FLIGHT PLAN

1. TYPE	2. AIRCRAFT IDENTIFICATION	3. AIRCRAFT TYPE/ SPECIAL EQUIPMENT	4. TRUE AIRSPEED	5. DEPARTURE POINT	6. DEPARTURE TIME PROPOSED (Z)	6. DEPARTURE TIME ACTUAL (Z)	7. CRUISING ALTITUDE
X VFR IFR DVFR	N123DB	C150/X	115 KTS	CHICKASHA AIRPORT	1400Z		5500

8. ROUTE OF FLIGHT
Chickasha direct Guthrie

9. DESTINATION (Name of airport and city)	10. EST. TIME ENROUTE HOURS	10. EST. TIME ENROUTE MINUTES	11. REMARKS
Guthrie Airport Guthrie, OK		35	

12. FUEL ON BOARD HOURS	12. FUEL ON BOARD MINUTES	13. ALTERNATE AIRPORT(S)	14. PILOT'S NAME, ADDRESS & TELEPHONE NUMBER & AIRCRAFT HOME BASE	15. NUMBER ABOARD
4	45		Jane Smith Aero Air Oklahoma City, OK (405) 555-4149	1

16. COLOR OF AIRCRAFT	
Red/White	CLOSE VFR FLIGHT PLAN WITH McAlester FSS ON ARRIVAL

FAA flight plan form.

Actually, filing a flight plan is a piece of cake because you've already developed your own comprehensive flight plan. All you need to do is tell the FAA about it. How? You can telephone it in or file it online. However, be aware that filing a flight plan doesn't mean a thing unless you activate it. So just before or after you take off on your cross-country solo you must contact an FSS to "open" your flight plan. And, of course, don't forget to "close" your flight plan once you reach your destination. If you must, you also can modify or even cancel your flight plan by radio or phone.

Enjoying Your Cross-Country Flight

In all the reports and calculations it could become difficult to remember the purpose of a cross-country trip is to have fun while going from here to there. Even your first cross-country solo won't be all work and no fun. So enjoy it!

Pilots seem to gain a greater perspective on their lives by seeing their small world in the context of the larger world. That home you live in is one of a thousand or maybe a million homes that you'll fly over. That workplace with all of its frustrations is just one small building among many buildings. Snarled traffic below looks like a parade from 3,000 ft. AGL (above ground level).

Your cross-country trip will help you see your flying and maybe even your life in a new light. It did for me and for many pilots I've asked. For example, Frank Kingston Smith, author of *Week-End Pilot V69* (Vintage Books, 1974) and many other fascinating aviation books, went from pessimism and poor health to a sheer joy of life with accompanying good health by simply learning to fly. He's said that he probably paid for his first aircraft with savings from fewer visits to the doctor.

So enjoy your cross-country flying—your first solo trip and the hundreds to come. It's good for your health and your outlook.

The Least You Need to Know

- As you plan your solo cross-country trip, ask your instructor and the FSS for assistance.
- You can learn how to use the E6B flight computer by following the instructions that come with it.
- Make sure your plane is not overweight and that all weight is balanced according to the manufacturer's guidelines.
- Use DUAT or the FSS to help you plan and file your cross-country flight plan.
- Your cross-country trip can help you see your flying—and possibly your life—from a fresh perspective.

Chapter 11

Passing the Test

In This Chapter

- Mental and emotional preparation to make test taking easier
- Tips for passing the knowledge test with "flying" colors
- What to expect during the practical exam and the checkride
- Displaying your knowledge of aviation

On the scale of things most folks hate, tests are right up near the top—next to root-canal work. Even students who have taken hundreds of tests still feel anxiety when someone says, "Ready? Begin!" And anxiety is intensified when the test is taken at 2,000 ft. AGL (above ground level)!

Not to worry. Taking a test is an opportunity for you to show what you know. Once it's passed, you'll have additional confidence in your flying skills and in yourself. So let's take a look at how millions of pilots over the years have successfully passed their FAA knowledge and practical tests.

Getting Ready for the Tests

If you've taken many tests, you know there are certain techniques and methods to make taking them easier. Some involve memory aids, but many are about your attitude toward the test. Here's a refresher course on taking tests.

Watch Your Attitude

How you feel about a test can dramatically affect how you do on it. If it's a do-or-die test, your anxiety can get in the way of your thinking, fogging otherwise clear answers. So remember to emotionally as well as mentally prepare yourself for a successful test.

What's the worst thing that can happen? You can fail the test! You can be so anxious that you do something you otherwise know is wrong. You're nervous. And you're excited. Psychologists suggest that if you are emotionally prepared to accept either a positive or negative outcome, you can more easily focus on making it positive. Failing a test on the first attempt really isn't the end of the world. Learn what you can from the experience and do better next time.

Of course, what you're working toward is a positive result. Fortunately, your instructor wants to help you pass the test. So do the examiners. So do I. Everyone is rooting for you. Keep a positive attitude and, combined with your knowledge and skills, you will succeed.

Remembering What You Forgot

Tests can be intimidating. All those questions, so little time, and your mind just went blank. Fortunately, people who take numerous tests learn how to use memory aids that help them retain and recall needed facts. Here are some tips.

One key to remembering things is relevance. I call it peg learning. If you come up with a new fact that you want to remember you need to have an easy-to-get-to place in your brain where you can later find it. Pegs are simply primary categories onto which secondary facts can be "attached." For example, new facts about clouds are attached to the "weather" peg. You also can think of the hierarchy as an outline with headings and subheadings. As new facts are added—"nimbus" in a cloud name means "moisture"—you mentally associate it with "weather" and you can more easily recall it later.

Another key to memory is thinking visually. If you can visualize the fact, you can more readily remember it. For example, **strat**us clouds are **straight.** You can even group associated facts by visualizing them. New facts about a specific flight instrument can be visually remembered by associating the facts with the instrument as you see it in your memory. Then you will more easily recall the fact by either looking at the instrument or visualizing it in your mind.

Acronyms—words formed by the first letter of several words—can be useful memory aids. Your ground-school and flight instructors probably will offer you a few to help you remember things. You also can come up with some of your own. For example, remembering which way a magnetic compass swings (causing a reading error) is made easier by remembering "ANDS." It stands for **A**ccelerate **N**orth, **D**ecelerate **S**outh, meaning accelerating causes the compass to give a more northerly heading than is true, and decelerating gives a more southerly heading. Use anything you can come up with to help you remember facts that you'll need for the test and for flying.

Many ground schools and multimedia training programs offer additional test-taking tips and memory aids. There's much to learn and remember as you become a sport pilot—just as there was much to learn when you first began to drive. It won't be long before you ace the tests and get your certificate!

Passing the Knowledge Test

The sport-pilot knowledge test is a computerized test with 30 questions covering aerodynamics, airspace, aeromedical issues, regulations, navigation, and weather topics. You have 90 minutes to complete the test, giving you 3 minutes per question. Attempt to answer all 30 in one hour and leave the final half hour to work on any questions you didn't feel as comfortable answering the first time through.

A passing score is 70 percent, or 21 correct answers. You should go for a higher score just to be sure. One hundred percent is achievable. Here are some tips:

- Your ground or flight instructor must endorse your logbook before you can take the knowledge test.
- Review all study materials and take sample or practice tests just prior to your knowledge test appointment.
- Make sure you take photo identification with you when you take the test.
- You will have approximately 1½ hours to complete the test and you will receive your score immediately after completion.
- All questions have equal value, so answer the easier ones first.
- Read and answer each question in your mind before looking at the multiple-choice answers provided on the test.
- Remember that your first answer is usually the best.
- Read all notes and footnotes on any example figure in the test because they can hold clues to the answers to the question you're on, or other questions later on.

Wing Tips

If you don't yet have a flight instructor before you take your knowledge test, you can get your ground-school instructor to endorse your logbook. Some multimedia ground schools also will endorse you if you send them sample tests you have passed.

- You may bring an E6B slide computer or calculator and a plotter to the test, but no other aids.
- Relax! You can always take the test again if you don't get a passing score this time.

There are numerous excellent ground schools and computerized courses to help you pass your knowledge test. You also can take sample tests online for free at www.sportys.com. Refer to Appendix B for more information.

Passing the Practical Exam

The second test that sport and other pilots take is called the practical test. It's a combination of oral questioning and practical demonstration (flying). Once you've finished training and your instructor has reviewed all flight maneuvers with you, he or she will endorse your logbook to indicate you are ready for the practical test.

Here's a fact that will help you sleep better: You've already passed a practice version of the practical test! The three-plus hours of test preparation you just completed with your instructor is designed to be very similar to what the sport-pilot *examiner* will test you on. Your instructor puts his or her reputation on the line by endorsing you for the practical test. Instructors are somewhat judged by their success rate of getting students certified on their first try. If you've been recommended for the practical test by your instructor, chances are great that you're going to pass.

The oral component of the examination continues throughout the test. When you make an appointment with the examiner, he or she probably will give you an assignment. Typically, you must plan a cross-country trip to a specific airport and prepare a flight plan. The purpose of this assignment is to demonstrate your knowledge of the rules of flying.

Once you meet with the examiner and you've introduced yourselves, the examiner will ask you about the cross-country flight you've planned for the two of you. You'll pull out the appropriate sectional chart and airport facility directory to describe your planning of the flight. Along the way your examiner will ask you open-ended questions, ones that require a descriptive answer beyond yes or no. Answer the question clearly, but don't go into related topics unless asked. The examiner will ask you to clarify answers as needed.

Flying Words

Your FAA-approved **examiner** will be called by a variety of names, all of them respectful. For example, he or she might be called a sport-pilot examiner (SPE), designated pilot examiner (DPE), check pilot, or "the boss." Remember, this is a job performed by professionals who typically have flown thousands of hours in a variety of planes. Respect them, and they will be fair with you.

The examiner wants you to exhibit your aeronautical knowledge: how planes fly, what rules govern flying, and what you can and cannot do as a sport pilot. The examiner will especially be interested in your ability to read and interpret a sectional chart. You'll be asked questions like "Why did you choose this route?", "Why did you select your specified altitude?", and "What points or landmarks have you selected along your course and why?"

Knowledge Test

Your pilot examiner is testing you by "the book," *Sport Pilot Practical Test Standards* (PTS), an FAA publication that tells the examiner what the applicant (that's you) must know or illustrate before a sport-pilot certificate can be issued. Your instructor might have a copy you can use, or you can purchase one through the FAA. It's important you get a copy of the PTS and review it extensively with your instructor.

The oral questioning typically gets into aeromedical issues. The most important are alcohol, drugs, and vertigo. As you probably learned in ground school, you cannot legally fly an aircraft if your alcohol blood level is greater than .04 percent—about half the limit imposed by most states on automobile drivers. Nor can you legally fly if you've consumed alcohol within the previous 8 hours. The reason for these stringent rules is not just because you're operating an airplane. It's also because altitude increases the disabling effects of alcohol. The same goes for drugs, both prescription and nonprescription. Also, because of the variations in air pressure during a flight, it's a good idea not to fly if you have a head cold because the differential pressure can give you an extreme headache.

Vertigo is the sensation of dizziness caused by spatial disorientation. It happens when your mind doesn't know up from down. If you've ever played a childhood game where you're blindfolded and spun around, you know what vertigo is. It can happen when flying if you can't see the horizon or other reference points, and occurs when you get into clouds. As a VFR pilot you're *never* supposed to get into or even near clouds. However, a fast-moving weather front or inattention could get you into a cloud and you must know how to get out of it. How? By reading and trusting your instruments.

Wing Tips

The examiner wants to pass you as much as you want to be passed. "The paperwork is easier," said one. You won't get tricky questions. Instead, you'll get questions that will help you illustrate your developed knowledge of safe flying. If you don't understand a question, the examiner expects you to ask for clarification.

During your oral questioning the instructor will ask you about alcohol, drugs, vertigo, and other aeromedical issues. Know what they are. In addition, the practical exam will include some flying by instruments only to make sure you know how to use them to get out of trouble.

Don't think you'll remember everything you need to know to answer all the questions? No problem. The oral exam is actually an open-book test. You can refer to the plane's operating handbook or even FAA publications, including the legend on a sectional chart, as needed to respond to the examiner's questions. Don't rely on publications, but know that you can refer to them during the exam if necessary. You will use these publications in real-life flying.

Passing the Flying Part of the Practical Exam

Once your sport-pilot examiner is comfortable with the thought of flying with you, it's time to get airborne. The questioning part actually continues as you describe what you're doing and the examiner asks additional questions during your flight.

What will the flight exam cover? Just about everything you've learned thus far. Though the examiner uses the *Sport Pilot Practical Test Standards* as a guideline, he or she will combine maneuvers into a single directive to help you illustrate what you've learned. For example, the examiner might simulate an emergency ("You just lost your engine. What are you going to do?") to help you illustrate a wide variety of flying skills.

Remember, you can practice your flight examination using flight-simulation programs. Microsoft Flight Simulator, for example, includes a "Private Pilot Checkride" under flight lessons. It's more comprehensive than what you will face for the sport-pilot certificate, but offers a good opportunity to test your flying skills at home. See Chapter 5 for more.

What will the flight exam, sometimes called the checkride, cover? Here's what's typical:

- Preflight inspection
- Pretakeoff (start, run-up, taxi)
- Takeoff and climb
- Radio communications, including opening a flight plan (if you don't have a radio this will be tested by oral questioning)
- En route flying using pilotage and dead-reckoning navigation skills
- Ground-reference maneuvers
- Short- and soft-field takeoffs and landings

- Ability to quickly read and interpret your airplane's instruments
- Ability to maintain altitudes and headings within specific ranges
- Handling simulated emergencies
- Ability to fly safely

What should you do if you get an examiner who seems to have an attitude? Be patient. Most examiners take their job very seriously and want to put a little pressure on you to see how you respond. They want to help you realize that safety is more important than ego. So be patient and be thankful that the examiner is willing to give you this opportunity to learn about yourself.

CAUTION

Stall Warning!

What is the major reason why student pilots fail their checkride? Inappropriate flying caused by nervousness. Doing something really dumb when you know better. Relax!

Getting Your Ticket

Hopefully, when you land from your checkride there will be *two* certified pilots in your aircraft—the examiner and *you!* The examiner will tell you right then whether you passed or not.

When you land from your checkride there will be two certified pilots in your sport plane (pictured here, a Sinus).

The examiner will also give you a test debriefing after the flight, telling you what you need to work on. Few pilots get raving reviews from the examiner because examiners know that *all* pilots actually are *student pilots*, learning more skills as they learn to fly. If you listen carefully to your debriefing you will get sage advice from an experienced pilot on how you can fly safer and more efficiently in the future. If the examiner chooses to share this wisdom with you, don't make excuses or defensive remarks. Instead, listen carefully and say "yes" and "thank you."

What's next now that you have a sport-pilot certificate? Chapter 12 offers a self-training course that can help you develop your flying skills as you have some fun.

By the way, congratulations!

The Least You Need to Know

- Test-taking involves both your mind and your emotions, and smart student pilots prepare themselves on both levels.
- The knowledge test determines what you know about aerodynamics, airspace, aeromedical issues, regulations, navigation, and weather.
- The question-and-answer portion of the practice exam demonstrates your knowledge of flight planning and preparation.
- The flight portion of your exam gives you the opportunity to show an experienced pilot that you can fly your sport aircraft safely.

Part 3 Expanding Your Horizons

You've earned your wings!

Now it's time to test them. This third part includes a couple of really enjoyable chapters on how to have some fun with your flying. You'll soon discover that piloting an aircraft means much more than getting from here to there. You have many new—and fun—options.

You also have a wide future. You can continue as a sport pilot, adding endorsements and skills—or you can move on up to a private, instrument, or even commercial certificate. You can make a career out of flying. Or you can simply find new ways of paying your flying expenses.

Who knows where your new wings will take you?

Chapter 12

Flying for Fun

In This Chapter

- Organizations that connect you with other sport pilots
- Getting more comfortable with your flying
- Camping, fly-ins, and other recreational pursuits
- Flying for business

This is your frequent-flier rewards chapter! You've worked hard—and had some fun—getting your sport-pilot certificate. You're now ready to put it into action and get up into the sky without having an instructor breathing on your shoulder.

The sky is the limit on the many things you can do to have fun flying your sport aircraft! Some are obvious and some are not. I guarantee you'll find something in this chapter that tells you, "Hey, I gotta try this!"

Let's go flying for fun!

Associations for Sport Pilots

You've probably noticed that once you're involved in an activity, you soon discover there are thousands of others enjoying it, too. Whether you're collecting coins, climbing mountains, or learning a new language, you soon find other crazy folks who've been doing it for years.

Flying is no different. Yes, the sport-pilot certificate is a new thing, but many thousands of pilots are already primarily sport or recreational fliers—and most would love to meet you and share their knowledge. You'll find most of them quite helpful. Meeting them will broaden your flying experiences as well as your friendships. Let's meet a few of them.

EAA

The Experimental Aircraft Association (EAA) began more than 50 years ago when a group got together in Milwaukee, Wisconsin, to help each other build their own planes. By then, people had been building aircraft from plans for about 30 years, so the hobby wasn't new. They shared information and, as interest grew in flying, added more and more members. The EAA now boasts more than 170,000 members around the world.

The EAA initially focused on "homebuilt" or "experimental" aircraft, planes that were built from plans. FAA regulations allowed these aircraft to be constructed and certified under a separate set of rules that are different from those required for the aircraft industry, such as Piper and Cessna. And those rules hold today. If the planes are built from kits, the builder must do at least 51 percent of the work to qualify as an experimental aircraft. If you're interested in building your own plane, the EAA is an excellent place to start getting advice.

The EAA has expanded from purely owner-built general-aviation aircraft to include vintage aircraft, warbirds (older military aircraft), ultralights (small, light-weight aircraft, usually pilot only), aerobatic planes, and rotorcraft (helicopters). Over the past few years, the EAA has been instrumental in developing the new sport-pilot and light-sport aircraft proposal, and getting it moved through the FAA and other governmental bodies.

Besides their primary website (www.eaa.org), the EAA runs a website specifically for sport pilots (www.sportpilot.org).

The EAA is extensively involved in all phases of recreational aviation. Besides lobbying in Washington, the EAA sponsors or cosponsors numerous air shows throughout the United States, including the granddaddy of them all: the EAA AirVenture (www.airventure.org). Held at their headquarters in Oshkosh, Wisconsin, AirVenture attracts about *2,800* aircraft in late July each year—everything from lawnmowers with wings to stealth fighters. In recent years the planes have included a Concorde jet, a fully restored B-29 bomber, and replicas of the *Wright Flyer* (the first airplane) and the *Spirit of St. Louis* (arguably the most famous aircraft). If you can't make it to Oshkosh, there are numerous regional shows as well, announced in EAA publications.

The EAA publishes Sport Pilot *and other magazines that include excellent articles for the new sport pilot.*

Wing Tips

Basic membership in the EAA currently is $40.00 a year—a real bargain. You also can join one of the nearly 1,000 chapters to meet and talk planes with other sport pilots near you. Some of the services available to members include focused magazines (including the new *Sport Pilot*), flight-planning services, insurance services, travel discounts, and other opportunities. For further information, contact the EAA online at www.eaa.org or call 1-800-JOIN-EAA (1-800-564-6322). The mailing address is EAA Aviation Center, PO Box 3086, Oshkosh, WI 54903.

AOPA

The Aircraft Owners and Pilots Association (AOPA) is older and larger than the EAA. Since 1939, the AOPA has been a major voice for general aviation. It currently has more than 400,000 members, including sport, recreational, private, and commercial pilots and instructors. Though their primary market is pilots with a private or higher certification, they have reached out to embrace the newest category, sport pilots, with new programs and new opportunities.

Wing Tips

Membership in the AOPA is just $39.00 a year and includes publications and numerous benefits. For further information, contact the AOPA online at www.aopa.org or call 1-800-USA-AOPA (1-800-872-2672). The mailing address is AOPA, 421 Aviation Way, Frederick, MD 21701.

The AOPA is increasing its focus on student pilots for all certificates. Its *Flight Training* magazine, for example, is top-notch and includes articles and advertisements aimed at helping new and wannabe pilots feel more comfortable in aviation.

The AOPA has stressed flying safety for many years, developing training that has helped private aviation become an extremely safe sport. The AOPA sponsors conventions, seminars, fly-ins, and other events that spread the word about safe flying. In addition, it is a strong voice in Washington for making sure pilots have a say in legislation.

The AOPA publishes Flight Training *magazine and other excellent resources for new pilots.*

USUA

The United States Ultralight Association (USUA) was formed in 1985 when ultralights were becoming quite popular in the United States. It has become the primary voice for ultralight pilots and manufacturers, encouraging knowledge and safety. The USUA has regional chapters, as well, to help bring together ultralight pilots and those who want to know more about this fun way to fly.

Ultralights are smaller aircraft, designed to be light and easy to fly. With the exception of two-seat ultralight training aircraft, most ultralights are single-place aircraft that weigh under 254 pounds without the pilot. Think of them as flying motorcycles.

Ultralights are built and flown under their own federal rules, called "Part 103," referring to CFR-103 (also known as FAR Part 103) covering "Ultralight vehicles." In the United States, the major group for ultralight flyers is the United States Ultralight Association (USUA). In Canada, it's the Ultralight Pilot Association of Canada (UPAC). Europe, too, has ultralight aircraft and associations with slightly different rules and requirements.

Contrary to some rumors, the sport-pilot certificate does not exclude ultralight pilots. The new sport-pilot designation was established to fit an expanding market between the ultralights and the private pilots. Ultralight pilots who want to move to light planes can use their flight experience to get the new sport-pilot certificate faster. Private pilots who are looking for lower-cost aircraft or have medical restrictions that keep them from flying can easily become sport pilots. The recreational pilot certification program of a dozen years ago attempted to do this, but included some self-defeating rules that stunted its growth. The new sport-pilot certificate was designed to overcome these limitations while offering safe flying opportunities to newbie, ultralight, and noncurrent private pilots. Thus far it is succeeding.

Wing Tips

If you're interested in flying ultralights or would like to know more about them, visit the USUA online at www.usua.org or call 301-695-9100. The mailing address is United States Ultralight Association, PO Box 667, Frederick, MD 21705. The EAA also has information and resources for ultralight pilots.

Official Sky Inspector

So you now have your sport-pilot certificate and you're itching to go flying. Any old excuse will do. I'll cover the most popular ones in the next two sections. Meantime, here is the most important one: honing your flying skills.

Remember, all pilots are really student pilots—until they quit learning. Your sport-pilot instructor has given you the tools to fly safely, but you're not yet an experienced pilot. Even though you may legally take passengers flying, you might decide to wait until you have more flying time in your log before you do so.

The pilots with the highest accident rates are those who have just received their pilot certificate. It's similar to new drivers who have the skills to drive safely, but don't have the experience needed to keep out of harm's way. That takes plain old practice. Fortunately, practicing flying is even more fun than practicing driving.

Until you're more comfortable with flying and have learned to make needed skills your responsive instincts, you probably will not plan many longer flights. In fact, you might decide to simply "fly the patch" or fly in the vicinity of your home airport. That's a good idea. Practice touch-and-goes, fly the airport pattern, then venture out farther. If you haven't flown above 5,000 ft. above ground level (AGL), give it a try. Just remember that sport pilots can't legally fly higher than 10,000 ft. above mean sea level (MSL) or 2,000 ft. AGL, whichever is greater. You can inspect clouds *at a safe distance.*

Flying requires, by definition, stretching your comfort level. You probably weren't fully comfortable making your first solo flight, but you learned what you can and cannot do. Now that you have your sport-pilot certificate, you continually will be adjusting your comfort level with new skills and experiences. Learn a little, test a little, learn some more. That's one of the fun parts of flying. Just make sure you don't push yourself too far toward dangerous mistakes. Remember, this is *sport* flying.

Another fun thing you can do is wash your aircraft. Just as you do when buying a new car, you might decide to wash and even wax your new aircraft frequently. Not only will you be maintaining it, you will be learning more about it. Besides, it's a great excuse to get out of Saturday yard work!

Fun Things You Can Do with Your Airplane

As you fly more and talk with people who have flown, you'll discover that an airplane is just like any other mode of transportation. You can do many things with it besides simply fly the patch.

To get your mind working, here are a few of the more popular excuses, er, reasons, why people fly sport aircraft. Try them all.

Camping

Thousands of people have discovered the versatility of sport aircraft in choosing and using remote campsites. A sport pilot skilled in soft-field landing techniques can gently set a plane down in a quiet meadow away from the subdivision campgrounds. Tents that attach to the underside of a high-wing plane are available, and they offer easy access to both the cockpit and the outside world. A sport plane can quickly overfly the Friday afternoon commuting campers, and the pilot and passenger can be fishing in a cool stream before a motor home finds a level campsite in an RV parking lot.

If you're interested in camping on the wing, you'll find books and directories on this fun pastime in major bookstores and at pilot shops. There might even be dozens of such camping spots near you. Also, many smaller grass-field airports offer camping sites. Just remember to get sufficient training and experience on soft- and short-field landings before you attempt air camping. Get permission before landing anywhere except public airports.

Wilderness Flying

If you're into wilderness trekking, trail hiking, or other natural pastimes, consider how your sport aircraft can get you there and back. You can get there twice as fast as you can by car and enjoy more time at your endeavor.

Yes, there are airfields even in national parks and adjacent to wilderness areas. They require advanced piloting skills, but you will soon have them and can enjoy more of the great outdoors. Just remember that some wilderness and natural areas have fly-over and landing restrictions that you must obey. Sectional charts will help you identify remote airfields and the Airport/Facility Directory will tell you the rules. In addition, books are available on wilderness flying.

Boating by Plane

Had to sell your boat to buy your sport aircraft? Pilots living in areas with navigable waters can do both by installing floats to land on lakes and rivers.

Of course, you'll need to get your logbook endorsed for seaplane (a.k.a. floatplane) operation, which requires additional instruction and practice. However, it can combine the best of both worlds, offering you access to great fishing and recreational locations right on the water.

Social Events

Flying can be a very social avocation. You could fly just yourself and a passenger, but you're joining a fraternity of many thousands who enjoy not only flying but talking about it. If you get heavily into aviation you'll soon find that many of your closest friends are pilots.

Fly-ins are the most popular social events for pilots. Fly-ins can involve a few friends meeting for breakfast or a picnic together at a small airport, or can turn into big get-togethers with thousands of participants coming in from neighboring states or even across the country. Fly-ins are simply excuses to go flying and meet other like-minded people. You can find out more about fly-ins through clubs and national and regional aviation magazines. On any given weekend there's probably a fly-in within a couple hundred miles of where you live. If not, call your flying friends and get one started.

Joining the EAA, AOPA, and other groups will motivate you to find local chapters and participate in various charity events. Sport pilots cannot take people up for charity flights (donations going to a charity), but they can participate in other ways to help their favorite cause. Once you've upgraded your wings to a private-pilot certificate (covered in the next chapter), you can donate aircraft time to charity flights as you wish.

Of course, there are national and regional conventions that you *must* attend. Planning for such events can be fun and instructional as you apply what you've learned about cross-country flying toward a specific goal. Just remember to get any needed endorsements to your sport-pilot certificate before you need to fly in controlled airspace.

Using Your Plane for Business

Technically, you cannot fly your sport aircraft for pay. You can't carry passengers or freight for money. However, you *can* accept remuneration of their fair share of costs (fuel, oil, etc.). To fly passengers for profit you'll need to step up to a commercial certificate.

But you *can* use your sport aircraft in your business, if you follow the FAA and IRS rules. For example, if you need to fly commercial airlines or drive to locations as part of your job or business, you can fly your own sport aircraft to the same location and deduct the business costs. It's just like getting mileage for your car.

I don't know what business you're in, if any, or how you might use your sport plane for business purposes, so I advise you to talk with an accountant before attempting to expense plane travel. However, you might find that using your plane for business can help you better afford a sport aircraft. At the least you'll need to track these expenses:

- Fuel costs
- Replacement oil
- Maintenance
- Insurance
- Hangar or tie-down costs
- Landing fees
- Plane value and depreciation
- How and how much you use the aircraft for business

It's similar to what you need to do for declaring a car as a business expense. If you need further help, contact your accountant, the AOPA, the EAA, or discuss this with other pilots who use their planes for business purposes.

There is so much to know about flying that you will *never* learn it all. Fortunately, learning can be much of the fun of owning and flying a sport plane. Next, let's consider how far you can take your flying.

The Least You Need to Know

- The EAA, AOPA, and USUA are valuable resource associations for those who want to have fun flying.
- You will soon learn how to make up plausible excuses for flying your sport plane.
- You can use your plane to camp, get into the wilderness, boat, and even join others for social time.
- Many sport pilots share their flying costs with their business.

Chapter 13

Flying Higher

In This Chapter

- Spreading your wings: adding endorsements to your sport-pilot certificate
- Upgrading to a private-pilot certificate
- How to accumulate new ratings
- Making a profession out of flying
- What's ahead for sport flying

Learning to fly is just the beginning of your aerial journey. You now have the basic skills and knowledge to make flying a life-long hobby or even a career. Many flyers find that the sport-pilot certificate fills the bill perfectly, and they simply remain at that level. Others want to build on what they've learned. It's really up to you.

Many professional airline pilots started just about where you were before you picked up this book. They, too, wanted to know what flying was all about and decide if it was for them. Then, through practice and training, they moved from private pilot to commercial pilot and then to air transport-pilot (ATP) certification. This chapter shows you how you can follow their flight path as far as you want to take it.

Sport-Pilot Endorsements

The major differences between sport-pilot and private-pilot certification is that sport pilots can start off with fewer training hours and lower-cost aircraft, then add endorsements as their interest and training expand. The sport-pilot certificate gets you flying faster!

Let's take a look at how sport pilots can spread their wings.

Tower-Controlled Airspace Endorsement

Chapter 3 covers controlled and uncontrolled airspace. Specifically, it outlines the requirements for flying in Classes A, B, C, D, E, and G airspace. You learned that sport pilots cannot fly in Class A airspace (above 18,000 ft. mean sea level (MSL) and that they can't fly in Class B, C, or D (tower-controlled) airspace without an official endorsement in their logbook that says they can.

Why is this so? It's because flying in these controlled airspaces is more complex, requiring an understanding of air traffic control (ATC), radio communications, and other more advanced topics than pilots in Class E controlled or Class G uncontrolled airspace need. As a sport pilot you can legally fly in Classes E and G all day long (no night flying, remember) and that might be enough for you. If it isn't, it's time to get some more training.

If you want to add a tower-controlled airspace endorsement, all you need to do is prove to a flight instructor that you can do it. That means reviewing the requirements and limitations of these tower-controlled airspaces, learning more about communicating with ATC, making sure your aircraft is equipped to enter controlled airspace, and showing your instructor that you know this stuff. You already had to know the basics of controlled airspace for your knowledge test, so you might need just a refresher course. Your instructor will go with you as you fly into, land, and take off at airports in Class B, C, or D airspace.

Frankly, some sport pilots decide to get this endorsement out of the way quickly. If you'll be flying in, near, or through tower-controlled airspace as a student, consider opting to get the endorsement as soon as you get your solo permit. It should take you only a couple of extra hours of training, so you might as well do it while you're focused on being a student pilot.

Type Certification

Another restriction of the sport-pilot certificate is that you are permitted to fly only aircraft of the make and model of whatever you took your test in. That is, if you get your certificate in a Kitfox sport plane, then that's the only plane you're allowed to fly. If you want to fly a Zodiac XL sport plane, you must receive training and an instructor's endorsement to be able to fly the Zodiac.

Typically an endorsement requires that a sport-pilot instructor (SPI) give you a lesson or two in the plane you want to fly. If you're relatively proficient, you might be able to get your endorsement in a single flight.

Other Aircraft Categories

Your initial sport-pilot certificate permits you to fly a specific type (model) of an ASEL (airplane, single-engine, land) only. To expand your certification into flying other categories of sport aircraft, all you have to do is receive the appropriate training, fly with an instructor to verify your proficiency, and receive your instructor's endorsement on your sport-pilot certificate. No new knowledge test or practical exam is required.

Most new pilots are happy to fly only the ASEL. But did you know your sport-pilot certification allows you to take off and land on water, too? With additional training and an endorsement, you can add ASES (airplane, single engine, sea) to your certification. And best of all, any ASEL can become an ASES with the addition of pontoon floats, which means you can turn your landlocked aircraft into a water bird and fly away!

You can easily add a seaplane rating and fly a floatplane, such as this Kitfox.

Or you might want to try your hand at flying a powered parachute, a powered hang glider, or another category of aircraft without a fixed wing (see Appendix B). The point is, once you have your sport-pilot certificate, you can use it to expand your knowledge, skills, and endorsements as far as you want—and can afford—to go!

Many sport pilots enjoy the exhilaration of flying a powered parachute such as this Pegasus.

Single-place rotorcraft (helicopters) like this Mosquito are a blast to fly!

Private-Pilot Certificate

For most of the past century, the entry level for new pilots was the FAA private-pilot certificate. Then came the ill-fated recreational-pilot certificate, which hardly got off the ground for various design reasons. Today's sport-pilot certificate is on its way to opening the door to flying for millions of potential pilots at relatively low cost.

Then what? For many sport pilots the next logical step is to the private-pilot certificate. Why? What are the advantages? What is needed to make it happen? Let's take a closer look.

Advantages

The private-pilot certificate removes some of the limitations imposed on sport pilots. First, you are automatically trained for flying in controlled airspace. And you don't need to get an endorsement for airplanes of the same category and class. For example, if you're a private pilot for airplane, single engine, land, you can fly any ASEL and are not limited to a specific make and model. However, endorsements are still required for high-performance and complex airplanes.

Of course, you'll need endorsements or ratings for aircraft that are functionally different. You'll need a rating for flying a multiengine or a seaplane, for example.

One other limitation that private pilots don't have is international flights. Because the sport-pilot certificate is not internationally recognized, you can use it to fly only in the United States. With a private-pilot certificate you can fly in Canada, Mexico, or wherever else that's under the International Civil Aviation Organization (ICAO) rules. In addition, private pilots can fly at night and with lower visibility requirements than sport pilots.

With these benefits come additional training requirements and costs. The private-pilot certificate costs at least twice as much to get as the sport-pilot certificate. Also, the aircraft you'll be flying, with the exception of much older models, will be more expensive to buy, rent, or lease than sport aircraft. Fortunately, you can take your private-pilot training in a sport aircraft; you just can't take your sport-pilot certificate in any craft that doesn't qualify as a sport aircraft. In addition, the lower medical requirements for sport pilots—one of the advantages of being a sport pilot—could keep many sport pilots from becoming private pilots.

Training

Training for your private-pilot certificate is similar to that for the sport-pilot certificate, only there's more of it. Instead of 20 hours of instruction, your private-pilot certificate will require a minimum of 40 hours of instruction—with 60 or more hours typical. In addition, the knowledge test has more questions and the checkride is more comprehensive than that for the sport-pilot certificate.

Fortunately, you'll be able to apply your sport-pilot flight instruction and some of your logbook time toward your private-pilot certificate requirements. So getting your "private" could involve about the same effort again as you put into getting your sport-pilot certificate.

For the time being, there are many places where you can get a private-pilot certificate, so choosing a flight school or certified flight instructor (CFI) is relatively easy. And now that you're a smart aviation consumer, you know how to get top value for every dollar you spend on flight instruction.

Instrument Rating and Others

Once you have a private-pilot certificate you can add a rating or two. For example, many private pilots want to be able to fly under instrument flight rules (IFR), especially in places where the weather isn't always that great. With an instrument rating you can fly anytime and anywhere the big commercial jets can.

Let's take a closer look at the instrument rating for your private or higher certificate.

Advantages

The most obvious advantage to adding an instrument rating is that you no longer are limited to visual flight rules. You can fly from here to there using IFR—as long as you have the training and your plane has the equipment for IFR flight.

IFR flying means that ATC helps you stay clear of other aircraft in the area, called separation. You must fly a specified path and follow directions, but this allows you to fly under conditions that keep VFR pilots on the ground. An instrument rating especially makes sense if you travel for business and need to be somewhere on time no matter what the weather.

Training

To get an instrument rating tacked on to your certificate, you'll need to log 50 or more hours of cross-country flight time. Then you'll need 40 hours of instrument flight training, of which at least 15 of the hours must be instrument flight training with a CFII (certified flight instructor who can teach instrument flying). You'll have to pass a knowledge test and the practical test for the instrument rating. There's more fine print, but those are the basic requirements.

Wing Tips

All the primary flight schools that offer ground instruction or knowledge-test training also offer training toward the instrument rating. Check out King Schools, Jeppesen, Cessna Training Centers, Sporty's Pilot Shop, and other training providers for specific information (see Appendix B).

Commercial and ATP Certificates

The big airplanes that take you coast to coast—and even the smaller connecting planes—require pilots to have a commercial-pilot or airline transport-pilot (ATP) certificate. That's reassuring!

If, after flying for a while, you decide you want to pursue a career in commercial aviation, you'll need one or both of these certificates, as well as ratings for instrument flying and for multiengine aircraft.

Advantages

The greatest advantage commercial pilots have is that they get paid for what they love to do—fly! Sure, it can become a "job" after a while, but few will trade it for a desk job.

To fly passengers for pay you must have a commercial-pilot certificate. An airline transport-pilot certificate is broader and is typically required for flying larger aircraft. In addition, both certificates allow for ratings to be added on for multiengine and various types of aircraft.

If you're considering a career as a professional pilot, I recommend you go to the best school you can afford. The better airlines want graduates from the better schools. Some even have their own schools to train pilots their way and build loyalty. Many of these schools offer low or free tuition for pilots who accept employment with the school's airline sponsor. Start your career by joining the AOPA and reading their *Flight Training* magazine to find out which schools are most respected in the industry.

Training

Chances are your local airport or flight school won't be able to train you as a career pilot. Fortunately, there are many places that can, and most of them are showcased on the Internet.

A good place to start is at www.jetcareers.com, a website for folks who want to be commercial aviators. It provides extensive resources on training (college vs. military vs. flight academies), who's hiring, how to get hired, and a chat room where you can talk with active airline pilots about their careers. It's a great aviation career resource!

How much will training toward an ATP certificate cost? Just as costs vary with the particular college, costs for your commercial-pilot training in flight school can be minimal ($20,000 and lots of work and study) or in the stratosphere ($100,000 or more). Just as with college, you can obtain scholarships to help you out or even pay your way. Talk with professional pilots and ask them for advice. Decide on what your flying goals are (airlines, business jets, freight, international flight, etc.) and find a mentor to help you reach them.

Becoming an Instructor

Many pilots, especially those who want to be paid to fly, become instructors. You can be an FAA-certified flight instructor (CFI) by passing additional knowledge and flight tests, and then use your job to "build air time" toward higher certificates and ratings.

CFR-61, Subpart H, covers the requirements for becoming a flight instructor for various types of certificates and ratings. For example, you can be an instructor for the sport-pilot certificate but not for training private or commercial pilots. In other words, a person licensed as a sport pilot may instruct sport pilots only. The flight-instructor certificate is not a pilot license, but is an addition to the license you already hold.

Advantages

Like commercial pilots, flight instructors get paid to fly. However, not everyone who loves to fly is an effective teacher. If you have the desire to teach others, this can be a very rewarding career that you can do full-time or even part-time. Many excellent flight instructors do it because they truly enjoy and are good at teaching flying basics. They have no aspirations to fly passenger jets to San Francisco or freight to Bangkok.

In addition, popular independent flight instructors can earn a very good primary or supplemental income by offering their services through local airports or fixed-base operators (FBOs). An independent flight instructor can make a thousand dollars a month in extra cash working weekends only.

Training

In addition to earning a pilot certificate, an instructor needs an additional FAA certificate that authorizes him or her to teach others how to fly. This certificate requires a specific number of hours as the pilot in command of that type of aircraft as well as additional training. There are courses for instructors just as there are for students.

If you're interested in a career as a flight instructor, ask your instructor for additional information and advice. Most will be glad to share career info with you, just as they've shared their knowledge and love of flying.

The Future of Sport Flying

Sport flying is relatively new, the product of many great aviation resources working hard toward lower-cost flying. You are now part of a century-old industry that continually proves that change is good.

In the coming years, sport flying will become increasingly popular as more people find out how easy—and how relatively inexpensive—it is to fly. Anticipating the thousands of new sport pilots, the general-aviation industry has already introduced many new models of light-sport aircraft. As they become increasingly popular, you will see even lower costs and more opportunities to fly on a budget. Just as the automobile required mass production to bring it to the masses, so light-sport aircraft will add to the ranks of sport pilots.

The Least You Need to Know

- Once you have your sport-pilot certificate, you can stretch your wings with endorsements.
- Your next logical step in aviation is the private-pilot certificate, which gives you many more flying opportunities.
- You can take flying as far as you want—including as a commercial pilot or a flight instructor.
- As new models of light-sport aircraft are introduced, sport flying will become increasingly popular and inexpensive.

Part 4

Choosing Your Sport Plane

Congratulations! You're a sport pilot! Now what?

Your new sport-pilot certificate won't do you much good without a sport plane, but which one? How much will it cost to fly? How can you get the best plane for the buck? Where?

This part shows you how to find, fund, borrow, and even build your own sport plane. Your options are almost infinite. I'll tell you what they are and how to get the most for every dollar you spend on sport flying. Along the way I'll share some money-saving tips that will help you keep down the cost of going up. You'll also learn how to save hundreds or even thousands of dollars by doing some of your own sport-plane maintenance.

Ready to spread your wings? Let's go shopping for *big* toys!

Chapter 14

Sport Planes

In This Chapter

- A look at the new light-sport aircraft (LSA)
- Making sure that LSAs are safe
- What you can fly and what you can't
- Consider older and experimental aircraft

If you were a private pilot, you could not fly a Boeing 747. Not only don't you have an ATP (airline transport-pilot) certificate, but you don't have training on flying larger and more complex aircraft. The same goes for sport pilots: Sport pilots can fly only sport aircraft that fit the definition of light-sport.

Fortunately, the rules for new light-sport aircraft are as dramatically reworked as the sport-pilot certification rules. It's as though the FAA threw out many of their preconceived ideas about how complex a plane needs to be, and started over with simpler rules. The result is lower-cost flying!

What Are the New Light-Sport Aircraft?

A light-sport aircraft is larger than an ultralight and smaller than most private-aviation aircraft. It borrows from both types, offering simplicity with safety. It's a low-performance, low-energy aircraft limited to two occupants (pilot and passenger). It's absolute fun!

The FAA has been working with the aircraft industry and trade groups for more than three years to come up with a new category of aircraft (and pilots) to meet an expanding need. People want to fly simple aircraft for about the cost of other recreational vehicles. The new rules could carry over to, and eventually change, other pilot certificates and aircraft manufacturing. For now, it's a bold new step that will dramatically impact general aviation for many years.

The best way to define light-sport aircraft is to list their limits. Here's how the FAA defines the limits of LSAs:

- 1,320 lbs. (599 kg.) maximum certified gross weight (1,430 lbs. if float-equipped)
- Two-occupant seating (pilot and one passenger)
- Single, nonturbine engine only
- Fixed-pitch or ground adjustable propeller (not adjustable while flying)
- Maximum cruise airspeed of 138 mph (120 knots) and stall speed of 51 mph (45 knots)
- Fixed (not retractable) landing gear
- Unpressurized cabin

It's that simple. The limits were determined by the rules that restrict what a sport pilot may fly. These limits resulted in what many sport pilots were asking for: a simple airplane. In the 1930s and 1940s a number of manufacturers came out with simple aircraft, names that are legends, such as Cessna, Piper, Taylorcraft, and Aeronca. They flew "low and slow." Planes then became more and more complex, leaving the idea of a simple aircraft behind. Fortunately, flying is returning to its roots—and adding a little pizzazz. LSAs fly at *twice* highway speed. Let's take a closer look at the most important of the limits.

Wing Tips

You are permitted to have landing gear that can be "repositioned" if your plane is equipped with floats to operate on land and water.

Weight Limit

The performance of aircraft is greatly affected by weight. A heavier aircraft requires a larger engine and wings. Also, the weight limit tends to restrict the distance the aircraft can fly, because each gallon of fuel weighs about 6 lbs., deducted from the useful load the airplane can carry.

LSAs are limited to a maximum certified gross weight of 1,320 lbs., or 599 kg. Gross weight means that everything is included: you, your passenger, luggage, fuel, lunch, etc. It's also called the maximum takeoff weight. Ultralights are limited by their number of seats (one in most models, two in trainers) and empty weight (without pilot or gas). Gross weight makes more sense because it gives the designers a specific takeoff weight that they can work with, rather than an approximation depending on how heavy the ultralight pilot is. The figure of 599 kg is similar to that used by the "ultralight" class of aircraft in Europe.

Seating

LSAs have seating for two, a pilot and a passenger, making them friendlier than pilot-only ultralights. You can take a friend up with you—or you can take lots of luggage or even extra fuel.

Like other small general-aviation aircraft, LSAs come in two seating configurations: side by side and tandem (one behind the other). Both are popular for different reasons. Most aircraft with tandem seating are high wing as well, offering both the pilot and passenger clear visibility out of either side of the aircraft. Side-by-side seating is found in both high- and low-wing aircraft.

Engine

Engines in sport aircraft can be two-stroke, four-stroke, or whatever. They just have to conform to the limits and other good-sense requirements. One of the requirements is that the engine is a reciprocating engine. Gas turbine engines are not allowed.

There is no horsepower limit for the engine, but the basic lightweight design of the plane will result in it using an engine of about 100 horsepower or less. Some of the engines in sport planes are ones that were originally developed for homebuilts and ultralights, such as the Rotax line. Others are new, downsized engines produced by manufacturers such as Lycoming and Continental, who also make engines for larger aircraft. One of the advantages of buying a finished aircraft rather than building your own is that the engine decision has already been made for you, though you might have an option or two.

Maximum speeds, too, are critical to the definition of LSAs. That's because sport aircraft are designed to be simple and safe. Increasing the maximum airspeed of an aircraft can greatly complicate an otherwise simple plane. The FAA limits are reasonable. Your craft must be rated by the manufacturer for no more than a "maximum continuous power" or V_H. It's not the airplane's highest speed (called V_{NE} or never-exceed speed), but the maximum speed in level flight. For LSAs that number is 120 *knots* or 138 *mph*.

Flying Words

Which should you use: knots or mph? Most regulations and manufacturers present speeds in **knots** or nautical miles per hour. If you become a commercial pilot, you will use knots almost exclusively. However, many sport and recreational pilots prefer **mph** or miles per hour because that's what they use when driving. Use whichever you wish—as long as you identify whether it is knots or mph. ATC (air traffic control) uses only knots, so you must remember to use that measurement during radio communications. To convert knots into mph, simply multiply knots by 1.15. To convert mph into knots, multiply mph by .87.

Stall speed is important, too, because that's the speed at which the aircraft lands. The stall speed needs to be 45 knots (51 mph) or lower. Without flaps it can be 51 knots (59 mph) or lower. The point is that these simple aircraft should have low landing speeds to make them easier and safer to land.

Certification vs. Consensus

One of the biggest changes in the new SP/LSA world is how aircraft are determined to be airworthy, or officially considered safe enough to fly. As you've learned, small aircraft are inherently safe, and the manufacturing focus has been on making them safe. However, the rules have become very restrictive over the years, making it quite expensive for an aircraft manufacturer to get FAA approval on a plane. Yet the result isn't an inherently safer aircraft. Planes fly just fine; it's the pilots who need to be made airworthy!

So the rules have been changed and the cost of manufacturing safe and airworthy aircraft is going down. The rule change involves the difference between certification and consensus. Let's take a closer look.

Aircraft Certification

The FAA (and, previously, the Civil Aviation Authority [CAA]) has regulated aircraft manufacturing for more than 50 years, working hard toward making all aircraft as safe as they can be. In addition, the FAA requires periodic inspections, certified mechanics, and other rules that ensure public safety. To their credit, aircraft that are properly maintained and repaired last a very long time. Many pilots fly small aircraft that are older than they are.

The flip side is that if cars were required to follow the same rules, new vehicles would cost $100,000 or more, and engine overhauls would be required, by law, at, say, every 100,000 miles. Driving would be much more expensive, and not necessarily that much safer.

All civil (nonmilitary) aircraft require a current airworthiness certificate stored in a visible location somewhere in the plane. It includes information about the manufacture and certification of the craft. To get an airworthiness certificate the plane must be built in an FAA-certified factory to approved plan standards or, if homebuilt, inspected and tested by an FAA official. Certifying a new aircraft design and the factory in which it is built can be very expensive (read: many millions of dollars). That's why few really new designs are coming out of aircraft plants today. Most are simply upgrades and enhancements to designs that have been certified for years.

So how did light-sport aircraft get around the need for certification?

Consensus Standards

Engineering has evolved tremendously over the past 100 years, and standards for metal, construction, and machinery have stood the tests of time. One of the organizations that has standardized much of this engineering is ASTM (American Society for Testing and Materials) International, a standards association that tests and publishes standards for just about anything you can think of. It helps standardize materials so that you can buy something by the ASTM standard rather than a brand name, and you get a consistent product with reliable results.

Light-sport aircraft manufacturers have agreed to design and build their planes using a new set of LSA-specific standards published by ASTM International. These are called consensus airworthiness standards, meaning that everyone agrees to use specific grades and types of materials as well as construction standards when building their aircraft. The manufacturers then give owners standards for how to maintain these craft to keep them airworthy.

Wing Tips

If you'd like to see it, ASTM standard WK627, "Specifications for Airworthiness of Light-Sport Aircraft," is available at www.astm.org. It's an engineer's bedtime story!

So, What's the Bottom Line?

As you can imagine, the cost of manufacturing airplanes to these new consensus standards is much lower than for FAA certification. That's one of the great benefits of the new SP/LSA rulings: Aircraft are about half as expensive to make. And, as more planes are made, costs will come down even further. You might soon see assembly lines of airplanes just like you see of cars.

But are they *safe?* Yes! They still are much safer than the pilots who fly them! Even awkward-looking aircraft become efficient flying machines when airborne and in their own element. There still are rules and regulations for maintaining light-sport aircraft. The rules just aren't as stringent as for an aircraft that takes 500 people to 35,000 ft. MSL (mean sea level). They are safe enough!

New Light-Sport Aircraft

There's an amazing array of new light-sport aircraft in the marketplace and many more models coming out in the next year or two. If LSA rules are so new, where did these aircraft come from? Good question!

Allegro.

Buse Air.

Kolb Sport 600.

Loehle 5151.

Murphy JDM-8.

Murphy Maverick.

Tetras.

X-Air Hanuman.

Some of the new LSAs started life as kit planes, designed and manufactured so that amateur homebuilders could assemble them in 200 to 500 hours and fly them as experimental aircraft. During the three-year process of developing the LSA rules, some of these kit-plane manufacturers decided to offer finished aircraft, completing the assembly themselves. Of course, the assembled craft are more expensive than kits, but they're still much less expensive than standard certified aircraft.

Wing Tips

Light-sport aircraft is a brand new category of planes, official since September 1, 2004. Some of the model specifications will be modified during the first year, and others, such as fuel capacity, can be selected by the buyer. Contact the LSA manufacturer (see Appendix B) for the latest specifications and options.

Europe has had what they call ultralight aircraft for a few years now. There are aircraft made in various EU (European Union) countries that fit in the new LSA category. Some manufacturers are making slight modifications to their design to make sure they fit into this new market. Here are some examples of new LSAs that actually have been around a while.

Zodiac XL

The Zodiac XL is a low-wing, side-by-side, light-sport aircraft with tricycle gear. It has a gross weight of 1,232 lbs. with an empty weight of 690 lbs., meaning you can pack it with 542 lbs. of pilot, passenger, fuel, luggage, and whatever. It has two 12-gallon fuel tanks for a range of about 600 miles excluding reserve. That's nearly 5 hours of flying. (Of course, you'll always make sure you have 30 to 60 minutes of fuel reserve—just in case.)

Zodiac XL.

Takeoff and landing distances are important to many pilots who fly from shorter fields. The Zodiac XL has a takeoff roll of 490 ft., a landing distance of 500 ft., and a climb rate of 980 feet per minute (fpm). Specifications are with the 100-hp Rotax

912S engine. Alternately, the 110-hp Jabiru 3300 engine is available for about the same takeoff and landing specs and a climb rate of 1,245 fpm.

The Zodiac XL and other LSAs are designed and built by Zenith Aircraft Co., Mexico Airport, PO Box 650, Mexico, MO 65265. Phone: 573-581-9000. Website: www.zenithair.com.

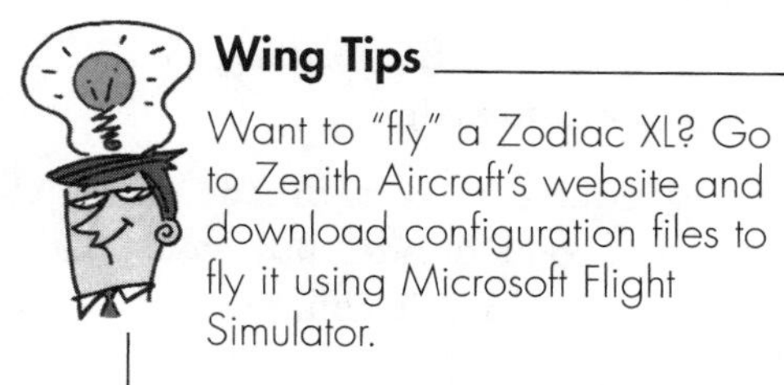

Kitfox Sport

For sport pilots who like the style and ground visibility of high-wing aircraft, the Kitfox Sport is very popular. Yet, it isn't slow as older aircraft are. With an average useful load of 532 lbs., it can carry two passengers, lots of fuel (20+ gallons), and some luggage, too. Cruise and stall speeds meet LSA requirements.

Takeoff and landing rolls are relatively short at 275 ft. each, meaning this is a plane designed for short-takeoff and landing (STOL) flying. It gets off the ground quickly. That's great if you're flying out of a short field. However, it also means taxiing too fast can make you airborne before you realize it. The rate of climb is very good, too: 1,300 fpm.

The Kitfox Sport actually is the latest version in the Kitfox series. The kit version is called the Series 7, and the Sport version has most of the same features, fully assembled.

The Kitfox Sport and other models are built and sold by SkyStar Aircraft Corp., 3901 Aviation Way, Caldwell, ID 83605. Phone: 1-800-554-8639. Website: www.skystar.com.

ATEC Zephyr

A popular EU entry is the ATEC Zephyr, designed and manufactured in the Czech Republic. The Zephyr is a low-wing, side-by-side, tricycle-gear LSA with a T-tail (elevators at the top of the tail). The speeds and flight specifications are similar to other LSAs.

What's different about the Zephyr is that it uses carbon fiber construction to be more streamlined. Also, it has a very high glide ratio: 16:1. Many small planes have a glide ratio of about 9:1, meaning they will glide for 9 miles for every 1 mile they are above ground level (AGL).

The North American distributor of the ATEC Zephyr is ATEC Aviation, 15526-95A Ave., Surrey, BC (Canada) V3R 7S7. Phone: 604-581-0041. Website: www.atecaviation.com.

Of course, there are many more new light-sport aircraft on the market. This is just an introduction to show you what's available. For more information, visit www.sportflyingguide.com.

Classic LSAs

I use the term "classic LSA," but what we're going to talk about are not certified as the "new LSA." They are aircraft that have been around for years and are certified under the FAA standard rules. However, they do meet the limitations assigned to sport pilots.

Because the new LSA consensus standards are an *alternate* method of getting an aircraft certified, you still can fly planes that were built under FAA standard certification—if they meet the other requirements for sport pilots to operate them.

What does that mean? It means that there are dozens of proven aircraft designs and models built over the past 60 or more years that you can fly with your sport-pilot certificate! You don't have to wait until just the right new model rolls out.

Piper J-3 Cub

One of the most popular recreational aircraft of all time qualifies as a light-sport aircraft: the Piper J-3 Cub. Designed in the 1930s, the Piper Cub is no longer in direct production, but you can still get a modern version known as the Taylorcraft F-19.

Piper J-3 Cub.

The Piper Cub is a two-place (tandem), high-wing, fabric-covered taildragger built from 1938 to 1947. Its offspring, the Super Cub (not sport-pilot eligible), was produced into the 1980s. If you're not in a hurry, the Cub is your friend as it cruises at about 75 mph, depending on whether it has the Continental 40 or 65 hp engine. For the record, there are more than 40 older Piper models that technically qualify as eligible for sport pilots.

By today's standards, the Cub is a very slow aircraft. However, if you're not in a hurry and you're looking for nostalgia, the Cub is a great airplane for sport pilots. I tell you how and where to find them in the next chapter.

Aeronca Champion

After World War II many wartime aircraft manufacturers thought that returning servicemen would be clamoring to continue flying, so the industry was shifted from warbirds to funbirds. From 1945 to 1949, the Aeronautical Corporation of America (Aeronca) built a number of planes that now qualify as LSAs. After Aeronca folded, other manufacturers took over and reproduced the same design for many years.

The Aeronca Champion (affectionately known as the Airknocker or Champ) was one of the more popular models and is still widely available—and flyable—more than a half century later. The performance specifications are a little more impressive than the Piper Cub, but still are in the category of "low and slow." You can buy a Champ for less than a Cub and the prices don't go down, so they've been popular with new student pilots for many years.

By the way, there are over 25 models of Aeronca aircraft that qualify as LSAs. They are a good option.

Luscombe Silvaire

Another oldie but goodie is a classic metal-covered aircraft built by various companies from 1946 to 1960: the Luscombe Silvaire. What makes them look so retro is that they are metal-covered rather than fabric-covered (though some early models had fabric-covered wings). Only models 8A and 8B qualify for sport-pilot operation.

If you decide that one of these classic birds is for you, make sure it meets the weight limit for LSAs. Because the weight of a Silvaire is very near the class limit, if someone upgraded the plane with additional instruments, you might find that it's too heavy to qualify.

CAUTION

Stall Warning!

These standard-certified airplanes must be certified to not exceed sport-pilot limitations. You cannot simply take the back seat out of an over-the-weight-limit plane to fly it within the weight limit.

There are many other older aircraft that qualify for sport-pilot operation. Cruise speed typically isn't what makes them ineligible, it's usually their gross weight. Fortunately, you can check a plane's certification records to determine the gross weight.

Experimental Aircraft

As I've mentioned, homebuilt or "experimental" aircraft have been around for decades. The first aircraft were all homebuilt. Even today, a century later, there are thousands of experimental aircraft at varying stages of completion in garages across the country.

Airborne Edge Trike.

Hundreds of homebuilt or experimental aircraft plans and kits qualify under the sport-pilot rules. That means you can build your own aircraft, then fly it under your sport-pilot certificate. In addition, a new type of homebuilt plane will become available called the "experimental" LSA. The new rules don't require that you construct a "major portion" (interpreted as at least 51 percent) of the experimental LSA. You now can build less than 51 percent using quick-build kits.

I tell you more about building your own sport pilot-eligible airplane in Chapter 18. You also can learn more through the Experimental Aircraft Association (EAA) (www.eaa.org). The EAA publishes an extensive resource and catalog called AeroCrafter that comes with a CD.

The Least You Need to Know

- Know the limits of the new sport-pilot and light-sport aircraft (SP/LSA) rules so you can choose the best plane for you.
- The new consensus standards dramatically reduced the cost of manufacturing aircraft without reducing safety.
- Many new LSAs are on the market and many more are coming as people discover sport flying.
- Classic and even homebuilt aircraft can qualify for sport-pilot operation.

Chapter 15

Finding Your Sport Plane

In This Chapter

- Selecting the sport plane that's right for you
- Questions to ask yourself and others
- Figuring out how much money it will take to fly your plane
- Making sure you get the most value for your aviation dollars

Now that you've earned your sport-pilot certificate, you're probably anxious to get your own airplane! Not so fast. There's more you need to know.

The last chapter introduced you to the new light-sport aircraft (LSA) and other planes a sport pilot may fly. The next few chapters show you how to buy, share, build, and maintain your new wings. *This* chapter shows you how to choose the right plane to meet your needs. You want to make the best decision so you get the most from every dollar you spend on sport flying.

Getting What You Want

Advertising is designed to push us toward buying something we probably don't need and can't afford. For example, millions of dollars are spent on ads to show you what it would be like to drive your car in places no one really drives, such as desolate desert roads or closed-course test tracks. The reality is that you'll probably drive bumper to bumper in a line of commuters. But commuting isn't sexy. It doesn't sell cars. It's reality.

What's reality for planes? What should you know before you go shopping for your first light-sport aircraft or other sport pilot-eligible airplane? You need to decide how you're going to use it. How can you do that? By asking questions of yourself and others, and then considering your options. Let's get started.

Esqual VM 1.

Pipistrel.

Polaris.

Asking Questions

You can run out and buy or lease the first LSA that has the right paint job, but you might soon become dissatisfied with your wings—which means you won't fly it as much as one that's equipped with features that really matter to you. The trick to choosing almost anything is learning from your first one to select your second one, but that can get expensive. The purpose of this chapter is to give you advice from other aircraft owners on what to select—and what to avoid—on your first plane.

The process starts by asking yourself lots of relevant questions and getting the answers that most fit your needs. One of the reasons so many *used* airplanes are out there is that the first owners weren't satisfied with their planes when they were new. That's because the new owners didn't ask the right questions—or know what questions they should ask—before choosing. You're not going to make that mistake. You're going to keep and enjoy your sport plane for many years.

So let's get to the questions. The first ones aren't about the plane, but about how you intend to fly. Getting to the answers will take some thought as you estimate the way you'll use your plane next year, three years from now, and well into the future. Fortunately, you have a history of using vehicles (cars, boats, RVs, etc.) to give you a starting point. Here are some questions to ask yourself:

- A year from now, how many hours of flying do you realistically expect to do each week?
- Will your flying be entirely for pleasure, for business, or for both? How many hours of each?
- Is your primary purpose in flying to view the ground from above or to travel from here to there?
- Where will you be flying? Local? Regional? Interstate? National?
- Who will your passenger(s) be? Spouse? Partner? Children? Friends? Associates? Clients? Will they soon tire of flying and leave you alone in the sky? If so, is that okay?
- Because of where you live, will your flying be seasonal or year-round?
- Because of where you live, will you be limited in the number of nearby airports to which you can fly?
- Can you legitimately share the cost of your sport plane with a business?
- Are the airport runways you will typically use short, long, grass, or paved?
- Does your home-base airport have adequate hangar space for rent at a reasonable cost, or will you use a tie-down parking spot?

- Is it smarter to own a sport plane with fold-up wings so you can tow the craft home and park it in your garage between flights?
- Will you be doing many cross-country trips? If so, will you fly primarily by pilotage (looking out the window), dead reckoning (navigation radios), or GPS?
- Are you a larger pilot (over 200 lbs.) who needs a little more room and a little more power in your plane?
- Will you be doing any landings on water (requiring additional endorsements and equipment)?
- How comfortable do the seats need to be?
- Will you be taking much luggage with you as you fly?
- Will you use your sport plane for camping, wilderness flying, fishing or hunting trips, or other recreational sports?
- Are you a social person who wants to go to every fly-in within fuel range?
- Do you expect to trade in your sport plane within a couple of years for a plane that flies faster or holds more passengers?
- Do you have support within your family toward your goal of flying?

Wing Tips

I recommend that you record your answers to these questions and even prioritize them so that you can keep your goals in mind as you select your wings. Making the right choice of your first sport plane can not only cut costs, but greatly enhance every hour you fly it.

The list of questions could go on for pages. These are the most important and they will help you think through *how* you will fly before you decide *what* to fly.

Considering Your Options

What options do you have? One of the *advantages* of the new light-sport aircraft rulings is that it limits your options. If you eventually want more options, you can step up to higher-performance aircraft and a private-pilot certificate. But in order to fly under your sport-pilot certificate you *must* fly a plane that qualifies for the limitations a sport pilot must adhere to. While the rules might limit your options, you have a lot less information to process, which is an advantage for the fledgling pilot.

When selecting general or private aircraft you have options regarding weight, power, seating, cruise speed, range, landing gear, propeller, and avionics (aviation electronics). A sport plane, by definition, limits most of these options for you. Limiting them makes flying a little safer and selecting a sport plane a little easier.

The major decision you'll have to make is high-wing or low. As you consider various types of sport planes, you might be told that one is better than the other. There really is no "best" wing configuration. Instead, there are reasons why you should select one over the other—as well as reasons why "it don't matter."

High-wing aircraft offer better ground clearance and visibility for rough-field landings, and are easier to board (especially in the rain). In addition, most planes with folding wings (for towing behind a car) are high-wing planes. Of course, high-wing aircraft offer a clearer view of the ground below and are a favorite with those who do aerial photography and sightseeing.

Low-wing aircraft offer better ground stability (because the center of gravity is lower), better visibility in turns, and greater ease when filling fuel tanks. Low-wing aircraft also offer greater crash protection if you ever have to land where you shouldn't.

The only other configuration issue that you can decide is tricycle or tail gear. All sport planes must be "fixed gear," meaning that you cannot retract them after takeoff to enhance aerodynamics. The landing gear is important only during takeoff and landing, so let's take a quick look at the advantages and disadvantages of each. As I've mentioned, ASES sport pilots are permitted to fly a float plane that allows the floats to be "repositioned" for landing on solid runways.

Aircraft with fixed tricycle gear have two wheels below the cabin and one below the nose. This arrangement provides for greater visibility when taxiing and during the initial takeoff roll. The primary disadvantage is that the nose gear is more susceptible to damage than other types of fixed-gear planes.

Aircraft with fixed tail gear (called taildraggers) have two wheels below the cabin and one below the tail of the plane. Because this configuration makes the cabin slope backward, it is more difficult to taxi in a taildragger. On takeoff, the tail soon lifts off the ground and gives the pilot better visibility. Meantime, the pilot taxies in an S-pattern to see the taxiway better. Tail wheels can take more abuse than nose wheels, so they are selected for rough-field landings. However, taildraggers are a little trickier to land than a tricycle-gear plane, because the tail could swing around in what's called a ground loop.

Tricycle-gear aircraft are increasingly popular because they're easier to take off and land with, but with a little training, you can fly a taildragger just as well. Taildraggers are the configuration of choice for unimproved and barely improved landing fields.

One more factor about gear configurations: cost. With just a small pivoting wheel, taildraggers are less expensive to manufacture. However, the difference really isn't that much. Some of the new LSAs can easily be changed from tricycle to taildragger and back.

What's in *Your* Wallet?

Another important consideration when choosing your sport plane is how much it's going to cost. And, just as with cars, you have initial as well as ongoing costs to consider. The initial cost is how much you pay for the plane (including any loan interest or fees). The ongoing costs for flying include hangar or tie-down rent, insurance, and maintenance. Operating costs are fuel and oil. If you're renting, you have no initial cost, but your ongoing costs (rent) are higher. If you're in a flying club (see Chapter 17), you'll pay a smaller initial fee and lower rents. The next three chapters cover the specifics of buying, renting, and sharing.

Wing Tips

The most expensive components on some aircraft are the avionics. Knowing how you will fly dictates how much avionics you will need. For example, you can buy a handheld nav-com radio and a GPS unit for under $1,000—or you can spend more than $5,000 on a full dual-channel nav-com system.

So the best place to start is to determine how much discretionary income you have for your new-found hobby. Do you have minimal money saved up but can spend a couple hundred dollars a month on flying? Or do you have a larger chunk to put down to keep monthly costs to a minimum?

Initial Costs

Again, the initial costs depend on how you "own" your wings: rent, lease, partner, or buy. For most folks, the initial investment dictates ownership form. That is, if you really don't have enough saved up for a down payment or initial lease payment, you're stuck with renting. If you do have more in the piggy bank, your options grow. In addition, if you have good credit, your options increase because you can get a low-interest loan on your wings.

So let's talk about the prices of sport planes. Depending on what you're looking for, you can find a dependable airplane priced from $10,000 to $100,000. That's quite a range, so let me break it down:

- Used ultralights (these all qualify for sport pilots) can be purchased for $10,000 or even much less.
- Kits that qualify for sport pilots require you to invest from 200 hours to many hundreds of hours of building time. Costs for these start at about $10,000 and go up to about $40,000, depending on the engine you select.

- You can build a sport plane from plans for under $20,000 and a lot of sweat equity.
- Used experimental aircraft that qualify as LSAs can be found for $15,000 to $50,000.
- Used general-aviation aircraft that qualify for sport pilots (Aeronca, J-3 Cub, Luscombe, etc.) sell for $15,000 to $30,000 or more.
- Quick-build experimental LSA kits (you add the finishing touches) can be purchased for $35,000 to $50,000.
- Ready-to-fly planes built under the new LSA rules are priced from $40,000 to $80,000.
- Top-of-the-line LSAs are available with avionic packages for $80,000 to $100,000—about half the price of many new FAA-certified aircraft.

Those are the ballpark figures. For more specifics on current prices, get a copy of *Trade-A-Plane* (www.trade-a-plane.com), *AeroTrader* (www.aerotraderonline.com), or visit Pilotmarket (www.pilotmarket.com) and start learning. I tell you more about buying your sport plane in Chapter 16.

Operating Costs

Operating costs are simply those that change as you fly more. Fuel and oil are operating costs. Scheduled maintenance is an operating cost if it's required based on how many hours your plane has flown. A meter on the control panel will tell you how many hours the engine has been in use and you must perform maintenance on it at regular intervals.

Did you know that you legally can perform some or even all of your own aircraft maintenance? You can do all of your own maintenance if you build a craft that is certified "experimental." You can do some of the maintenance if you buy a new LSA and get an LSA-maintenance certificate, requiring some training and a test. Chapter 19 gives you the specifics.

How can you minimize operating costs? Don't fly! Alternately, make sure you select a fuel-efficient aircraft, learn how to "lean" it for greatest fuel efficiency (directions are in the plane's operating handbook), and keep your plane in optimum mechanical condition. Most pilots keep an aircraft expense log, similar to an automobile expense log, to help them track and manage operating expenses.

Wing Tips

How fuel-efficient are sport planes? About as fuel-efficient as smaller cars! Depending on how you fly, how efficiently you operate your aircraft engine, whether you carry a passenger, and other factors, you'll find that you'll get 20 to 35 miles per gallon of fuel. Some of the ultralights get 50 mpg or more. Yes, avgas (aviation fuel) is more expensive than auto gas, but it's much more fun to empty a tank! Many sport planes may be legally operated on auto fuel, and some *must* use auto fuel. This is another example of the various factors you need to consider when making your choice of a sport plane.

Ongoing Costs

Ongoing costs are those that continue whether you fly or not. They include plane storage (hangar or tie-down rent), insurance, and time-based inspections called annuals.

The one you have the most control over is plane storage. If you have more than one airport nearby, shop around for the lowest hangar rent. Or you can opt for an outdoor parking spot to which you attach your aircraft's wings and tail, called a tie-down. Tie-downs, of course, are much cheaper than hangar rent. However, in areas of high winds or hail, the smartest move might be a storage hangar. Hangar rent can range from $100 to $500 a month or more, depending on the size of the hangar and whether it is shared with other planes.

Wing Tips

There are hundreds of private airports around the country that are not included in the A/FD (Airport/Facility Directory) or other directories. You might find them marked on sectional charts or discover them through other pilots. You sometimes can find low-cost parking or storage on these private strips.

Another option is to choose a plane with folding wings and park your plane in your garage or driveway between trips. It's a little less convenient, but can be much less expensive. New LSAs and experimental aircraft with fold-up wings typically take less than a half hour to make flight-ready. Some can be set up safely in just a few minutes. Any car that can tow an 800-lb. load can pull your empty LSA.

Insurance can be the biggest ongoing cost. If you own a plane, you'll need it whether you're flying or not. There are two types of aviation insurance: hull and liability. Typically, hull insurance is the most expensive. It covers damage to a plane caused by accidents, wind, and hail. Your plane's hull insurance is based on the replacement value of your plane, and the premium goes down if you have a hangar or garage in which to store the plane. Liability insurance covers losses you might incur through injury or damage to other people or their property. If you rent aircraft, you might decide to carry aircraft rental insurance instead (discussed in Chapter 17). You must have liability insurance, but hull insurance is optional.

Insurance brokers and agents will give you cost estimates based on your specific needs. Refer to aviation magazines listed in Appendix B for contact information. You'll see ads for many insurance services in flying magazines published by aviation associations to which you belong.

Another ongoing cost is the price of reading materials such as new sectional charts (refreshed every six months), the A/FD and other airport directories, and flying magazines. Contact the FAA (www.faa.gov) or Sporty's Pilot Shop (www.sportys.com) for these and other pilot resources. To keep the skies friendly, you need to know what's new.

Unexpected Costs

Hopefully, you won't have any unexpected costs. But you might. Like what? Typically, major maintenance or a repair that isn't covered by insurance. One way of avoiding major maintenance and repair costs is shopping smart.

I get into how to buy your wings in the next chapter. Meantime, know that ongoing maintenance has been done on any used aircraft you're considering. Unlike cars, airplanes must have maintenance logs that tell you what's been done and when. You'll especially want to know about airworthiness directives (ADs) or other notifications from the manufacturer that have been issued for the plane you're considering. The directives and other notifications will tell you what should have been fixed to maintain the airplane's airworthiness. You can find out what directives have been issued for certified aircraft by contacting the FAA (www.airweb.faa.gov/ad).

Making Decisions

Selecting a sport plane is similar to selecting a car. You have similar options and each is interrelated with other options. Fortunately, the FAA already has made some of the major decisions for you—such as weight and capacity. You've got many more choices when selecting a car.

The first and most important aspect of deciding on a specific airplane is knowing what you want from it. Make sure you've answered the questions presented earlier in this chapter. Spend some time talking with other pilots, not about makes and models so much as how and why they fly. You could discover some new ways to use your new wings.

Rally.

Remos G-3 Mirage.

Texan.

Second, become an informed consumer. You probably shop for a new car by comparing features and prices and looking for the best relative value. It's the same with deciding about a sport plane. Read the magazines, especially *Sport Pilot*, to find out what's new. Also visit www.sportflyingguide.com online for the latest resources. Refer to *AeroCrafter* (www.aerocrafter.org) and other directories of recreational aircraft.

Third, make sure you try before you decide. The new LSA manufacturers and used-plane owners will let you inspect and fly the aircraft before you decide to buy it. Even if it means you have to jump on a commercial plane to visit a candidate, consider doing it. You certainly wouldn't choose a new or used car without a test drive.

Wing Tips

Many of the new light-sport aircraft manufacturers offer videos and books on their planes. Invest a few bucks in packages from the leading manufacturers to learn what's new. Many kit and plan airplanes also have reasonably priced information packages. See Appendix B for more information.

That's your introduction to choosing a plane, covering how to figure out what you want, how much you can afford, and how to make smart aviation decisions. The next few chapters get more specific about how to buy, share, build, and rent your wings. Enjoy!

The Least You Need to Know

- To get the most from your flying dollars, make sure you ask yourself and others the right questions.
- Many of the decisions for selecting a sport plane are already made for you by the FAA.
- The expenditures of sport flying include initial, operating, ongoing, and unexpected costs.
- Choosing a sport plane is similar to choosing any vehicle—make sure you do your homework before you buy!

Chapter 16

Buying Your Sport Plane

In This Chapter

- Should you buy your own sport plane?
- Where to look for aircraft in your price range
- How to decipher an airplane ad
- Inspecting sport planes for fun and profit
- Financing options
- Closing the deal on your purchase

Possession is nine tenths of the fun!

At least that's what many aircraft owners say. They enjoy the power of having a plane at their disposal whenever they wish. On alternate days, of course, these same owners curse the high price of ongoing expenses that go up even when their planes don't.

What's the answer for the sport pilot? Should you buy your own plane or shouldn't you? For some pilots, plane ownership is a cost-effective eagle. For others, it's a very expensive albatross. Your decision to buy or not to buy must be based on facts more than feelings if you hope to join the friendly skies of sport flying. This chapter shows you how to make the smartest decision for *you*.

Shopping Around

Before you decide whether you want to buy a sport aircraft, let's take a closer look at how and why to do it. Then you'll learn some of the jargon of buying a plane.

The selection process begins with a search of all available sources. Surprisingly, there are probably hundreds of sport planes on the market in your area. In addition, there are many thousands more if you're willing to do a little traveling. Where? Let's go find out!

Where to Look

Before you decided to get into sport flying, you probably noticed only a few planes for sale. But as you learned to fly, you discovered that nearly *every* plane is for sale. Narrowing the field is going to be your biggest challenge. Let's take a look at the many resources of new and used sport aircraft.

- **Aircraft dealers.** Plane manufacturers are like car makers in that they prefer to have dealers sell their vehicles for them. Nearly all plane builders use authorized dealerships where you can inspect the newest models and trade-ins. Some of these dealers are "authorized," meaning they get first choice on new models and are authorized to do repairs. Some are "independent" dealers, selling any brand they want; they might or might not have a service department. Both authorized and independent aircraft dealers typically sell used aircraft on a consignment basis, taking a fee from the owner if they sell the plane. Because aircraft dealers are based at airports, that's the first place to start looking for new and used sport aircraft.
- **Auctions.** Aircraft auctions are a good source for used planes—if you know what you're looking at. Most first-time plane buyers don't attend auctions without taking along an experienced aircraft owner or broker who can help them select and buy the right plane. You'll find aircraft auctions advertised in the classified section of major city newspapers and flying publications.
- **Online.** You can find thousands of aircraft for sale—including many sport planes—online. The most popular source is eBay Motors (www.ebaymotors.com), the world's largest auction. As this book is being written, a quick search of the aircraft category shows 167 planes available this week—everything from a $1,000 basket case to a half-million-dollar zoom machine. There are lots of sport planes mixed in there. AeroPrice (www.aeroprice.com) is another good resource for buying airplanes. They offer buying, selling, and appraisal services to help you get your money's worth.

- **Publications.** There is a variety of aviation publications, and many of them focus on helping pilots buy and sell aircraft. The granddaddy is *Trade-A-Plane* (www.trade-a-plane.com), published since 1937. It's a monthly and is available at some larger private airports and through bigger newsstands. *AeroTrader* (www.aerotraderonline.com) is another monthly buy-sell publication for planes. In addition, check the ads in *Sport Pilot* magazine (www.sportpilot.org) and *Flight Training* (www.aopa.org). Numerous regional aviation publications such as *The Oklahoma Aviator* (www.oklahomaaviator.com) also have classified ads for buying and selling aircraft. Even closer to home, check out the classified ads in your favorite metro newspaper, and you'll probably find lots of sport aircraft for sale nearby.

AeroTrader *is one of many periodicals that bring aircraft buyers and sellers together.*

- **Bulletin boards.** Most small airports have a bulletin board for pilots. You'll find ads, services, events, and even personal notes tacked up. Check out airports in your area for for-sale ads. Also walk around an airport's tie-down area because many owners simply post a "For Sale" sign in the window of their plane.
- **Airport personnel and other pilots.** One of the easiest ways to discover what's for sale at your nearby airport is to ask the FBO (fixed-base operator) or airport manager. They typically know what's for sale. They also might offer some valuable advice on selecting the right plane—and avoiding the wrong one. Ask other pilots, too. Most pilots will be very helpful if you simply tell them you're a new pilot looking for help in selecting your first plane. People *love* to help.

Deciphering Plane Ads

You'll discover many aircraft for sale through ads or signs. If you've ever tried to read some of these communications, you know they're confusing because they use various acronyms and contractions, called aviation shorthand. Let's take a look at the wording in a typical ad and how to decipher it:

> Kitfix 6, LSA-ready, 350 TT, 40 SMOH, Rtx 912, NAV/COM, GPS, ELT, XPDR, all ADs, Aug. ann.

It translates: Kitfox [manufacturer] 6 [model] that qualifies as a sport plane. It has 350 hours total time on the airframe and 40 hours since a major overhaul. The engine is a Rotax [manufacturer] 912 [model]. It has navigation and communication radios [manufacturer and model not identified], a global positioning satellite system, an emergency locator transmitter, and a transponder. All airworthiness directives (ADs) have been completed and an annual inspection was completed last August. Of course, the ad will also include a price and who to contact.

This particular ad answers many of your primary questions, but leaves a few more (nav-com system components, damage history, condition) that you can clarify if and when you contact the owner.

Think of shopping for a plane as being similar to shopping for a car. You have a list of what you're looking for and you compare each ad with your list, looking for ones you can disqualify. What's left is a field of candidates. From the seller's prospective, the purpose of a classified ad is to tell you enough to answer most of your primary questions, but not so many that you can make a decision to buy based on the ad. Most plane sellers want you to contact them for more information. Consider each conversation with an aircraft owner an opportunity to learn more about planes.

> **Wing Tips**
>
> A few more ad terms include Cont (Continental engine), Lyc (Lycoming engine), FRME (factory remanufactured engine), STOH (since top overhaul), STOL (short takeoff and landing aircraft), and TTAE (total time airframe and engine).

How can you decipher airplane ads for yourself? Most aircraft ad publications include a cheat sheet of acronyms and contractions used in ads. You'll also learn by contacting the owners and asking for an explanation. They're not trying to trick you, they're trying to keep the cost of the ad low by using aviation shorthand. You'll quickly catch on.

Checking It Out

Once you've narrowed the field to a handful of planes, you'll want to make an inspection, then take a test flight to be sure the plane is what you think it is. No surprises, please. Of course, the inspection will be more stringent for used aircraft than for new ones. And the older the plane, the more time and energy you'll want to spend on checking it out. If you have *any* doubts, hire an airframe and power-plant (A&P) mechanic to perform a thorough inspection before you buy (more about them in Chapter 19).

Take your time and inspect the fuselage, power plant, documentation, and flight characteristics before buying any sport plane (shown here, a KP 2U Sova).

What will you be inspecting? The fuselage, including wings and tail, mechanical systems, logs, ADs, owner reports, and aircraft appraisals. Let's go through them one at a time.

Fuselage

The first inspection you'll make is a *very* thorough preflight inspection, checking the fuselage, wings, tail, landing gears, and control surfaces for wear or damage. Examine the outside and as much of the inside of the plane as possible. Check for rust, deterioration, and loose rivets. If the skin is metal, check for serious dents and creases. Inspect the paint for underlying corrosion. If the plane is fabric-covered, have a mechanic test the fabric for strength. Also inspect controls for free and easy operation, instruments for proper operation, and electrical systems for condition and obvious additions and repairs. Make sure you examine all tubing and hydraulic lines for age and wear.

Mechanical Systems

Open or remove the engine cowling and inspect the unit for the condition of incoming controls and fuel lines. Inspect the carburetor and gasket. Check the intake and exhaust manifolds for leaks and general condition. Make sure that necessary parts such as the magnetos, starter, alternator, oil sump, fuel pump, and carburetor are attached securely and in good condition, with no loose components. Then inspect the propeller and hub for cracks and nicks, especially on the leading edge. Make sure the prop is securely mounted. Check the brakes and connection lines to make sure they're in good condition and secure. Inspect the tires for damage, wear, and proper air pressure.

Logs and Airworthiness Directives (ADs)

The maintenance logs for your aircraft could be clean for new aircraft or very long for older ones. In addition, the logs for LSAs look different from those for larger private aircraft. The airframe and engine logbooks note the inspections and repairs that have been made to the plane. They also should record maintenance to specific ADs on the craft. Separately, you should research to find out what ADs have been issued for this plane, then verify that each has been satisfactorily fixed. Some ADs require ongoing and regular inspections and repairs, adding to the overall cost of the aircraft.

If the aircraft you're inspecting has FAA standard certification, owners are required to perform AD maintenance or repairs as directed. If it follows consensus standards, the manufacturer will notify owners of required ADs. So make sure you know what the ADs are for any aircraft you buy *before* you buy it.

If you're buying an experimental (homebuilt) aircraft, the paperwork is slightly different. For example, the airworthiness certificate in the plane will be clearly marked "experimental." Make sure that you know enough about the model and the builder to make an informed decision about buying and maintaining it. ADs are not issued for experimental airplanes. If in doubt, ask the EAA (Experimental Aircraft Association) (www.eaa.org).

Wing Tips

Want to find out what ADs have been issued for a specific make and model of plane? Check online at www.airweb.faa.gov/ad. Also, AD research services can be found online (search for "airworthiness directive") or through flying magazines. ADs for the new LSAs are available from the manufacturer.

Reports and Appraisals

Just as there are for cars, there are consumer reporting services that tell you more about specific makes and models of aircraft, even the latest models. You can find such a service in various ways. First, ask the owner or dealer to suggest aviation report and appraisal services, keeping in mind that some won't recommend ones that say negative things about what they're selling. A good place to start is Aviation Consumer (www.aviation-consumer.com), though it currently covers few of the new LSA aircraft. Many smaller aircraft are covered in the *Ultralight Aircraft Shopper's Guide* annual (www.ultralight-aircraft.com), now updated to include many sport planes. In addition, appraisal services can help you determine if the asking price is a fair one. Plan to spend a few hundred dollars on such an appraisal, but that can be an investment that saves you time and money.

Wing Tips

Want a *free* aircraft appraisal? Call an aircraft loan service (found in leading aviation magazines) and ask for it. Many will give you a comprehensive appraisal at no cost for the opportunity to handle your loan.

Closing the Deal

Made your decision? Know what plane you want and just need to pull together the money?

Actually, that's backward. Let's go shopping for financing first, then make your deal. You'll save time and money in the long run.

Financing Your Wings

Maybe you can simply write a check for your new wings. If not, keep reading because there are many ways to save money on financing your sport aircraft.

First, try your favorite bank. You might be surprised to learn the bank that holds your car loan also lends on aircraft, too. Many lenders do. Being a customer in good standing can get you a preferred rate—or at least less hassle. You might need to educate your loan officer a little about the model you're buying, but most are very willing to make low-cost loans with secured collateral.

If you're buying your sport aircraft through a dealer, ask about house financing. The dealer might have a loan package all set up with a preferred aviation lender that can get you the lowest rates. Just as car loans often involve loan fees, so do plane loans, so be on the lookout, because such fees can drive up the total cost of your financing. Ask for the effective annual percentage rate (APR), which includes all interest charges and fees. Be aware that most lenders won't lend on kits, because kits have no collateral to resell until you finish building it.

By reading ads in various flying magazines you'll find a plethora of lenders just waiting for an opportunity to lend you money for your first or next aircraft. Call them. Compare rates and services. Learn from every contact you make.

Of course, many aviation loans are available online. As you must do with any online financial transaction, make sure you know who you're dealing with (ask about referrals, recommendations, accreditation) and proceed with caution. However, you might find that borrowing online is just as easy and safe as borrowing from your local bank—and sometimes you can save yourself time and money. Some of the primary aviation lenders online include AirFleet Capital (www.airfleetcapital.com), Beacon Credit Services (www.beaconcredit.com), MBNA Corp. (www.mbna.com), and National Aircraft Finance Co. (www.airloans.com). If you're a member of the Aircraft Owners and Pilots Association (AOPA) (www.aopa.org) or the Experimental Aircraft Association (EAA) (www.eaa.org), check out their websites for preferred lenders.

There's one more financial resource to try: the owner. Some aircraft owners who have free-and-clear title opt to sell their craft on an installment contract at an interest rate higher than they can get if they deposit their money in the bank. If you prove you're a worthwhile credit risk and put at least 20 percent down in cash or trade, you might find the fastest and fairest terms through the aircraft's seller.

The application you fill out for plane financing is identical to the one for a car loan, so get a copy and look it over to make sure you know the answers to all the questions. Going to a loan application meeting prepared can save time.

Taking Title

If you buy a car on loan, the lender gets title, and the title is registered with your state government. The lender gets title to your plane, too, except the registrar is the Federal Aviation Administration.

CAUTION

Stall Warning!

Make sure the plane you buy is available for sale. That is, the possessor of the plane might not be its legal owner. The title might be held by a lender, a corporation, a partner, or a relative of the "owner." You can check with the FAA to find out who the registered owner is. If you're using a lender, the lender will do a title search to make sure the title is clear of any problems that would preclude transfer to the lender. Both EAA and AOPA also have title-search services.

When you buy a plane, you'll fill out an aircraft registration application with the name(s) of the owner(s) of the plane, the registration number (for certified aircraft it's the N-number), make, model, serial number, and relevant signatures, and, of course, you pay a registration fee. You'll also need a bill of sale signed off by the seller and any lien holders.

Taking Possession

There are a couple more pieces of paper that need to be completed during the purchase of your sport aircraft. The first is an aircraft bill of sale which the seller should have. If not, you can get one through your lender, or directly from the FAA, and prepare it yourself.

Once you've registered your aircraft with the FAA you receive a new Certificate of Aircraft Registration with your name and address on it (and/or any lender's information).

As you take possession of your new/used plane, make sure you get all available records, including mechanical, flight, maintenance, and other logs. In fact, make sure you've carefully reviewed them *before* plunking down your money. Otherwise you might discover something that affects the plane's airworthiness—and value—too late to do much about it. A careful consumer is a smart consumer.

Now that you've read all about buying your plane, maybe you've decided that you need more options. The next few chapters offer them: sharing, building, and renting your wings. Even if you've decided to buy, keep reading anyway to learn more about the absorbing world of sport flying.

The Least You Need to Know

- Start looking for your sport plane at local and regional airports to save a long-distance trip.
- Smart aviation consumers know how to read classified-ad shorthand—and ask when they don't know.
- Make sure you adequately inspect airplane candidates, or hire an experienced mechanic or pilot to do so for you.
- If you are financing your sport plane, make sure you thoroughly complete the loan application for the best credit rating you can get.
- Don't forget the required FAA paperwork, similar to that needed when you buy and register a car.

Chapter 17

Sharing Your Sport Plane

In This Chapter

- Why rent your wings?
- The advantages and disadvantages of sharing a plane
- Signing up for a flying club
- Buying a block of time from an aircraft owner

The easiest way to own a plane is to own it by yourself. Your plane is always waiting. You don't have to worry about someone else using it—or abusing it. You don't wind up paying someone else's bills. It's simple: one plane, one pilot.

The easiest way, however, is also the most expensive way to fly a plane. When you own your own plane, you have no one to share with you the initial and ongoing costs of flying. In fact, you might not be able to buy the plane you want because you simply can't quite afford it—alone.

Fortunately, you have options! Many thousands of pilots share their wings—and the costs—as rentals, in partnerships, co-ops, and clubs. It's really not that tough and, if you go into the arrangement with both eyes open, it can work out well for everyone. Let's take a closer look at your relationship options.

Renting as an Option

You might be surprised to learn that not every pilot owns his or her aircraft. In fact, renting and other nonownership options for aircraft are approximately the same as those in the housing market—and for similar reasons. About two thirds own and one third don't.

The most popular reason for renting housing and aircraft is the cost. With classic sport planes (older aircraft that fall under new sport-pilot rules) priced at $10,000 (ultralights) to $30,000 (Piper Cub, for example) and new LSAs (light-sport aircraft) heading north from there, prices are higher than many folks can plunk down at one time. Even the down payment (typically about 20 percent with good credit) could be beyond your current reach. Renting is a good option.

Or maybe you have the down payment but your credit score isn't quite high enough to get you preferred interest rates. You want to save while you repair your credit, but don't want to put off flying.

Also, you might not know exactly what you want to buy yet. You might prefer to go on a few "dates" with attractive planes, looking for one that's compatible. You might discover that the ugly duckling you first passed up might be the best catch after all.

Finally, you might be in transition. Maybe you don't want to get into a long-term financial commitment until you've settled down in a new job or location. In the meantime, you want to fly.

So there are many good reasons to consider renting your wings as the best option. Perhaps it's a stopgap measure that holds you over until the day you can buy your own. Or you might decide that renting is a good long-term option, because you never intend to buy a plane of your own. No matter what you want from flying, making an informed decision can help you enjoy flying more. That's the goal.

CAUTION

Stall Warning!

Falling in love with flying can sometimes challenge other relationships you have, especially if you all of a sudden want to spend thousands of shared dollars on your new love. You could find resistance, particularly if others don't share your enthusiasm. Taking any relationship, including flying, a little slower might be a better option for all of your relationships.

Comparing Flying Costs

When does it make sense financially to rent rather than buy? The rule of thumb is: If you don't fly at least 100 hours a year—about two hours per weekend—ownership is more expensive than renting. Of course, much depends on what you're buying. If it's a brand-new aircraft, that number could be closer to 150 hours a year. On the other hand, the cost threshold for a simple sport plane could be 50 hours a year. The plane's cost, hangar or tie-down rent, insurance, and the fuel to take you flying are all factors in making the calculation.

When calculating how many hours you plan to fly each year, remember that in many locations you cannot fly year-round under VFR (visual flight rules). Clouds or fog can keep you on the ground for months. Snow on the ground won't stop you, but falling snow will—and you might need a sport plane with a heater to fly during some months. In other parts of the country, thunderstorms or high winds can ground you.

If you haven't already done so, calculate the costs of flying (see Chapter 15) to determine what it will cost you to own and operate a plane, how often you will use it, and what you expect to use it for. Then you can make a more informed decision on whether to rent or buy.

Finding the Right Wings

The cost of renting a plane can be as varied as the price of any other consumer product, especially when many smaller and independent FBOs (fixed-base operators) have overhead costs that are lower than municipal airport FBOs. It costs smaller FBOs less to rent airplanes. As a smart sport pilot you can take advantage of the disparity in fees by shopping around for low-cost rentals. Following is a list of suggestions.

Finding and renting the perfect sport plane for your needs, such as this Titan Tornado, can make flying even more fun.

Choose your wings. Decide, either through personal observations or those of other pilots, what type of plane you prefer to rent. Sport-pilot regulations do limit your choices, but you still have options, including whether you prefer to rent a low-and-slow classic sport plane or an at-the-limit newer LSA.

Choose your home base. Outline on a sectional chart or road map an area that's within easy driving distance. The farther you have to drive for your wings, the less time you have to fly.

Contact rental sources. Call or visit FBOs, new- and used-plane sales offices, leasing offices, and other aircraft rental sources. You can find their locations and phone numbers in the telephone book, classified ads in metropolitan newspapers, airport bulletin boards, or from other pilots.

Ask the right questions. There are many questions you need answered before you decide to rent a specific sport plane. Here are some starters:

- Ask the rental manager about the make, model, year, and equipment of sport pilot-eligible rental planes they offer.
- Ask the rental price per hour, per day, and minimum charges.
- Find out what the cost would be if you flew two hours to a destination, kept the plane overnight, and flew it back.
- Is the plane rented *wet* or *dry?*
- Is insurance included in the rental fee? If so, what's covered? Is your passenger and luggage covered? Is supplemental rental insurance needed for adequate coverage?
- How are rental planes reserved and are there alternate aircraft if the specific plane isn't available?

Flying Words

Renting a plane **wet** means that the cost of fuel is included in the rental fee. If **dry,** the pilot pays for the fuel directly and tops off the tanks when done.

Once you've narrowed down your rental options to a few candidates, you can arrange to see the plane and meet the rental manager. You want to find out whether the plane meets your needs—and the rental manager wants to know if you're a safe pilot.

The rental manager will ask to see your sport-pilot certificate, medical certificate, or valid driver's license, and your pilot logbook. For obvious reasons, the rental manager wants to know how many hours you've flown and in what type of equipment, who instructed you, what endorsements you have, how long you've been flying, and where. The manager wants to make sure you'll be a good customer rather than an insurance claim.

Your have similar goals, too. You want to make sure the plane is in good flying condition, that it's adequately maintained, that you're comfortable flying it, and that there will be no surprises at 3,000 ft.

Toward those goals, you probably will get—and pay for—a checkride in any craft you select. The checkride begins with a thorough preflight inspection. Ask about any problems you see. It's someone else's plane, but it's *your* safety and *your* responsibility. As part of the preflight inspection, take a close look at the plane's operating handbook for stall, best rate of climb, best angle of climb, and cruise speeds. Also ask the manager or a check pilot about any idiosyncrasies the plane might have. It's smarter to learn about them on the ground.

The checkride might be relatively short, depending on how you're planning to use the rental plane. If all you want to do is "fly the patch" (fly near the airport), that's probably all you'll need to do for the checkride, with special emphasis on landings. If, however, you'll be taking the craft on a long cross-country trip, your checkride will be more complex. The rental manager just wants to make sure you'll bring the plane—and yourself—back in the same condition you took it.

Wing Tips

Remember, if you're renting a make and model you're not endorsed to fly, an additional endorsement will be required. This will be included as part of the checkride procedure.

Fortunately, if you ever rent another aircraft from this rental manager, the paperwork and your checkride probably will be much easier. In fact, renting the same craft might require only a phone call to reserve the plane.

Flying Partnerships

The controversy of sole ownership versus partnership began more than 100 years ago when Wilbur and Orville Wright flipped a coin to see who would fly their shared airplane at Kitty Hawk. It's still a trade-off. You can share the plane and its expenses or you can have both of them to yourself.

As covered in Chapter 16, the advantages to individual ownership include exclusive use of your plane, lower aircraft insurance rates, and predictability. The obvious disadvantages are the higher cost of operation and the finite amount of capital available for purchasing the best plane.

The advantages of flying partnerships are numerous. A partnership allows you and a fellow pilot (or two or more) to pool cash and buy a better plane than you could on your own. It also helps reduce operating costs by sharing them with another pilot. The disadvantages to a partnership include potential conflict over times when the pilots want to use their plane and the chance that damage caused by another pilot will curtail your flying until repairs are made and paid for.

Even with these disadvantages, there are many long-term successful flying partnerships that have worked for decades. Let's learn a few lessons from them.

Choose Your Partner Carefully

Look for common flying goals and interests. Make sure your finances approximate each other so that one partner isn't carrying the burden if another partner has some financial difficulties. Develop a list of what you want from flying and from a partnership before you go looking for a partner. Unlike marriage, a flying partnership is a logical decision rather than an emotional one.

Plan the Use of Your Plane

Make sure your partner(s) or candidates agree on how the plane will be scheduled. One could have weekends free and the other not, which makes scheduling easier. If there's a scheduling conflict, how is it resolved? Do the partners agree to pay an equal share of all expenses or just those incurred when the plane is on the ground? If you take it up, do you pay for your own fuel and oil, always leaving it full for the next time? If you both fly weekends only, can you have one of you fly Saturdays and the other on Sundays or alternate weekends?

Decide on How to Hold Title

Will the plane, hangar rent, and other liabilities be in the name of both partners or an entity? If an entity, will it be a partnership that allows a membership to be transferred (with approval), a limited liability company (LLC), an S corporation, or some other legal entity? Work this all out in advance to make your partnership runs smoothly. (More about writing the agreement in a moment.)

Meet Regularly

It's a good idea to meet with your partner(s) once a month to pay bills, work out the next month's flying schedule, and discuss any upcoming expenses such as annual maintenance or required repairs. You also can discuss anything about flying in general, or clean up any problems to keep your partnership friendly.

Put Your Agreement in Writing

You can use an attorney or a simple partnership form (available at stationery stores) to draw up a binding agreement that covers potential problems and their solutions. The agreement can answer who owns what, who pays for what, when they pay, how shares can be sold without dissolving the partnership (if at all), how to handle disagreements, and what to do if a partner falls behind in sharing costs.

If a flying partnership sounds like a good option for you, delve into it further through the Aircraft Owners and Pilots Association (AOPA) (www.aopa.org), Experimental Aircraft Association (EAA) (www.eaa.org), or by reading *Aircraft Partnership* by Geza Szurovy (McGraw-Hill, 1998), available through local and online bookstores.

CAUTION

Stall Warning!

Before you sign any legal document that binds you financially, consider hiring an attorney to help you decipher your rights and obligations. A hundred dollars might save you thousands.

Flying Clubs

Flying clubs have been around for more than 75 years, offering memberships that allow you to fly a wide variety of aircraft by paying dues and a reduced rental fee. As sport flying grows, you will see many more of these flying clubs across the United States. They are very popular in Europe. Meantime, many long-time flying clubs are adding sport planes to their hangars.

Joining the Club

The concept is simple: You pay monthly membership dues for the right to fly aircraft the club owns at a price much lower than normal rental fees. All the terms are spelled out in the flying club membership agreement and each one is a little different.

Flying clubs come in all shapes and sizes. They range from clubs with just a few members sharing a single plane (similar to a partnership) to regional clubs with hundreds of members and as many as 50 aircraft. Some clubs are developed by aircraft dealers for their current and former students. Other clubs are independent, nonprofit organizations with a waiting list for memberships.

Finding a Local Flying Club

Flying clubs are found at airports, often with their own office or hangar. Larger clubs often have their own websites (such as West Valley Flying Club, www.wvfc.org) for prospects and members. Ask among your pilot friends and you might get a referral to a flying club that offers sport planes.

You can find out more about flying clubs in your area by visiting general-aviation airports around you and asking the airport manager or FBO. Meantime, let's take a look at the most common types of flying clubs.

Three Kinds of Flying Clubs

The oldest and most common type of flying club is called a shareholder club. Members purchase a share in the club with their initiation fee and actually own a percentage of what the club jointly owns. The club takes care of maintenance and other fixed costs out of monthly dues. Members pay the variable costs (fuel, for example) with an hourly rental fee.

A leaseback flying club works a little differently. It has a minimal initiation fee because the planes are actually owned by investors who purchased them for lease back to the club. Monthly dues are usually about the same as a shareholder club. The hourly rental fee can be slightly higher, but it is still less than an FBO's rental fee.

The major difference between a shareholder and leaseback flying club is what you get for your initiation fee. Shareholders actually own a share of all the aircraft. That means your membership costs more—and has some resale value. It's an asset.

A variation on the leaseback flying club is the cooperative flight center. Depending on how the co-op is set up, the primary advantage is that you can buy an aircraft with a relatively low initial investment (under $5,000) as the main asset of a "flight center." Other pilots in the area then can become members and rent the aircraft through you at reduced costs. Because it is a business, there are some tax advantages to this structure in addition to cost savings. For further information, contact Flight Management Services (www.letsfly.org) or check aviation magazines for ads on other co-op ownership programs.

Deciding Which Club to Join

Before you head off to join the first sport-flying club you run across, here are some questions to ask yourself and the prospective club:

- What flying clubs are within an hour of my home?
- Where do they operate?
- Are they independent or dealer-affiliated?
- Are the clubs shareholder or leaseback?
- How many members belong to the clubs?
- What type of planes does the club have?
- Are there sport planes in the lineup?
- Who handles maintenance and how often?
- What is the overall condition of the aircraft?
- Do I know any of the members? What do they like/dislike about the club?
- What is the initiation fee?
- What are the monthly membership dues?
- What are the hourly rental fees?
- Do rental fees include fuel and insurance?
- If I decide to leave the club, may I sell my share? How?
- What will this club require from me?
- Are there many sport pilots among the membership?
- How long has this club been in operation?
- Who are the club's officers?
- Are memberships available or is there a waiting list?

If you're interested in starting your own flying club, get a copy of *Forming and Operating a Flying Club* through the FAA (www.airweb.faa.gov). It's publication ACOO-25 and it's free. Computer software packages are available for managing flying clubs. One is MyFBO (www.myfbo.com), which handles financial and aircraft records, including scheduling planes for members.

Buying Flying Time Blocks

Let me give you one more cost-effective option that many pilots haven't considered: buying a block of time. You simply find an aircraft owner who's willing to let you fly his or her aircraft for a specified number of hours during a specified period.

The advantage to the aircraft owner is obvious: He or she gets some money to cover ongoing expenses. The advantage to you is that you get a known aircraft at a cost lower than standard rental fees.

For example, if you decide you would like to fly a specific sport aircraft and the owner is willing to let you fly it, you can negotiate a price and a block of time. If your goal is to fly 100 hours over the next year (about two hours every weekend) and the cost is agreed upon at $35 an hour, you pay $3,500 up front and work out an amicable flying schedule. However, if you fly only 50 hours during that year, you don't get a refund. You end up paying $70 an hour for your 50 hours.

Wing Tips

Some flying clubs, if allowed in their bylaws, sell blocks of flying time to nonmembers. It won't hurt to ask!

How can you find out more? Ask your flight instructor, pilot friends, local FBOs, nearby aircraft dealers, and others about buying some flying time. As part of the deal you probably will need to purchase aircraft renter's insurance and pay for all fuel and oil used on top of any hourly fees. Again, it can be cheaper than walk-up-and-pull-out-your-wallet renting.

As sport flying becomes increasingly popular, you'll see more opportunities for flying at costs that are less than what you'd pay if you owned your own plane. In the meantime, there are many flying clubs out there that are either dedicated to sport pilots or have added sport planes to their hangars so you can keep down the cost of going up.

The Least You Need to Know

- Renting your wings as you need them can be the least expensive way of flying.
- Partnerships can be an effective way to cut flying costs—if you find the right partner.
- Make sure your partnership agreement is in writing and understood by all partners.
- Flying clubs have served aviation for many years, sharing the costs—and joys—of flying among many.
- Also consider buying a block of flying time from aircraft owners, dealers, and FBOs.

Chapter 18

Building Your Sport Plane

In This Chapter

- Deciding whether to build your own plane
- Finding the right model at the right price
- The different materials you can work with
- Installing all the components needed for safe flight

You say you have your heart set on a new plane, my friend, but you don't think you can afford it? You feel that purchasing a plane—new or used—is beyond the elasticity of your budget? You tell me that you don't want to rent and fly an unfamiliar airplane? You say you can't afford to pay a mechanic, who's got a fancy piece of paper on the wall, $100 to change spark plugs? You insist that you have more time than money and you'd rather do it yourself?

Tell you what I'm going to do. Step this way, my friend, and I'll introduce you to the mystical, magical, money-saving world of building your own flying machine. This here's the "Right Brothers School of Do-It-Yourself Aviation!"

Seriously, building your own airplane as a way to get airborne on a tight budget is rapidly growing in popularity. In fact, over 20,000 aircraft are currently registered as amateur-built. Many folks have built more than one. If you have basic fix-it skills, you probably can, too. This chapter offers an overview of how you can build your own *safe* and *fun* plane.

Custom-Built Basics

Airplanes built by their owners are called by a variety of names: amateur-built, home-built, experimental, and others. I and many other people prefer "custom-built" because you're building the plane yourself, for yourself. Within certain limits you can modify the plane to fit your own needs and tastes. It's *your* personal aircraft!

Why would anyone want to build a plane? Many reasons, actually. By doing the work yourself (an unpaid laborer) you will save lots of money developing what's often called "sweat equity." You'll also know exactly what you're getting as you put each piece together; you'll probably be even more careful than the aircraft worker assembling a plane for an unseen customer. One more *big* reason: You'll be able to *legally* do maintenance and repair on your aircraft, saving you big bucks.

The Rules

Of course, to build, maintain, and fly a custom-built aircraft, you'll need to follow some rules. There always are rules. Though the Wright brothers were the first folks to build and fly their own plane, it wasn't until 1947 that the FAA allowed "home-built" aircraft to be certified for flight. Not much after that, Paul Poberezny founded the Experimental Aircraft Association (EAA) (www.eaa.org), the leading resource for people who build what are legally called "experimental" aircraft and popularly known as homebuilt or custom-built aircraft.

How do experimental aircraft get around the FAA certification process? They don't. They fall under a special rule, CFR-14-21.191(g), that covers how experimental or amateur-built aircraft can be built and operated. In simple language, it says that such aircraft are built with the sole intent of enhancing the builder's education and recreation, and that the builder must have done a *majority* (at least 51 percent) of the airframe construction, not including the engine, propeller, interior, and so on. You'll hear this referred to as the "51-percent rule."

Nearly a decade ago the FAA issued an advisory circular (AC-20-139) that reaffirmed and clarified the rules for building experimental aircraft, including what a manufacturer can and cannot do in building an aircraft kit for you to assemble. So any experimental/amateur-built/custom-built you build from scratch or a kit must comply with these FAA regulations if you want to get it legally certified as airworthy. Without FAA certification, it's a funny-looking car.

Fortunately, those who offer aircraft kits work with the FAA to make sure their planes, if built according to directions, not only comply with the 51-percent rule, but also are airworthy. In fact, the last stage of construction is having your aircraft checked out by an FAA designee and signed off as airworthy. Believe me, the designee isn't going to sign you off until he or she is thoroughly convinced that you've built an airworthy aircraft.

Sources

So where can you get plans or kits to build your custom aircraft? Actually, as you move into the world of experimental aircraft, you'll find hundreds of valuable resources and dozens of manufacturers vying for your attention—and dollars. None of them are getting rich, but many have successfully sold plans and kits that are now up and flying.

If you haven't guessed already, one of the leading resources for custom-built aircraft is the EAA. It not only helps those who want to build their own airplanes, it also works with manufacturers to develop and promote safe aircraft. Rather than add a few hundred pages to this book, I recommend you get the latest edition of *AeroCrafter* (www.aerocrafter.org), subtitled "The complete guide to building and flying your own aircraft." It's comprehensive and includes contact information, specifications, and pricing on hundreds of experimental aircraft plans and kits. It also notes which planes fall under the new sport-pilot rules as well as which ones can be built under the 51-percent rule. It also includes valuable articles on selecting engines and other components. The latest edition includes a searchable CD to help you make model and feature comparisons.

CAUTION

Stall Warning!

Building your own kit aircraft doesn't mean you automatically get to fly it. You still must have a pilot's certificate to fly any aircraft. And part of the aircraft construction process requires that the plane be checked for safety before you ever fly it. There are no shortcuts to safe flying.

Investment

So how much is all this going to cost? How much do you want to spend? You can buy a set of plans for under $100 and build an airworthy plane totally from scratch. Or you can spend $40,000 or more on quick-build kits that will have you flying in no time.

Actually, it's the investment in time that will keep you on the ground. If you're building from plans, you might need to invest 2,000 hours in construction—that's two years of very intense weekends! On the other hand, a simple quick-build kit can cut that to about 200 hours and get you flying in just a few months. The less you do, the more you pay.

Because of the time and money required to construct a custom-built aircraft, here are two good rules to follow:

- Make sure you know exactly what plane you want before you buy and build it.
- Make sure that others in your life (spouse, partners, kids) support your decision to give up some of your time and money to fulfill your dream.

You're going to spend lots of time—and money—in the garage or hangar. Be sure you make an informed decision and know all costs before you proceed.

Need Some Help?

Among the many benefits the EAA offers is a mentor program for those who are building their first custom aircraft. You can ask to be assigned to a member who lives nearby or one who has experience building the model you want to build. If you're lucky, you'll find both mentors in one. It's a great benefit to have a knowledgeable person to call if you run into problems. In addition, most kit manufacturers offer customer assistance and even builder newsletters to help you through any problems.

The EAA runs local chapters throughout the world. You'll find that many of them meet once a month and that members often will answer questions during the month if you get into technical trouble. Think of local chapters as Experimental Aircrafters Anonymous.

Choosing a Custom-Built

How can you choose the right plans or kit for your custom-built aircraft? Many new flyers spend years researching the models and features they want. You don't have to take that long. Using resources mentioned earlier, you can do your research and come up with a plane that meets your goals and your finances in just a few weeks.

Of course, the plan you select isn't the one you'll keep forever. You'll someday want to build your second custom craft, then maybe your third. In fact, some flyers find out they love building as much as flying, starting a new project soon after the last one is done. Just remember that, to someday sell your experimental plane, you'll need to carefully document every step of the process so the next owner is comfortable that you've done it right. That's what *you* would want if you were to buy an experimental-class aircraft.

Selection Process

Chapter 15 covers the selection process for sport aircraft that are already built. It helps you decide what your requirements are and how to meet them with a manufactured aircraft. Choosing a custom aircraft to build is a similar process, with a few added elements.

The most important question you need to answer is "how much of this do I want or need to do?" The answer will help you decide whether you'll build from plans, standard kits, or quick-build kits. If you have lots of do-it-yourself skills and experience and plenty of time, you might consider building from plans. Otherwise, you might decide to build from a kit.

Another important question that many experimental aircraft builders have to answer is "what skin do I prefer?" An airframe can be covered in various ways, including with a metal skin, a fabric skin, and a composite (fiberglass) skin. Fabric is cheaper and lighter, but metal holds up longer. Composite materials are light and stable, but more expensive. There are pros and cons to each. Of course, the decision could be made for you if you fall in love with a model that happens to be fabric-covered. Stay objective for as long as you can. And don't be afraid to ask other home builders for their opinions and preferences.

Note that resources such as *AeroCrafter* include specifications and characteristics such as wing span, fuel capacity, maximum gross weight, stall speed, and so on. This information can help you decide which aircraft best meet your flying requirements.

Plans

Some experimental aircraft are available only as plans, and no manufacturer makes a kit for them. If you select one of these plans, you'll wind up gathering all the parts yourself from various suppliers that serve the experimental aircraft hobby (see Appendix B).

Plans can be as simple as low-cost reprints of aircraft plans that have been around 50 years or more. Or the plans can include full-size templates for major components that you trace on to the material before cutting it out. The cost of such plans range from free to $1,000. You typically get what you pay for.

Those designers who provide plans and drawings for a price usually offer an information pack that you may buy to help you decide whether to purchase the full plan set. These information packs run about $20 to $50, depending on whether a video or other helpful resources are included. Besides magazines such as *Kit Planes* (www.kitplanes.com, or available at larger newsstands), you'll find information on plans in *AeroCrafter*, mentioned earlier in this chapter. Once you've narrowed your interest to one or two plans, you can buy an information pack to help in the final decision.

One of the earliest and most popular homebuilt aircraft plans is the Pietenpol Air Camper. It's still being built and still flying!

Kits

The complexity of kits runs the gambit from you-do-everything to almost complete. In addition, most kit manufacturers offer subassemblies—sort of a build-on-the-installment-plan process. You can buy the fuselage kit, then the wing kit, followed by the tail kit, finally adding the engine kit.

The Sonex can be built from plans or from a kit.

If you're buying any kit, especially one that you'll buy and build in installments, make sure the manufacturer is reputable, the design is proven, and that you can upgrade as needed without rebuilding the whole plane. If you're building your custom aircraft over an extended period, such as a few years, it's especially important that the manufacturer be in business and offer the appropriate kit when you decide to get your next subassembly. Experienced kit builders will help you find long-term kit manufacturers. Orphans can be expensive to finish.

How much time should you plan for building your custom plane from a kit? The manufacturer will tell you what's typical. Expect it will take from 500 to 1,000 hours for many of the planes that meet the sport-pilot requirements.

Stall Warning!

Don't forget to factor in *all* costs as you estimate the price of your custom sport plane. That means including the cost of preparing your kit for shipment (called crating) as well as the cost of shipping it to you—unless you decide to go pick it up!

Wing Tips

The FAA maintains a listing of eligible kits that comply with FAR requirements for experimental aircraft. Contact the FAA (www.faa.gov) for the latest list.

Quick-Builds

Due to recent rule changes and clarifications, some aircraft kits can be constructed using quick-build kits while still complying with the 51-percent rule. Make sure the quick-build kits you select comply with FAA regulations for experimental aircraft.

Quick-build kits or subassemblies can dramatically cut the amount of time you spend in your garage working on your plane. In fact, many can reduce assembly time by half or more. Yes, you can buy a standard kit for the fuselage and tail, and then purchase a quick-build kit for the difficult wings. Just make sure the manufacturer and model you select offer this option.

How much time is needed to construct from a quick-build kit? From 100 to 500 hours is typical. However, the plane might not comply with the 51-percent rule, meaning that you won't be able to register it as an experimental aircraft unless it's the new experimental LSA.

The Rans S-7 is a very popular aircraft that can be built from a standard or quick-build kit.

Working with Materials

There are five materials most often used to build experimental aircraft: wood, steel tubing, fabric, sheet metal, and composites. Most custom-built planes use two or more of these materials. Once you've selected a specific plan or kit, you'll have little choice of materials you'll use, so it's a good idea to know what you're getting into.

Wing Tips

Where can you get your aircraft construction materials? Check Appendix B as well as ads in homebuilt aircraft publications. The largest suppliers include Aircraft Spruce & Specialty Co. (www.aircraftspruce.com), Wag-Aero Group (www.wagaero.com), and Wicks Aircraft Supply (www.wicksaircraft.com).

Many of the older designs use wood for the main airframe and the wings because wood's easy to work with. The wood frame is then covered with a fabric followed by a stiffener, called dope. Finally, the surface is painted.

Newer aircraft designs use steel tubing for the airframe, followed by a covering of sheet metal riveted in place. Some models mix mediums by using sheet metal to cover the fuselage and fabric for the wings and tail.

Some of the newest designs use what are called composite materials for the skin. These typically are a combination of foam and fiberglass to make a strong and smooth surface that is more aerodynamic.

The popular Sting sport plane is made of carbon-based composite materials.

What is the better material for custom aircraft? They all have their advantages and disadvantages. If you're building from plans, wood and fabric is preferred by many because they're easier for amateur builders to use. If you're an excellent welder or have a small machine shop, you might prefer to work with steel tubing and sheet metal. If you have experience with fiberglass molding, composites might be your best choice. Economically, wood and fabric are cheaper materials than metals, but they might not last as long. Composites typically are the most expensive, but offer lower wind resistance.

Which material should you use to build your custom aircraft? Whatever the manufacturer uses or recommends. If your heart is set on using a specific material or combination, you'll need to shop for plans or kits that use it.

Wing Tips

The EAA offers "Sport Air Workshops," weekend training courses that teach you about the various building materials and allow you to work with them. These workshops let you sample before you buy. Check for these workshops at www.eaa.org.

Remember to include the cost of any special tools required for your project. You might need wood, metal, or composite tools to build your plane. Make sure a comprehensive list of needed tools is included with the plan or kit information package.

Engines and Props

If you're building your own light-sport aircraft, plan to spend one third to one half of your budget on the engine, sometimes called the power plant. The exact cost depends on how much of a mechanic and a machinist you are. You can buy ready-to-install power plants designed specifically for light-sport and ultralight aircraft, or you can modify smaller automotive and snowmobile engines to power your plane.

Propellers are easier to choose because LSA regulations limit the type of props you can install on these aircraft. We'll take a look at props after a discussion of aircraft engines.

Engine Basics

Engines are engines. However, there are some major differences between the engines that power cars and ones that power airplanes. The greatest difference is redundancy.

If an aircraft engine goes out at 3,000 ft AGL (above ground level), it's not as though you can pull over to a cloud and call AAA. You'll have to land somewhere—hopefully safely. That's why most aircraft use engines with some redundancy. For example, larger aircraft have dual-magneto systems with two magnetos, two wires, and two spark plugs for each cylinder. You actually fly using both systems, but if one goes out you can switch over to the other and continue flying, albeit at slightly lower efficiency. Many light-sport aircraft use dual-magneto systems, too, for the same safety reasons.

Two types of engines can be used: two-stroke and four-stroke. Smaller engines such as the ones on lawnmowers often are two-stroke engines, simpler in design, lighter, and cheaper to buy. Four-stroke engines are more complex (your car has a four-stroke engine) and more expensive, but develop more power. Many ultralight aircraft are powered by two-stroke engines. Sport planes can be powered by either type of engine. The decision typically is based on cost; two-stroke engines are simpler and less expensive.

Choosing the Right Engine

The plan publisher or kit manufacturer will tell you which engines are approved for installation in its craft. Because of the LSA weight and speed limitations, the options are fewer than you'd have for other experimental aircraft. Even so, you have choices to make.

Some of the leading manufacturers of engines for sport planes include (alphabetically) Franklin, Gobler-Hirthmotoren (G-H), Jabiru, and Rotax. The most common models are from Rotax and Jabiru. In the coming years, larger aircraft engine manufacturers such as Teledyne Continental and Textron Lycoming will probably add engines that meet LSA requirements. In addition, engine manufacturers that power ultralights and snowmobiles might add larger models closer to the LSA limits.

An important consideration in selecting a plane's engine is the horsepower rating. Though LSA engines don't have a horsepower limit, they do have a cruise speed limit, which means the horsepower rating can't be much over about 100 hp or the plane will go too fast for the LSA speed limits.

Automotive and other engines have been adapted to experimental aircraft, which is the topic of another thick book and lots of opinions. If your plane's plans call for a modified auto engine, do your homework and ask lots of experienced builders to find out what works and what doesn't before investing time and money into this option.

Installing the Engine

Many of the kits offered refer to the engine kit as "firewall forward" kits. The firewall is the wall between the engine and the pilot and the engine is hung on it. So the engine is installed or mounted on the firewall, and then all the electrical and fuel connections are made to feed it.

Make sure the engine you select has proven to be compatible with the aircraft you've selected. In most cases, the aircraft designer has already done this. In cases where you're experimenting with a truly experimental aircraft, you might need additional testing and documentation to assure the FAA that your new combination is safe to fly.

Propellers

The propeller on your LSA is actually a set of wings, designed as rotating airfoils. The selection of an appropriate propeller for your sport plane is relatively easy because the FAA regulations give you few options. To be legal the propeller must be fixed-pitch or ground-adjustable. That means you can't change its angle while you're flying as you can on some high-performance aircraft.

That's okay. At the speeds you'll be flying, having an adjustable propeller won't make that much difference in performance. Even so, you should choose a propeller that's designed for the best performance you can get from that engine. Your best choice is to install the propeller that comes with the kit or is recommended by the plan manufacturer. Don't try to be creative.

Two blades or three? Leave that, too, up to the aircraft designer and make sure you buy and install whatever the plane manufacturer recommends. Experienced builders of experimental aircraft have been known to design and fly custom props, but it typically takes some engineering and woodworking skills to make it work safely.

One more point: Many smaller aircraft engines operate at a higher speed (revolutions per minute or RPM) than is most efficient for the propeller to turn. These engines use a reduction unit that delivers the correct power, in RPMs, to the prop. Make sure you know if your aircraft engine needs one, which one, and how to install it.

Flight Instruments

Chapter 2 introduced you to the seven primary flight instruments you'll find in smaller aircraft:

- Airspeed indicator
- Altimeter
- Magnetic compass
- Attitude indicator (optional)
- Turn coordinator (optional)
- Heading indicator (optional)
- Vertical speed indicator (optional)

Which of these should you have in your custom-built sport plane? The minimum instruments *required* for VFR (visual flight rules) flight include airspeed indicator, altimeter, and magnetic compass. In addition, you should have some engine instruments including a tachometer, fuel quantity indicator, fuel pressure gauge, oil temperature indicator (for four-stroke engines), and an oil pressure indicator (for four-stroke engines). Remember, that's a minimum. The more you know about your sport plane's engine and flight conditions, the better sport pilot you can be.

A basic six-instrument panel (excluding the compass and engine instruments) will cost you $1,000 to $2,000. You can go up from there. In addition, there are newer digital electronic panels that start at about $3,000 and go up. Way up! Most builders buy and install a set of the primary six along with engine gauges (oil pressure, temperature, tachometer, etc.) and call it enough. Remember, it is not only the cost that counts; it's also the weight. Add too many gadgets and you could end up with a plane that's fancy but won't be able to carry a passenger!

Fortunately, installation of basic instruments and engine gauges is straightforward, especially with the kits that are constructed from proven designs. The only variation you might have is the placement on the instrument or control panel, though most builders opt for the standard two rows that you see in commercially manufactured aircraft (Cessnas and Pipers for example).

In addition, your sport plane can have navigation and communication radios. Remember, as a VFR pilot operating in uncontrolled airspace, you're not legally required to have nav-com equipment. However, it's in your best interest to at least have a handheld communications radio and a GPS unit. In fact, many sport pilots who fly classic sport planes that didn't come with nav-com systems install mountings for portable GPS receivers and handheld com radios. You can buy these two portable units for less than $1,000—much less than an installed nav-com system—and remove them when you park your plane so you don't "lose" them.

Wing Tips

Can you use a portable GPS receiver as your primary navigation system? Certainly! They're dependable (as long as they have good batteries or a power connection) and accurate. If you're looking for redundancy, consider installing a VOR (VHF omnidirectional range) or other navigation system as a backup. Alternately, some handheld coms offer navigation features as well.

The Least You Need to Know

- If you have more time than money, you can legally build and fly your own sport plane.
- Many pilots build their own experimental aircraft to learn more about planes and to test their own skills.
- Make sure the kit you select is designed to be airworthy, providing you follow directions.
- You can install your own engine, electronics, and instruments to cut costs and have more fun flying.

Chapter 19

Maintaining Your Sport Plane

In This Chapter

- Save time and money by performing basic maintenance on your sport plane
- Complying with airworthiness directives (ADs)
- Special repair and inspection certificates you can earn
- Maintaining your experimental aircraft

As you've learned, airplanes are about as safe as cars. In fact, there are more safety rules for planes than for cars. Many cars are driven without maintenance until they finally stop. You can't do that with planes. You must maintain them following FAA rules and regulations.

However, that doesn't mean you're at the mercy of expensive aircraft mechanics. *You* can do many things to keep the cost of flying down. And, if you're willing to take a class or two, you can be your own LSA mechanic! This chapter tells you how new FAA rules can save you time and money as a smart sport pilot.

Basic Aircraft Maintenance

If your car has a problem you can, if you wish, fix it yourself. That's not the case with most general-aviation aircraft. For the protection of yourself, passengers, future owners of your plane, and people on the ground, the FAA requires that all repairs on certified production airplanes be done by or under the supervision of an FAA-certified mechanic. Exceptions to these rules are covered later in this chapter. But for now, let's look at the rules.

One of the advantages of building your own sport plane is that you get to do the maintenance yourself. Aviation writer Dan Johnson enjoys flying this GT 400.

Flying Words

Airframe and power-plant (A&P) mechanics are licensed to work on the airframe, the engine, or both. An A&P mechanic can also perform maintenance on the entire plane.

The rules for aircraft maintenance, repairs, alterations, and rebuilding are in CFR 14-43 (previously called FAR Part 43). It's dull reading, but tells you who can fix airplanes, what they can and cannot do, and how they keep track of their efforts. Without the help of an FAA-certified *airframe and power-plant (A&P) mechanic*, the owner is permitted to do little more than some preventive maintenance. So let's first look at what "preventive maintenance" means.

Preventive Maintenance

Preventive maintenance on aircraft involves simply replacing some components with exact replacement parts and doing some lubrication. Here are a few of the things a sport pilot can do on a noncommercial aircraft:

- Remove, repair, and install landing-gear tires.
- Replace or service some landing-gear components.
- Lubricate components that don't require disassembly.
- Replace defective safety wiring or cotter keys.
- Make simple fabric patches that don't require part removal.
- Refinish exterior surfaces that don't require disassembly or removal.
- Apply preservative or protective coating on components that don't require disassembly or removal.
- Repair upholstery and other decorative interior furnishings.
- Repair nonstructural cover plates or fairings.
- Replace seat belts.
- Replace prefabricated fuel lines.
- Clean fuel and oil strainers.
- Check battery fluid levels and test specific gravity.
- Replace batteries.

The FAA says you can perform these and some other preventive maintenance tasks yourself without supervision or certification. These tasks are those that don't change the flight characteristics of the aircraft, but do help keep it flying safely. Again, check CFR 14-43 for the specifics.

Required Maintenance

Certified aircraft used for private (noncommercial) flying require an annual inspection of airworthiness, referred to as "the annual." This must be done by or under the supervision of an A&P mechanic.

Yes, you can do some or all of the work, but an A&P mechanic must sign off that the work was done correctly. Many sport pilots do their own required maintenance under the direction of an A&P, especially pilots who have proven mechanical aptitudes and know a friendly A&P mechanic. Don't know which repairs you can and cannot do on your plane? Find a helpful A&P mechanic and ask. Some are more willing than others to oversee and certify work done by aircraft owners.

Wing Tips

How much does an annual inspection cost? It depends on the complexity of the aircraft and whether repairs need to be done. If you hire an A&P mechanic to perform and certify the inspection, plan on spending from $500 to $1,500 on the annual inspection. You can cut the costs by half or more if you're willing to do some of the tasks under the direction of the A&P mechanic.

Repairs

If your plane is excessively worn or damaged, making it no longer airworthy, chances are you'll need to hire an A&P mechanic to do the required work. If you have mechanical skills, an A&P mechanic may allow you to do the work under his or her supervision.

You probably aren't going to try to do an engine overhaul yourself—at least not the first one—but many aircraft owners can do repairs on the craft's metal or fabric skin under supervision.

Airworthiness Directives

The FAA keeps track of aircraft accidents, failures, and other problems, specific to individual makes and models. If the FAA sees a problem caused by a design or manufacturing fault on a certified aircraft, it will issue an airworthiness directive (AD) and require that owners have the component inspected and, if needed, repaired.

ADs include part replacements on specific model aircraft. If you're buying a used aircraft (see Chapter 16), you need to know about any ADs issued for the craft and verify that the issues have been addressed. To find out what ADs have been issued on any plane you own or are buying, contact the FAA (www.faa.gov).

Manufacturers of the new LSAs issue "safety of flight" bulletins as needed to make sure all aircraft they produce continue to be airworthy. The FAA requires compliance with the bulletins, but does not oversee their distribution or make sure they are complied with. It's up to you to comply to assure the plane's airworthiness, and it's up to you to research the bulletins for any used aircraft you're considering buying.

LSA-Repairman Certificate

The recent addition of FAA rules for sport-pilot certificates and light-sport aircraft manufacturing also changed the rules for LSA maintenance and repair. Borrowing from how experimental aircraft are maintained and repaired (see the next section), the LSA-repairman certificate allows the pilot to participate more now than in the past in the craft's airworthiness.

Let's take a closer look at how these new rules can help you keep down the cost of going up.

LSA Inspection

As with other general-aviation aircraft, sport aircraft are required to have an annual inspection, also known as a condition inspection. You can hire an A&P mechanic, a certified LSA repairman, or you can get certified and do it yourself.

What's required during the inspection? The aircraft manufacturer explains in the plane's operating handbook what the annual inspection is to include. Typically, all operating components must be inspected for damage, wear, and fatigue. Some disassembly might be required depending on the craft's design and whether the inspection process was considered when the plane was designed and built. For common inspections there might be a removable inspection plate at important inspection points, for example.

What is required to earn an LSA-repairman certificate for inspections, called the inspection rating? You must complete a 16-hour training course on the inspection requirements of the specific make and model of LSA you'll be working on. In addition, you must be on the manufacturer's contact list so you can be notified of any airworthiness directives or other documents that update owners on potential problems.

LSA Maintenance and Repair

You can do even more of your own maintenance and repair on LSAs if you're willing to get some more training. To qualify for the LSA-repairman certificate with a maintenance rating, you must complete an 80-hour training course on the maintenance requirements of the specific category of LSA you will maintain.

Becoming a certified LSA repairman with a maintenance rating not only allows you to inspect, maintain, and repair your own aircraft, you also can offer your services to other sport pilots. Yes, you can legally help pay for your flying by helping others! Just remember that you may work only on the category of plane you're certified for, such as fixed-wing, powered parachutes, powered hang gliders, and so on.

Contact the FAA (www.faa.gov) for additional information on requirements and certification for the new light-sport aircraft-repairman certificates and authorizations. Kit and finished LSA manufacturers, too, can help you train for the repairman certification and ratings.

Experimental Aircraft Maintenance

Chapter 18 gives you an overview on building your plane. You might have been surprised to learn that currently more than 20,000 amateur-built or experimental aircraft are licensed in the United States. And thousands more are parked in garages and hangars waiting for additional work.

One of the greatest benefits of building your own airplane within the experimental classification is that the FAA says, in essence, "If you can build it, you can fix it." In fact, that's a major reason why budget-conscious flyers decide to build their own plane from a plan or a kit. They can do their own annual inspections (called condition inspections) as well as ongoing maintenance and periodic repairs. It's up to the plane's owner to make sure it's airworthy.

Of course, that puts additional responsibility on the owner to make sure all inspections, maintenance, repairs, and modifications solve problems rather than create new ones. However, people who invest hundreds or even thousands of hours into building something know much more about their aircraft than those who buy and hire planes, and they care about keeping their craft up and running.

Fortunately, most experimental aircraft plan publishers and kit manufacturers are conscientious about informing their customers about the technical aspects of their planes. In addition, many manufacturers encourage and assist user groups who help each other in the construction, flying, maintenance, and repair of their craft.

Wing Tips

Can you buy someone else's experimental aircraft and maintain it yourself? Technically, yes. However, remember that it's totally up to you to not only make sure it's airworthy, but also to know just about everything there is to know about the craft. If you did not build it, you cannot perform the annual condition inspection—only the original builder or an A&P mechanic can inspect it. Review the builder's logs and records to make sure you know what you're getting into.

Again, I stress that if you are considering building your own aircraft—or buying one from the builder—contact the plan publisher or kit manufacturer (if still in business) and learn as much as you can about the plane you'll be flying. Also, join the EAA (Experimental Aircraft Association) and any clubs specific to your craft so you can keep informed. You'll find many resources for parts, services, technical assistance, and knowledgeable sympathy. You'll need all of them if you accept the challenge of flying and maintaining experimental aircraft.

Up, Up, and Away!

The purpose of the new sport-pilot and light-sport aircraft rules is to make flying fun, affordable, and safe for more people. That has been the goal of aviation for more than a century. It is my goal in writing this book.

It has been my sincere pleasure to share the friendly skies of sport flying with you. I hope you gain a greater understanding of yourself and the world around you as you learn more about the challenges—and the sheer fun—of sport flying! Please visit me at www.SportFlyingGuide.com.

Happy flying!

The Least You Need to Know

- Maintaining general aviation aircraft can be expensive if you must rely on A&P mechanics to do all the inspections, maintenance, and repairs.
- The new light-sport aircraft repairman and inspection ratings allow you to perform your own inspections and even make your own repairs once you've completed training. This applies only to certified factory-built LSAs or experimental (meaning homebuilt) LSAs.
- Aircraft certified under the FAA standard certification rules must be maintained and inspected by A&P mechanics and inspectors. Owner-pilots are allowed to assist under supervision of an A&P mechanic.
- Builders of experimental aircraft are allowed to do their own condition inspections and make their own repairs, if certified.
- Sport flying is the newest and most enjoyable addition to the captivating world of private aviation.

Sport Flying Rules

The following are additions and changes to the Federal Aviation Regulations (FARs) regarding sport pilots, as published by the *Federal Register*.

Part 61, Subpart J—Sport Pilots

61.301 What is the purpose of this subpart and to whom does it apply?

(a) This subpart prescribes the following requirements that apply to a sport pilot certificate:

(1) Eligibility.

(2) Aeronautical knowledge.

(3) Flight proficiency.

(4) Aeronautical experience.

(5) Endorsements.

(6) Privileges and limits.

(7) Transition provisions for registered ultralight pilots.

(b) Other provisions of this part apply to the logging of flight time and testing.

(c) This subpart applies to applicants for, and holders of, sport pilot certificates. It also applies to holders of recreational pilot certificates and higher, as provided in 61.303.

61.303 If I want to operate a light-sport aircraft, what operating limits and endorsement requirements in this subpart must I comply with?

(a) Use the following table to determine what operating limits and endorsement requirements in this subpart, if any, apply to you when you operate a light-sport aircraft. The medical certificate specified in this table must be valid. If you hold a recreational pilot certificate, but not a medical certificate, you must comply with cross-country requirements in 61.101 (c), even if your flight does not exceed 50 nautical miles from your departure airport. You must also comply with requirements in other subparts of this part that apply to your certificate and the operation you conduct.

If You Hold	And You Hold	Then You May Operate	And
(1) A medical certificate,	(i) A sport pilot certificate,	(A) Any light sport aircraft for which you hold the endorsements required for its category, class, make and model,	(1) You must hold any other endorsements required by this subpart, and comply with the limitations in 61.315.
	(ii) At least a recreational pilot certificate with a category and class rating,	(A) Any light sport aircraft in that category and class,	(1) You do not have to hold any of the endorsements required by this subpart, nor do you have to comply with the limitations in 61.315.
	(iii) At least a recreational pilot certificate but not a rating for the category and class of light sport aircraft you operate,	(A) That light sport aircraft, only if you hold the endorsements required in 61.321 for its category and class,	(1) You must comply with the limitations in 61.315, except 61.315 (c)(14) and, if a private pilot or higher, 61.315 (c)(7).
(2) Only a U.S. driver's license,	(i) A sport pilot certificate,	(A) Any light sport aircraft for which you hold the endorsements required for its category, class, make and model,	(1) You must hold any other endorsements required by this subpart, and comply with the limitations in 61.315.

If You Hold	And You Hold	Then You May Operate	And
	(ii) At least a recreational pilot certificate with a category and class rating,	(A) Any light sport aircraft in that category and class,	(1) You do not have to hold any of the endorsements required by this subpart, but you must comply with the limitations in 61.315.
	(iii) At least a recreational pilot certificate but not a rating for the category and class of light-sport aircraft you operate,	(A) That light sport aircraft, only if you hold the endorsements required in 61.321 for its category and class,	(1) You must comply with the limitations in 61.315, except 61.315 (c)(14) and, if a private pilot or higher, 61.315 (c)(7).
(3) Neither a medical certificate nor a U.S. driver's license,	(i) A sport pilot certificate,	(A) Only a light sport glider or balloon for which you hold the endorsements required for its category, class, make and model,	(1) You must hold any other endorsements required by this subpart, and comply with the limitations in 61.315.
	(ii) At least a private pilot certificate with a category and class rating for glider or balloon,	(A) Only a light sport glider or balloon in that category and class,	(1) You do not have to hold any of the endorsements required by this subpart, but you must comply with the limitations in 61.315.
	(iii) At least a private pilot certificate but not a rating for glider or balloon,	(A) Only a light sport glider or balloon, if you hold the endorsements required in 61.321 for its category and class,	(1) You must comply with the limitations in 61.315, except 61.315 (c)(14) and, if a private pilot or higher, 61.315 (c)(7).

(b) A person using a current and valid U.S. driver's license to meet the requirements of this paragraph must—

(1) Comply with each restriction and limitation imposed by that person's U.S. driver's license and any judicial or administrative order applying to the operation of a motor vehicle;

(2) Have been found eligible for the issuance of at least a third-class airman medical certificate at the time of his or her most recent application (if the person has applied for a medical certificate);

(3) Not have had his or her most recently issued medical certificate (if the person has held a medical certificate) suspended or revoked or most recent Authorization for a Special Issuance of a Medical Certificate withdrawn; and

(4) Not know or have reason to know of any medical condition that would make that person unable to operate a light-sport aircraft in a safe manner.

61.305 What are the age and language requirements for a sport pilot certificate?

(a) To be eligible for a sport pilot certificate you must:

(1) Be at least 17 years old (or 16 years old if you are applying to operate a glider or balloon).

(2) Be able to read, speak, write, and understand English. If you cannot read, speak, write, and understand English because of medical reasons, the FAA may place limits on your certificate as are necessary for the safe operation of light-sport aircraft.

61.307 What tests do I have to take to obtain a sport pilot certificate?

To obtain a sport pilot certificate, you must pass the following tests:

(a) Knowledge test. You must pass a knowledge test on the applicable aeronautical knowledge areas listed in 61.309. Before you may take the knowledge test for a sport pilot certificate, you must receive a logbook endorsement from the authorized instructor who trained you or reviewed and evaluated your home-study course on the aeronautical knowledge areas listed in 61.309 certifying you are prepared for the test.

(b) Practical test. You must pass a practical test on the applicable areas of operation listed in 61.309 and 61.311. Before you may take the practical test for a sport pilot certificate, you must receive a logbook endorsement from the authorized instructor who provided you with flight training on the areas of operation specified in 61.309 and 61.311 in preparation for the practical test. This endorsement certifies that you meet the applicable aeronautical knowledge and experience requirements and are prepared for the practical test.

61.309 What aeronautical knowledge must I have to apply for a sport pilot certificate?

Except as specified in 61.329, to apply for a sport pilot certificate you must receive and log ground training from an authorized instructor or complete a home-study course on the following aeronautical knowledge areas:

(a) Applicable regulations of this chapter that relate to sport pilot privileges, limits, and flight operations.

(b) Accident reporting requirements of the National Transportation Safety Board.

(c) Use of the applicable portions of the aeronautical information manual and FAA advisory circulars.

(d) Use of aeronautical charts for VFR navigation using pilotage, dead reckoning, and navigation systems, as appropriate.

(e) Recognition of critical weather situations from the ground and in flight, windshear avoidance, and the procurement and use of aeronautical weather reports and forecasts.

(f) Safe and efficient operation of aircraft, including collision avoidance, and recognition and avoidance of wake turbulence.

(g) Effects of density altitude on takeoff and climb performance.

(h) Weight and balance computations.

(i) Principles of aerodynamics, powerplants, and aircraft systems.

(j) Stall awareness, spin entry, spins, and spin recovery techniques, as applicable.

(k) Aeronautical decision making and risk management.

(l) Preflight actions that include—

(1) How to get information on runway lengths at airports of intended use, data on takeoff and landing distances, weather reports and forecasts, and fuel requirements; and

(2) How to plan for alternatives if the planned flight cannot be completed or if you encounter delays.

61.311 What flight proficiency requirements must I meet to apply for a sport pilot certificate?

Except as specified in 61.329, to apply for a sport pilot certificate you must receive and log ground and flight training from an authorized instructor on the following areas of operation, as appropriate, for airplane single-engine land or sea, glider, gyroplane, airship, balloon, powered parachute land or sea, and weight-shift-control aircraft land or sea privileges:

(a) Preflight preparation.

(b) Preflight procedures.

(c) Airport, seaplane base, and gliderport operations, as applicable.

(d) Takeoffs (or launches), landings, and go-arounds.

(e) Performance maneuvers, and for gliders, performance speeds.

(f) Ground reference maneuvers (not applicable to gliders and balloons).

(g) Soaring techniques (applicable only to gliders).

(h) Navigation.

(i) Slow flight (not applicable to lighter-than-air aircraft and powered parachutes).

(j) Stalls (not applicable to lighter-than-air aircraft, gyroplanes, and powered parachutes).

(k) Emergency operations.

(l) Post-flight procedures.

61.313 What aeronautical experience must I have to apply for a sport pilot certificate?

Except as specified in 61.329, use the following table to determine the aeronautical experience you must have to apply for a sport pilot certificate:

If You Are Applying for a Sport Pilot Certificate With …	Then You Must Log at Least …	Which Must Include at Least …
(a) Airplane category and single-engine land or sea class privileges,	(1) 20 hours of flight time, including at least 15 hours of flight training from an authorized instructor in a single-engine airplane and at least 5 hours of solo flight training in the areas of operation listed in 61.311,	(i) 2 hours of cross-country flight training, (ii) 10 takeoffs and landings to a full stop (with each landing involving a flight in the traffic pattern) at an airport; (iii) 1 solo cross-country flight of at least 75 nautical miles total distance, with a full-stop landing at a minimum of two points and one segment of the flight consisting of a straight-line distance of at least 25 nautical miles between the takeoff and landing locations, and

If You Are Applying for a Sport Pilot Certificate With …	Then You Must Log at Least …	Which Must Include at Least …
		(iv) 3 hours of flight training on those areas of operation specified in 61.311 preparing for the practical test within 60 days before the date of the test.
(b) Glider category privileges, and you have not logged at least 20 hours of flight time in a heavier-than-air aircraft,	(1) 10 hours of flight time in a glider, including 10 flights in a glider receiving flight training from an authorized instructor and at least 2 hours of solo flight training in the areas of operation listed in 61.311,	(i) 5 solo launches and landings, and (ii) 3 hours of flight training on those areas of operation specified in 61.311 preparing for the practical test within 60 days before the date of the test.
(c) Glider category privileges, and you have logged 20 hours flight time in a heavier-than-air aircraft,	(1) 3 hours of flight time in a glider, including 5 flights in a glider while receiving flight training from an authorized instructor and at least 1 hour of solo flight training in the areas of operation listed in 61.311,	(i) 3 solo launches and landings, and (ii) 3 hours of flight training on those areas of operation specified in 61.311 preparing for the practical test within 60 days before the date of the test.
(d) Rotorcraft category and gyroplane class privileges,	(1) 20 hours of flight time, including 15 hours of flight training from an authorized instructor in a gyroplane and at least 5 hours of solo flight training in the areas of operation listed in 61.311,	(i) 2 hours of cross-country flight training, (ii) 10 takeoffs and landings to a full stop (with each landing involving a flight in the traffic pattern) at an airport, (iii) 1 solo cross-country flight of at least 50 nautical miles total distance, with a full-stop landing at a minimum of two points, and one segment of the flight consisting of a straight-line distance of at least 25 nautical miles between the takeoff and landing locations, and

If You Are Applying for a Sport Pilot Certificate With ...	Then You Must Log at Least ...	Which Must Include at Least ...
		(iv) 3 hours of flight training on those areas of operation specified in 61.311 preparing for the practical test within 60 days before the date of the test.
(e) Lighter-than-air category and airship class privileges,	(1) 20 hours of flight time, including 15 hours of flight training from an authorized instructor in an airship and at least 3 hours performing the duties of pilot in command in an airship with an authorized instructor in the areas of operation listed in 61.311,	(i) 2 hours of cross-country flight training, (ii) 3 takeoffs and landings to a full stop (with each landing involving a flight in the traffic pattern) at an airport, (iii) 1 cross-country flight of at least 25 nautical miles between the takeoff and landing locations, and, (iv) 3 hours of flight training on those areas of operation specified in 61.311 preparing for the practical test within 60 days before the date of the test.
(f) Lighter-than-air category and balloon class privileges,	(1) 7 hours of flight time in a balloon, including 3 flights with an authorized instructor and 1 flight performing the duties of pilot in command in a balloon with an authorized instructor in the areas of operation listed in 61.311,	(i) 2 hours of cross-country flight training, and (ii) 3 hours of flight training on those areas of operation specified in 61.311 preparing for the practical test within 60 days before the date of the test.
(g) Powered parachute category land or sea class privileges,	(1) 12 hours of flight time in a powered parachute, including 10 hours flight training, and at least 2 hours solo flight training in the areas of operation listed in 61.311.	(i) 1 hour of cross-country flight training, (ii) 20 takeoffs and landings to a full stop in a powered parachute with each landing involving flight in the traffic pattern at an airport,

If You Are Applying for a Sport Pilot Certificate With ...	Then You Must Log at Least ...	Which Must Include at Least ...
		(iii) 10 solo takeoffs and landings to a full stop (with each landing involving a flight in the traffic pattern) at an airport, (iv) 1 solo flight with a landing at a different airport and one segment of the flight consisting of a straight-line distance of at least 10 nautical miles between takeoff and landing locations, and (v) 3 hours of flight training on those areas of operation specified in 61.311 preparing for the practical test within 60 days before the date of the test.
(h) Weight-shift-control aircraft category land or sea class privileges,	(1) 20 hours of flight time, including 15 hours of flight training from an authorized instructor in a weight-shift-control aircraft and at least 5 hours of solo flight training in the areas of operation listed in 61.311,	(i) 2 hours of cross-country flight training, (ii) 10 takeoffs and landings to a full stop (with each landing involving a flight in the traffic pattern) at an airport, (iii) 1 solo cross-country flight of at least 50 nautical miles total distance, with a full-stop landing at a minimum of two points, and one segment of the flight consisting of a straight-line distance of at least 25 nautical miles between takeoff and landing locations, and (iv) 3 hours of flight training on those areas of operation specified in 61.311 preparing for the practical test within 60 days before the date of the test.

61.315 What are the privileges and limits of my sport pilot certificate?

(a) If you hold a sport pilot certificate you may act as pilot in command of a light-sport aircraft, except as specified in paragraph (c) of this section.

(b) You may share the operating expenses of a flight with a passenger, provided the expenses involve only fuel, oil, airport expenses, or aircraft rental fees. You must pay at least half the operating expenses of the flight.

(c) You may not act as pilot in command of a light-sport aircraft:

(1) That is carrying a passenger or property for compensation or hire.

(2) For compensation or hire.

(3) In furtherance of a business.

(4) While carrying more than one passenger.

(5) At night.

(6) In Class A airspace.

(7) In Class B, C, and D airspace, at an airport located in Class B, C, or D airspace, and to, from, through, or at an airport having an operational control tower unless you have met the requirements specified in 61.325.

(8) Outside the United States, unless you have prior authorization from the country in which you seek to operate. Your sport pilot certificate carries the limit "Holder does not meet ICAO requirements."

(9) To demonstrate the aircraft in flight to a prospective buyer if you are an aircraft salesperson.

(10) In a passenger-carrying airlift sponsored by a charitable organization.

(11) At an altitude of more than 10,000 feet MSL.

(12) When the flight or surface visibility is less than 3 statute miles.

(13) Without visual reference to the surface.

(14) If the aircraft has a V_H that exceeds 87 knots CAS, unless you have met the requirements of 61.327.

(15) Contrary to any operating limitation placed on the airworthiness certificate of the aircraft being flown.

(16) Contrary to any limit or endorsement on your pilot certificate, airman medical certificate, or any other limit or endorsement from an authorized instructor.

(17) Contrary to any restriction or limitation on your U.S. driver's license or any restriction or limitation imposed by judicial or administrative order when using your driver's license to satisfy a requirement of this part.

(18) While towing any object.

(19) As a pilot flight crewmember on any aircraft for which more than one pilot is required by the type certificate of the aircraft or the regulations under which the flight is conducted.

61.317 Is my sport pilot certificate issued with aircraft category and class ratings?

Your sport pilot certificate does not list aircraft category and class ratings. When you successfully pass the practical test for a sport pilot certificate, regardless of the light-sport aircraft privileges you seek, the FAA will issue you a sport pilot certificate without any category and class ratings. The FAA will provide you with a logbook endorsement for the category, class, and make and model aircraft of aircraft in which you are authorized to act as pilot in command.

61.319 Can I operate a make and model of aircraft other than the make and model aircraft for which I have received an endorsement?

If you hold a sport pilot certificate you may operate any make and model of light-sport aircraft in the same category and class and within the same set of aircraft as the make and model of aircraft for which you have received an endorsement.

61.321 How do I obtain privileges to operate an additional category or class of light-sport aircraft?

If you hold a sport pilot certificate and seek to operate an additional category or class of light-sport aircraft, you must—

(a) Receive a logbook endorsement from the authorized instructor who trained you on the applicable aeronautical knowledge areas specified in 61.309 and areas of operation specified in 61.311. The endorsement certifies you have met the aeronautical knowledge and flight proficiency requirements for the additional light-sport aircraft privilege you seek;

(b) Successfully complete a proficiency check from an authorized instructor other than the instructor who trained you on the aeronautical knowledge areas and areas of operation specified in 61.309 and 61.311 for the additional light-sport aircraft privilege you seek;

(c) Complete an application for those privileges on a form and in a manner acceptable to the FAA and present this application to the authorized instructor who conducted the proficiency check specified in paragraph (b) of this section; and

(d) Receive a logbook endorsement from the instructor who conducted the proficiency check specified in paragraph (b) of this section certifying you are proficient in the applicable areas of operation and aeronautical knowledge areas, and that you are authorized for the additional category and class light-sport aircraft privilege.

61.323 How do I obtain privileges to operate a make and model of light-sport aircraft in the same category and class within a different set of aircraft?

If you hold a sport pilot certificate and seek to operate a make and model of light-sport aircraft in the same category and class but within a different set of aircraft as the make and model of aircraft for which you have received an endorsement, you must—

(a) Receive and log ground and flight training from an authorized instructor in a make and model of light-sport aircraft that is within the same set of aircraft as the make and model of aircraft you intend to operate;

(b) Receive a logbook endorsement from the authorized instructor who provided you with the aircraft specific training specified in paragraph (a) of this section certifying you are proficient to operate the specific make and model of light-sport aircraft.

61.325 How do I obtain privileges to operate a light-sport aircraft at an airport within, or in airspace within, Class B, C, and D airspace, or in other airspace with an airport having an operational control tower?

If you hold a sport pilot certificate and seek privileges to operate a light-sport aircraft in Class B, C, or D airspace, at an airport located in Class B, C, or D airspace, or to, from, through, or at an airport having an operational control tower, you must receive and log ground and flight training. The authorized instructor who provides this training must provide a logbook endorsement that certifies you are proficient in the following aeronautical knowledge areas and areas of operation:

(a) The use of radios, communications, navigation system/facilities, and radar services.

(b) Operations at airports with an operating control tower to include three takeoffs and landings to a full stop, with each landing involving a flight in the traffic pattern, at an airport with an operating control tower.

(c) Applicable flight rules of part 91 of this chapter for operations in Class B, C, and D airspace and air traffic control clearances.

61.327 How do I obtain privileges to operate a light-sport aircraft that has a V_H greater than 87 knots CAS?

If you hold a sport pilot certificate and you seek to operate a light-sport aircraft that has a V_H greater than 87 knots CAS you must—

(a) Receive and log ground and flight training from an authorized instructor in an aircraft that has a V_H greater than 87 knots CAS; and

(b) Receive a logbook endorsement from the authorized instructor who provided the training specified in paragraph (a) of this section certifying that you are proficient in the operation of light-sport aircraft with a V_H greater than 87 knots CAS.

61.329 Are there special provisions for obtaining a sport pilot certificate for persons who are registered ultralight pilots with an FAA-recognized ultralight organization?

(a) If you are a registered ultralight pilot with an FAA-recognized ultralight organization use the following table to determine how to obtain a sport pilot certificate:

If You Are ...	Then You Must ...
(1) A registered ultralight pilot with an FAA-recognized ultralight organization on or before September 1, 2004, and you want to apply for a sport pilot certificate,	(i) Not later than January 31, 2007— (A) Meet the eligibility requirements in 61.305 and 61.23, but not the aeronautical knowledge requirements specified in 61.309, the flight proficiency requirements specified in 61.311, and the aeronautical experience requirements specified in 61.313, (B) Pass the knowledge test for a sport pilot certificate specified in 61.307 or the knowledge test for a flight instructor certificate with a sport pilot rating specified in 61.405, (C) Pass the practical test for a sport pilot certificate specified in 61.307, (D) Provide the FAA with a certified copy of your ultralight pilot records from an FAA-recognized ultralight organization, and those records must— (1) Document that you are a registered ultralight pilot with that FAA-recognized ultralight organization, and (2) Indicate that you are recognized to operate each category and class of aircraft for which you seek sport pilot privileges.
(2) A registered ultralight pilot with an FAA-recognized ultralight organization after September 1, 2004, and you want to apply for a sport pilot certificate,	(i) Meet the eligibility requirements in 61.305 and 61.23, (ii) Meet the aeronautical knowledge requirements specified in 61.309, the flight proficiency requirements specified in 61.311, and aeronautical experience requirements specified in 61.313;

If You Are ...	Then You Must ...
	however, you may credit your ultralight aeronautical experience in accordance with 61.52 toward the requirements in 61.309, 61.311, and 61.313, (iii) Pass the knowledge and practical tests for a sport pilot certificate specified in 61.307, and (iv) Provide the FAA with a certified copy of your ultralight pilot records from an FAA-recognized ultralight organization, and those records must— (A) Document that you are a registered ultralight pilot with that FAA-recognized ultralight organization, and (B) Indicate that you are recognized to operate the category and class of aircraft for which you seek sport pilot privileges.

(b) When you successfully pass the practical test for a sport pilot certificate, the FAA will issue you a sport pilot certificate without any category and class ratings. The FAA will provide you with a logbook endorsement for the category, class, and make and model of aircraft in which you have successfully passed the practical test and for which you are authorized to act as pilot in command. If you meet the provisions of paragraph (a)(1) of this section, the FAA will provide you with a logbook endorsement for each category, class, and make and model of aircraft listed on the ultralight pilot records you provide to the FAA.

Part 65—Certification: Airmen Other than Flight Crewmembers

Amend 65.85 by designating the existing text as paragraph (a) and inserting phrase "Except as provided in paragraph (b) of this section," at the beginning of new paragraph (a), and adding paragraph (b) to read as follows:

65.85 Airframe rating; additional privileges.

(b) A certificated mechanic with an airframe rating can approve and return to service an airframe, or any related part or appliance, of an aircraft with a special airworthiness certificate in the light-sport category after performing and inspecting a major repair or major alteration for products that are not produced under an FAA approval provided the work was performed in accordance with instructions developed by the manufacturer or a person acceptable to the FAA.

Amend 65.87 by designating the existing text as paragraph (a) and inserting the phrase "Except as provided in paragraph (b) of this section," at the beginning of new paragraph (a) and adding paragraph (b) to read as follows:

65.87 Powerplant rating; additional privileges.

(b) A certificated mechanic with a powerplant rating can approve and return to service a powerplant or propeller, or any related part or appliance, of an aircraft with a special airworthiness certificate in the light-sport category after performing and inspecting a major repair or major alteration for products that are not produced under an FAA approval, provided the work was performed in accordance with instructions developed by the manufacturer or a person acceptable to the FAA.

Amend 65.101 by revising paragraph (b) to read as follows:

65.101 Eligibility requirements: General.

(b) This section does not apply to the issuance of a repairman certificate (experimental aircraft builder) under 65.104 or to a repairman certificate (light-sport aircraft) under 65.107.

Amend 65.103 by adding paragraph (c) to read as follows:

65.103 Repairman certificate: Privileges and limitations.

(c) This section does not apply to the holder of a repairman certificate (light-sport aircraft) while that repairman is performing work under that certificate.

Add 65.107 to subpart E to read as follows:

65.107 Repairman certificate (light-sport aircraft): Eligibility, privileges, and limits.

(a) Use the following table to determine your eligibility for a repairman certificate (light-sport aircraft) and appropriate rating:

To Be Eligible For ...	You Must ...
(1) A repairman certificate (light-sport aircraft),	(i) Be at least 18 years old, (ii) Be able to read, speak, write, and understand English. If for medical reasons you cannot meet one of these requirements, the FAA may place limits on your repairman certificate necessary to safely perform the actions authorized by the certificate and rating, (iii) Demonstrate the requisite skill to determine whether a light-sport aircraft is in a condition for safe operation, and

To Be Eligible For ...	You Must ...
	(iv) Be a citizen of the United States, or a citizen of a foreign country who has been lawfully admitted for permanent residence in the United States.
(2) A repairman certificate (light-sport aircraft) with an inspection rating,	(i) Meet the requirements of paragraph (a)(1) of this section, and (ii) Complete a 16-hour training course acceptable to the FAA on inspecting the particular class of experimental light-sport aircraft for which you intend to exercise the privileges of this rating.
(3) A repairman certificate (light-sport aircraft) with a maintenance rating,	(i) Meet the requirements of paragraph (a)(1) of this section, and (ii) Complete a training course acceptable to the FAA on maintaining the particular class of light-sport aircraft for which you intend to exercise the privileges of this rating. The training course must, at a minimum, provide the following number of hours of instruction: (A) For airplane class privileges—120 hours, (B) For weight-shift control aircraft class privileges—104 hours, (C) For powered parachute class privileges—104 hours, (D) For lighter than air class privileges—80 hours, (E) For glider class privileges—80 hours.

(b) The holder of a repairman certificate (light-sport aircraft) with an inspection rating may perform the annual condition inspection on a light-sport aircraft:

(1) That is owned by the holder;

(2) That has been issued an experimental certificate for operating a light-sport aircraft under 21.191 (i) of this chapter; and

(3) That is in the same class of light-sport-aircraft for which the holder has completed the training specified in paragraph (a)(2)(ii) of this section.

(c) The holder of a repairman certificate (light-sport aircraft) with a maintenance rating may—

(1) Approve and return to service an aircraft that has been issued a special airworthiness certificate in the light-sport category under 21.190 of this chapter, or any part thereof, after performing or inspecting maintenance (to include the annual condition

inspection and the 100-hour inspection required by 91.327 of this chapter), preventive maintenance, or an alteration (excluding a major repair or a major alteration on a product produced under an FAA approval);

(2) Perform the annual condition inspection on a light-sport aircraft that has been issued an experimental certificate for operating a light-sport aircraft under 21.191 (i) of this chapter; and

(3) Only perform maintenance, preventive maintenance, and an alteration on a light-sport aircraft that is in the same class of light-sport aircraft for which the holder has completed the training specified in paragraph (a)(3)(ii) of this section. Before performing a major repair, the holder must complete additional training acceptable to the FAA and appropriate to the repair performed.

(d) The holder of a repairman certificate (light-sport aircraft) with a maintenance rating may not approve for return to service any aircraft or part thereof unless that person has previously performed the work concerned satisfactorily. If that person has not previously performed that work, the person may show the ability to do the work by performing it to the satisfaction of the FAA, or by performing it under the direct supervision of a certificated and appropriately rated mechanic, or a certificated repairman, who has had previous experience in the specific operation concerned. The repairman may not exercise the privileges of the certificate unless the repairman understands the current instructions of the manufacturer and the maintenance manuals for the specific operation concerned.

Part 91—General Operating and Flight Rules

91.1 Applicability.

(b) Each person operating an aircraft in the airspace overlying the waters between 3 and 12 nautical miles from the coast of the United States must comply with 91.1 through 91.21; 91.101 through 91.143; 91.151 through 91.159; 91.167 through 91.193; 91.203; 91.205; 91.209 through 91.217; 91.221; 91.303 through 91.319; 91.323 through 91.327; 91.605; 91.609; 91.703 through 91.715; and 91.903.

Amend 91.113 by revising paragraphs (d)(2) and (d)(3) to read as follows:

91.113 Right-of-way rules: Except water operations.

(d) * * *

(2) A glider has the right-of-way over an airship, powered parachute, weight-shift-control aircraft, airplane, or rotorcraft.

(3) An airship has the right-of-way over a powered parachute, weight-shift-control aircraft, airplane, or rotorcraft.

Amend 91.126 by revising paragraph (b)(2) to read as follows:

91.126 Operating on or in the vicinity of an airport in Class G airspace.

(b) * * *

(2) Each pilot of a helicopter or a powered parachute must avoid the flow of fixed-wing aircraft.

Amend 91.131 by revising paragraphs (b)(1)(i), (b)(1)(ii) and (b)(2), and by adding paragraphs (b)(1)(iii) and (b)(1)(iv) to read as follows:

91.131 Operations in Class B airspace.

(b) * * *

(1) * * *

(i) The pilot in command holds at least a private pilot certificate;

(ii) The pilot in command holds a recreational pilot certificate and has met—

(A) The requirements of 61.101 (d) of this chapter; or

(B) The requirements for a student pilot seeking a recreational pilot certificate in 61.94 of this chapter;

(iii) The pilot in command holds a sport pilot certificate and has met—

(A) The requirements of 61.325 of this chapter; or

(B) The requirements for a student pilot seeking a recreational pilot certificate in 61.94 of this chapter; or

(iv) The aircraft is operated by a student pilot who has met the requirements of 61.94 or 61.95 of this chapter, as applicable.

(2) Notwithstanding the provisions of paragraphs (b)(1)(ii), (b)(1)(iii) and (b)(1)(iv) of this section, no person may take off or land a civil aircraft at those airports listed in section 4 of appendix D to this part unless the pilot in command holds at least a private pilot certificate.

Amend 91.155 by revising paragraph (b)(2) to read as follows:

91.155 Basic VFR weather minimums.

(b) * * *

(2) Airplane, powered parachute, or weight-shift-control aircraft. If the visibility is less than 3 statute miles but not less than 1 statute mile during night hours and you are operating in an airport traffic pattern within 1/2 mile of the runway, you may operate an airplane, powered parachute, or weight-shift-control aircraft clear of clouds.

Amend 91.213 by revising paragraph (d)(1)(i) to read as follows:

91.213 Inoperative instruments and equipment.

(d) * * *

(1) * * *

(i) Rotorcraft, non-turbine-powered airplane, glider, lighter-than-air aircraft, powered parachute, or weight-shift-control aircraft, for which a master minimum equipment list has not been developed; or

Amend 91.309 by revising the section heading and paragraphs (a) introductory text, (a)(3), (a)(5), and (b) to read as follows:

91.309 Towing: Gliders and unpowered ultralight vehicles.

(a) No person may operate a civil aircraft towing a glider or unpowered ultralight vehicle unless—

(3) The towline used has breaking strength not less than 80 percent of the maximum certificated operating weight of the glider or unpowered ultralight vehicle and not more than twice this operating weight. However, the towline used may have a breaking strength more than twice the maximum certificated operating weight of the glider or unpowered ultralight vehicle if—

(i) A safety link is installed at the point of attachment of the towline to the glider or unpowered ultralight vehicle with a breaking strength not less than 80 percent of the maximum certificated operating weight of the glider or unpowered ultralight vehicle and not greater than twice this operating weight;

(ii) A safety link is installed at the point of attachment of the towline to the towing aircraft with a breaking strength greater, but not more than 25 percent greater, than that of the safety link at the towed glider or unpowered ultralight vehicle end of the towline and not greater than twice the maximum certificated operating weight of the glider or unpowered ultralight vehicle;

(5) The pilots of the towing aircraft and the glider or unpowered ultralight vehicle have agreed upon a general course of action, including takeoff and release signals, airspeeds, and emergency procedures for each pilot.

(b) No pilot of a civil aircraft may intentionally release a towline, after release of a glider or unpowered ultralight vehicle, in a manner that endangers the life or property of another.

Amend 91.319 by redesignating paragraph (e) as paragraph (h) and adding new paragraphs (e), (f) and (g) to read as follows:

91.319 Aircraft having experimental certificates: Operating limitations.

(e) No person may operate an aircraft that is issued an experimental certificate under 21.191 (i) of this chapter for compensation or hire, except a person may operate an aircraft issued an experimental certificate under 21.191 (i)(1) for compensation or hire to—

(1) Tow a glider that is a light-sport aircraft or unpowered ultralight vehicle in accordance with 91.309; or

(2) Conduct flight training in an aircraft which that person provides prior to January 31, 2010.

(f) No person may lease an aircraft that is issued an experimental certificate under 21.191 (i) of this chapter, except in accordance with paragraph (e)(1) of this section.

(g) No person may operate an aircraft issued an experimental certificate under 21.191 (i)(1) of this chapter to tow a glider that is a light-sport aircraft or unpowered ultralight vehicle for compensation or hire or to conduct flight training for compensation or hire in an aircraft which that persons provides unless within the preceding 100 hours of time in service the aircraft has—

(1) Been inspected by a certificated repairman (light-sport aircraft) with a maintenance rating, an appropriately rated mechanic, or an appropriately rated repair station in accordance with inspection procedures developed by the aircraft manufacturer or a person acceptable to the FAA; or

(2) Received an inspection for the issuance of an airworthiness certificate in accordance with part 21 of this chapter.

(h) The FAA may issue deviation authority providing relief from the provisions of paragraph (a) of this section for the purpose of conducting flight training. The FAA will issue this deviation authority as a letter of deviation authority.

(1) The FAA may cancel or amend a letter of deviation authority at any time.

(2) An applicant must submit a request for deviation authority to the FAA at least 60 days before the date of intended operations. A request for deviation authority must contain a complete description of the proposed operation and justification that establishes a level of safety equivalent to that provided under the regulations for the deviation requested.

Add 91.327 to read as follows:

91.327 Aircraft having a special airworthiness certificate in the light-sport category: Operating limitations.

(a) No person may operate an aircraft that has a special airworthiness certificate in the light-sport category for compensation or hire except—

(1) To tow a glider or an unpowered ultralight vehicle in accordance with 91.309 of this chapter; or

(2) To conduct flight training.

(b) No person may operate an aircraft that has a special airworthiness certificate in the light-sport category unless—

(1) The aircraft is maintained by a certificated repairman with a light-sport aircraft maintenance rating, an appropriately rated mechanic, or an appropriately rated repair station in accordance with the applicable provisions of part 43 of this chapter and maintenance and inspection procedures developed by the aircraft manufacturer or a person acceptable to the FAA;

(2) A condition inspection is performed once every 12 calendar months by a certificated repairman (light-sport aircraft) with a maintenance rating, an appropriately rated mechanic, or an appropriately rated repair station in accordance with inspection procedures developed by the aircraft manufacturer or a person acceptable to the FAA;

(3) The owner or operator complies with all applicable airworthiness directives;

(4) The owner or operator complies with each safety directive applicable to the aircraft that corrects an existing unsafe condition. In lieu of complying with a safety directive an owner or operator may—

(i) Correct the unsafe condition in a manner different from that specified in the safety directive provided the person issuing the directive concurs with the action; or

(ii) Obtain an FAA waiver from the provisions of the safety directive based on a conclusion that the safety directive was issued without adhering to the applicable consensus standard;

(5) Each alteration accomplished after the aircraft's date of manufacture meets the applicable and current consensus standard and has been authorized by either the manufacturer or a person acceptable to the FAA;

(6) Each major alteration to an aircraft product produced under a consensus standard is authorized, performed and inspected in accordance with maintenance and inspection procedures developed by the manufacturer or a person acceptable to the FAA; and

(7) The owner or operator complies with the requirements for the recording of major repairs and major alterations performed on type-certificated products in accordance with 43.9 (d) of this chapter, and with the retention requirements in 91.417.

(c) No person may operate an aircraft issued a special airworthiness certificate in the light-sport category to tow a glider or unpowered ultralight vehicle for compensation or hire or conduct flight training for compensation or hire in an aircraft which that persons provides unless within the preceding 100 hours of time in service the aircraft has—

(1) Been inspected by a certificated repairman with a light-sport aircraft maintenance rating, an appropriately rated mechanic, or an appropriately rated repair station in accordance with inspection procedures developed by the aircraft manufacturer or a person acceptable to the FAA and been approved for return to service in accordance with part 43 of this chapter; or

(2) Received an inspection for the issuance of an airworthiness certificate in accordance with part 21 of this chapter.

(d) Each person operating an aircraft issued a special airworthiness certificate in the light-sport category must operate the aircraft in accordance with the aircraft's operating instructions, including any provisions for necessary operating equipment specified in the aircraft's equipment list.

(e) Each person operating an aircraft issued a special airworthiness certificate in the light-sport category must advise each person carried of the special nature of the aircraft and that the aircraft does not meet the airworthiness requirements for an aircraft issued a standard airworthiness certificate.

(f) The FAA may prescribe additional limitations that it considers necessary.

Amend 91.409 by revising paragraph (c)(1) to read as follows:

91.409 Inspections.

(c) * * *

(1) An aircraft that carries a special flight permit, a current experimental certificate, or a light-sport or provisional airworthiness certificate;

Amend Appendix D to part 91 by revising the section heading and introductory text of Section 4 to read as follows:

Appendix D to Part 91—Airports/Locations: Special Operating Restrictions

Section 4. Locations at which solo student, sport, and recreational pilot activity is not permitted.

Pursuant to 91.131 (b)(2), solo student, sport, and recreational pilot operations are not permitted at any of the following airports.

Appendix B

Sport Flying Resources

Excited about sport flying?

Here are hundreds of resources for sport-pilot training, light-sport aircraft, as well as other products and services aimed at the new sport flying market. Also refer to www.SportFlyingGuide.com for the latest information and updates.

Sport Plane Manufacturers and Models

As of the publication date of this book, the following manufacturers have produced, have announced production, or are eligible for production of the listed models that qualify for flight by sport pilots. For the latest list, visit www.bydanjohnson.com or www.sportpilot.org. Also refer to the latest edition of *AeroCrafter* (www.aerocrafter.org).

American Fixed-Wing Manufacturers

Manufacturer	Model(s)	Telephone
Ace Aircraft	Corben Baby Ace/Jr. Ace	706-886-6341
Aerocomp	Merlin	321-453-6641
Aero Adventure	Aventura I and II, Tucan and Sova	321-635-8005

continues

American Fixed-Wing Manufacturers (continued)

Manufacturer	Model(s)	Telephone
Airdrome Aeroplanes	Fokker DR1, D-VI, D-VIII, Eindecker	816-230-8585
Capella Aircraft	Capella SS, Fastback, XLS	512-288-4161
Carlson Aircraft	Sparrow, Sport Special	330-426-3934
CGS Aviation	Hawk Classic/Arrow	440-632-1424
Earthstar Aircraft	Gull 2000, Odyssey	805-438-5235
Excalibur Aircraft	Excalibur, Excalibur Stretch	863-385-9486
Fisher Flying Products	Complete line of fixed-wing aircraft	701-493-2286
Flightstar	Flightstar IISL, IISC	860-875-8185
Golden Circle Air	T-Bird I and II	515-834-2225
Hummel Aviation	Hummel Bird, UltraCruiser	419-636-6700
Hurricane	Clip Wing, Hauler	904-935-0356
JDT miniMAX	Max 103, miniMAC 1100R, Z-Max, V-Max	574-773-2151
Just Aircraft	Escapade, Summit	208-454-3446
Leza AirCam	Drifter, Super Drifter XL	863-655-4242
Loehle Aircraft	P-40, 5151 Mustang (fixed gear), Spad	931-857-3419
M-Squared	Breese DS, Breese SS	251-957-1533
New Kolb Aircraft	Complete line of fixed-wing aircraft	606-862-9692
Preceptor Aircraft	N-3 Pup, Ultra Pup	828-286-1926
Progressive Aerodyne	SeaRey	407-292-3700
Quad City Ultralights Aircraft	Challenger I, II, Clipped Wing	309-764-9515
Quicksilver Manufacturing	Sprint, Sport, GT400/500	909-506-0061
RANS	S-6 Coyote, Sakota, Airaile, Stinger, S-7	785-625-6346
Rocky Mountain Wings	Ridge Runner	208-446-6699
Sky Raider LLC	Sky Raider I, II, and Super Sky Raider	208-465-7116

Manufacturer	Model(s)	Telephone
SkyStar	Kitfox Lite, Classic IV, Series 7	208-454-2444
Slipstream Industries	Genesis, Revelation	920-787-5886
Sonex Ltd.	Sonex, Waiex, Xenos glider	920-231-8297
Spectrum Aircraft (Aeroprakt)	Vista-Cruiser, Vulcan, Valor	863-655-9299
Thunderbird Aviation	SNS-8 Hiperlight	586-212-5862
Titan Aircraft	Tornado I, II, T-51	440-466-0602
Ultralight Soaring Aviation	Cumulus motorglider	618-833-3187
U.S. Light Aircraft	Hornet	760-789-8607
Weedhopper USA	Weedhopper II	601-918-8415
Zenith Aircraft	Zodiac 601XL, 701	573-581-9000

Foreign Fixed-Wing Manufacturers

Manufacturer	Model(s)	Telephone
Aeroprakt/Spectrum Aircraft (importer)	Vista, Vulcan, Valor	863-655-9299
Aeropro/Rollison Light-Sport Aircraft (importer)	EuroFox	812-384-4972
A.S.A.P.	Chinook, Chinook Plus 2, Beaver RX 550	250-549-1102
Atec Aviation Inc. (ATEC)	Zephyr	604-581-0041
B&F Technik/FK Planes	FK-9, FK-12	(49) 6232-72076
CFM Aircraft	Shadow, Streak Shadow	(44) 1728-832-353
CLASS Inc.	BushCaddy	450-452-4772
Comco Ikarus/Rollison	C22, C42	(49) 7572-600-80
Light Sport Aircraft (importer)		812-384-4972
Dyn'Aero	MCR 01/BanBi	386-740-7140
Euro ALA	JetFox	(39) 861-808-026

continues

Foreign Fixed-Wing Manufacturers (continued)

Manufacturer	Model(s)	Telephone
Evektor-Aerotechnik	SportStar	(42) 532-537-910
Fantasy Air	Allegro	(42) 2-602-293-309
Flight Design/ Flightstar Sportplanes (importer)	CT2K	860-875-8185
Fly Synthesis	Storch, Texan	(39) 431-99-105
Harper Aircraft (WD/Dallach)	Fascination	904-778-0021
ICP/Sky Rider (importer)	Amigo, Savannah	(39) 141-99-63-05 703-754-4959
Interplane	Skyboy	813-782-7900
Jabiru Aircraft	Jabiru	1-800-522-4781
Murphy Aircraft	Renegade, Maverick	604-792-5855
Randkar/Sky Rider (importer)	X-Air	703-754-4959
Remos/Rollison Light Sport Aircraft (importer)	G 4, G 3 Mirage	812-384-4972 (49) 8442-96-77-77
SkyRangert Aircraft Company/Best Off (importer)	Sky Ranger	304-754-6010
StingUSA LLC	TL Sting and Star	501-228-7777
Tecnam/Pacific Aerosystems (importer)	Sky Arrow, P-92, P-96	858-571-1441
Ultravia Aero The New Kolb Company (importer)	Pelican Kolb Sport	819-669-3144

Trike/Weight-Shift Manufacturers

Manufacturer	Model(s)	Telephone
Aeros International Lookout Mountain Flight Park (importer)	Velocity	706-398-3541
AirBorne Australia First Light Aviation (importer)	Outback, Redback, 912XT	607-256-9149
Air Creation	Buggy, GTE, Racer, Clipper	623-566-8068
Airsports USA	DFS Single & Dual	718-777-7000
Antares U.S. Corp.	Antares	907-350-6501
Butterfly Wings by GibboGear	BB Trike	863-679-6383
Concept Aviation	Prowler	865-693-1284
Cosmos/ Personal Flight	Phase II, Samba, Bison	509-682-6262
Flight Park	SkyCycle	706-398-3541
Kemmeries Aviation Lookout Mountain	Trike Zilla, Tukan	623-566-8068
Mainair	Blade, Rapier	352-542-2985
North Wing Design	Apache, Maverick, ATF	509-886-4605
Rainbow Aircraft	Cobra, Safari, DTA	310-251-7560
Ramphos	Ramphos	631-872-2332
Rossi Trikes USA/ Phoenix Trikes USA/ Aerial Adventure	Rossi GTL, Phoenix	270-881-1369
Stellar Aircraft	Astra	812-384-4760
TC Trikes	TC Trike	423-802-1193
WeTTrike Inc.	WeTTrike	601-947-9281

Powered Parachute Manufacturers

Manufacturer	Model(s)	Telephone
Aerochute International/ Easy Flight Powered Parachutes (importer)	Aerochute	618-664-9706
Alliant Aviation (formerly Destiny)	Destiny 2000, Sparrow	616-273-6223
Buckeye Industries	Brat, Breeze, Hornet, Dream Machine	574-892-5566
Gemini Industries	Gemini Classic, Twin	574-842-4185
Harmening High Flyers	High Flyer	815-784-5876
Heldeberg Designs	Blue Heron Marathon, Spirit	518-872-2638
Infinity Powered Parachutes	Infinity	269-659-9113
Para-Ski International	Freedom, Top Gun	1-888-727-2754
Phoenix Industries	ParaFlyer, Liberty, Phoenix X-Treme	574-892-4785
Powrachute	PC2000, Sky Rascal, Pegasus	620-429-1397
Six Chuter	Legend	509-966-8211
Skymaster Powered Parachutes	C-Max, Excel	262-966-2533
Summit Powered Parachutes	Summit II, SS	250-503-1033
Viking Aircraft	Viking I	850-233-4847

Standard Category Aircraft

According to the type certificates and published specifications, the following standard category ASEL aircraft meet the definition of a light-sport aircraft (LSA). In addition, there are 33 ASES standard-category aircraft that meet the requirements of LSAs. However, an individual aircraft of a certain type may have been modified by the manufacturer and, therefore, may not meet the criteria. Modifications are noted in these lists if known. Still, check the records of standard category aircraft to verify that a specific aircraft will qualify as an LSA before flying it. (Lists courtesy of www.sportpilot.org.)

Aeronca

C	C-2	C-3	PC-3	CF	K	KC	KCA
KF	KM	KS	50-C	50-F	50-S	50-TC	50-TL
60-TF	65-C	65-TC	65-TF	65-TL	65-TAF	65-TAL	YO-58
7AC	7BCM	L-3	L-3D	L-3J	L-16A	50-F	50-L
50-LA	50-M	65-CA	65-LA	65-LB	65-TAC	O-58A	O-58B
7CCM	7DC	11AC	11BC	L-3A	L-3B	L-3C	L-3E
L-3F	L-3G	L-16B					

Ercoupe

415-C	415-CD

Interstate

S-1A	S-1A-65F	S-1A-85F	S-1A-90F	S-1 Cadet

Luscombe

8	8A	8B	8C	8D

Piper

E-2	F-2	J-2	J-3	J3C-40	J3C-50
J3C-65	J3F-50	J3F-60	J3F-65	J3L	J3P
J4	J4A	J4B	PA-11	PA-15	PA-17
L-4	L-4A	L-4B	L-4C	L-4D	L-4H
L-4J	NE-1	NE-2			

Porterfield

35	35-70	35V	CP-40	CP-50	CP-55	LP-65	FP-65

Taylorcraft

BC	BC-65	BC12-65	BC12-D	BC12-D1	BC12D-85	BF
BC12D-4-85	BF-60	BF-65	BF12-65	BL	BL-65	DC-65
DCO-65	DF-65	DL-65	A	L-2	L-2A	L-2B
L-2C	L-2E	L-2F	L-2G	L-2H	L-2J	L-2K

Homebuilt Aircraft

Numerous models of experimental or homebuilt aircraft also fall within the requirements for sport pilots. Here are typical fixed-wing models. Contact the EAA (www.eaa.org) for additional information.

Manufacturer	Model(s)
Ace Aircraft	Baby Ace Model D
Acro Sport Inc.	Pober Pixie, Pober Super Ace
Aerolites Inc.	Aeromaster AG, AeroSkiff, Sport Bearcat
Air Domi	STOL Trophy TT 2000, Trophy 4000
Aircraft Sales & Parts	Chinook Plus
Airdrome Aeroplanes	E III Eindicker, Fokker DR1, D-VI, D-VIII
AmeriPlanes Inc.	Mitchell Wing T-10D
Arnet Pereyra Aero Design	Aventura HP, II, UL; Bucaneer II, SX; Sabre II; Zephyr II
Avid Aircraft Inc.	Mark IV STOL Wing
B&F Technik V. Gmbh	FK12 Comet; FK9 Mk III, TG
Bradley Aerospace	Bradley Aerobat
BX-Aviation	Cherry BX-2
Canada Model Craft	Champion V, CP 90 Pinoccio, Junior VI, Whiskey IV
Capella Aircraft Corp.	Capella SS, XS, XLS, XLS Super 100
Carlson Aircraft Inc.	Sparrow II, Sparrow Sport Special
CFM Aircraft	Shadow
CGS Aviation	Hawk Arrow, Hawk II Arrow, Hawk II Classic, Hawk Plus

Manufacturer	Model(s)
Classic Aero Enterprises	H-2 Honey Bee (biplane), H-3 Pegasus
Clifford Aeroworks	80% Spad 13
CSN	Corby Starlet CJ-1
Don S. Wolf	W-11 Boredom Fighter
Early Bird Aircraft Co.	Early Bird Jenny
Ehroflug GmbH	Coach II S
Eric Clutton Co.	FRED
Evans Aircraft	Wolksplane VP-1
Evektor-Aerotechnik	EV-97 Eurostar
Falconar Avia Inc.	ARV-1K Golden Hawk, Falconar F9A
Ferguson Aircraft Inc.	F-II
Fisher Flying Products	Avenger, Celebrity (biplane), Classic (biplane), Dakota Hawk, FP-202 Koala (similar to J-3), FP-404 (biplane), Horizon I, Horizon II, Super Koala, Youngster (biplane)
Flightstar Inc.	Flightstar Formula, IISC, IISL, Spyder
Fly Synthesis	Storch, Texan
Golden Circle Air Inc.	T-Bird II, Sonerai I, Sonerai II
Green Sky Adventures Inc.	Micro Mong (biplane), Zippy Sport
Hipp's Superbirds Inc.	J-4 Sportster, J-5 Super Kitten, Reliant SX, Reliant
Hummel Aviation	Hummel Bird
John W. Grega	GN-1 Aircamper
Joplin Light Aircraft	Tundra
Jurca Plans	MJ-2 Tempete
KAPPA as	KP-2U Sova (Owl)
Leading Edge Air Foils	Nieuport 11, Nieuport 12
Letov Air Division	ST-4 Aztek; Drifter XP503, DR447, MU582
Light Miniature Aircraft	LM-1-2P-W, LM-2X-2P-W Taylorcraft, LM-3X-W Aeronca Champ, LM-5X Super Cub, LM-5X-W Super Cup
Loehle Aircraft Corp.	5151 Mustang
Mini-Imp Aircraft Company	Mini-Imp
Murphy Aircraft Mfg. Ltd.	Maverick, Renegade Spirit (biplane)

continues

continued

Manufacturer	Model(s)
Nancy Peris	JN-1
New Kolb Aircraft Co.	Firestar II, Mark III, Slingshot
Nipper Kits & Components Ltd.	Tipsy Nipper Mk III/IV
Norman Aviation International Inc.	Nordic VI-912
Pazmany Aircraft Corp.	Pazmany PL-4A and PL-2
Peter M. Bowers	Fly Baby 1A
Pietenpol Aircraft	B4F Air Camper, Sky Scout
Popular Flying Association	Isaacs Fury II
Preceptor Aircraft Corp.	Ultra Pup, Super Pup
Progressive Aerodyne Inc.	StingRay
ProSport Aviation	Freebird
Quad City Ultralight Aircraft	Challenger II Special, Challenger II, Challenger Special
Quicksilver Aircraft Mfg. Inc.	MX II Sprint, MXL II Sport, GT 500
RagWing Aviation	RagWing Stork, PT2S, Ragabond
RANS Inc.	S-10 Sakota (aerobatic), S-12S Super Airaile, S-12XL Airaile, S-14 Airaile, S-4/S-5 Coyote I, S-6ES Coyote II, S-6S Coyote II, S-7 Courier, S-9 Chaos (aerobatic)
Replica Plans	SE-5A Replica
Rocky Mountain Wing LLC	Mi Fyter
Sapphire Aircraft Australia Ltd.	Sapphire LSA Mk II
SkyCraft International Inc.	ARV Super 2
Sky Raider LLC	Sky Raider I and II, Super Sky Raider
SkyStar Aircraft Corp.	Kitfox Classic 4
SlipStream Industries	Revelation, Scepter
Sonex Ltd.	Sonex
St. Croix Aircraft	Pietenpol Aircamper
Stolp Starduster Corp.	Starlet SA500, V-Star SA900
Sunrise Aircraft Corp.	SNS-8 Hyperlite
Synairgie	Jet Ranger, Sky Ranger

Manufacturer	Model(s)
Terry Taylor Co.	Taylor Monoplane
Titan Aircraft	Tornado 912, Tornado II
U.S. Light Aircraft Corp.	Hornet
Warner Aerocraft Co.	Spacewalker I/Revolution I
Zenith Aircraft Co.	STOL CH 701, Zodiac CH 601 (UL), Zodiac CH 601 HD

Sport Flying Websites

The best resource for the latest information and suppliers for sport flying is found in magazines such as *EAA Sport Pilot & Light Sport Aircraft* and *AOPA Flight Training*, described in Chapter 12. In addition, you'll find information at my website, www.SportFlyingGuide.com, as well as on the various websites. Note: Prefix the following URLs with "www":

aceaircraft.net (manufacturer)

aerocrafter.org (publication)

aeroplanner.com (flight planning)

aerotraderonline.com (publication)

aircraftspruce.com (parts)

airnav.com (pilot resources)

airweb.faa.gov (FAA)

all-about-sport-pilot.com (training)

aopa.org (organization)

aopa.org/flight_planner/ (flight planning)

asa2fly.com (publications)

astm.org (LSA construction)

aviation-consumer.com (buying assistance)

bydanjohnson.com (sport-pilot resource center)

chproducts.com (multimedia flying products)

duat.com (flight planning)

duats.com (flight planning)

eaa.org (organization)

embryriddle.edu (school)

faa.gov (Federal Aviation Administration)

flightlearning.com (training)

gaservingamerica.org (organization)

goldencircleair.com (manufacturer)

ipilot.com (pilot knowledge)

jeppesen.com (training)

kingschools.com (training)

kitbuiltplane.com (kit-builder resource)

kitplanes.com (publication)

lama.bz (LSA manufacturers association)

learntofly.com (training)

letsfly.org (cooperative)

myairplane.com (meeting place)

myfbo.com (software)

ninety-nines.org (women aviators)

oklahomaaviator.com (regional aviation publication)

pcaviator.com (computer flying)

rans.com (manufacturer)

skystar.com (manufacturer)

sportair-usa.com (manufacturer)

sportflight.com (flying adventures)

SportFlyingGuide.com (additional resources)

sportpilot.com (training)

sportpilot.org (organization)

sportpilots.com (additional resources)

sport-pilot-training.com (training)

sportys.com (supplies and training)

tnkolbaircraft.com (manufacturer)

trade-a-plane.com (publication)

uflyit.com (LSA sales)

ultralight-aircraft.com (manufacturer)

usapilot.com (organization)

usua.org (organization)

vansaircraft.com (manufacturer)

wagaero.com (parts)

wheretofly.com (flight planning)

zenithair.com (manufacturer)

If you would like your organization added to this list for future editions, visit www.SportFlyingGuide.com.

Appendix C

Sport Flying Glossary

51-percent rule FAA requirement that the majority (more than 50 percent) of an experimental aircraft be built by the owner.

100LL Aviation gasoline; 100 is the octane rating, LL stands for low lead.

above ground level (AGL) Altitude expressed as feet above terrain or airport elevation (see also *mean sea level*).

acrobatic flight Intentional maneuver involving an abrupt change in an aircraft's attitude. It is an abnormal attitude or abnormal acceleration not necessary for normal flight.

aeronautical chart Map used in air navigation. Plots topographic features, hazards and obstructions, navigation aids, navigation routes, designated airspace, and airports. Commonly used VFR aeronautical charts are sectional charts, VFR terminal area charts, and world aeronautical charts (WAC).

***Aeronautical Information Manual* (AIM)** Primary FAA publication of instructions to airmen about operating in the national airspace system of the United States. Provides basic flight information; ATC procedures; general instructional information on health, medical facts, factors affecting flight safety, accident and hazard reporting; and types of aeronautical charts and their use.

ailerons Movable control surfaces at the outer trailing edge of each wing. Control movement around the longitudinal axis of the aircraft.

airframe Structure of the aircraft.

airframe and power-plant (A&P) mechanic Mechanic who is licensed to work on the airframe, the engine, or both. An A&P mechanic can perform maintenance on the entire plane.

airfoil The wing, elevator, or rudder of an aircraft.

airport elevation Highest point of an airport's usable runways, measured in feet from mean sea level.

Airport/Facility Directory (A/FD) Publication containing information on all airports, seaplane bases, and heliports open to the public. Includes communications data, navigational facilities, and certain special notices and procedures.

airport radar service area (ARSA) See *Class C*.

air traffic control (ATC) FAA service providing separation services to participating airborne traffic. It includes clearances to land, take off, or taxi at airports with a control tower.

altimeter Highly sensitive barometer that shows an aircraft's altitude above mean sea level by measuring atmospheric pressure.

altimeter setting Local barometric pressure, usually provided to pilots by air traffic control. Used as a reference setting so that the aircraft altimeter indicates an accurate altitude.

altitude Height of a level, point, or object measured in feet above ground level (AGL) or mean sea level (MSL). Indicated altitude is the altitude as shown by an altimeter. Altitude as shown on a pressure or barometric altimeter is uncorrected for instrument error and uncompensated for variation from standard atmospheric conditions.

ammeter Instrument that measures electrical current.

approach/departure control Radar-based air traffic control, associated with the control tower at larger airports. Provides traffic separation services from outside the immediate airport area to a distance of about 40 miles.

Automated Flight Service Station (AFSS) Facility providing pilots with weather briefing and flight-plan filing by radio, telephone, and in person. Monitors flight plans for overdue aircraft and initiates search and rescue services. "Automated" refers to telephone call–handling equipment and computer information systems aiding pilot briefers.

Automated Surface Observation System (ASOS) Primary automated surface weather observing system in the United States, supporting aviation operations and weather forecasting. Sensors record wind direction and speed, visibility, cloud ceiling, precipitation, and so on. Data is sent automatically to the National Weather Service. At many locations, a computer-generated voice broadcasts the minute-by-minute weather reports to pilots.

Automated Terminal Information System (ATIS) Continuous broadcast on a separate ATC frequency of an airport's current weather (updated at least hourly). Eliminates controller requirement to read local weather data to each landing or departing aircraft.

Automated Weather Observing System (AWOS) Provides automated airport weather observations to pilots via a computer-generated voice. Less sophisticated than ASOS, usually installed using state funds.

avionics Aviation electronics that are typically found in the instrument panel of practically every airplane: communications, navigation, weather radar, and the like.

base or **base leg** Leg perpendicular to the final leg of the traffic pattern to the landing runway.

ceiling Height above the earth's surface of the lowest layer of clouds or obscuring phenomena that is reported as "broken," "overcast," or "obscuration," and not classified as "thin" or "partial."

certified flight instructor (CFI) Pilot holding a commercial pilot certificate who, after passing two written tests and a practical flight exam, is FAA-rated to give flight instruction. The flight instructor rating specifies the type of instruction authorized: for example, single-engine airplane, multiengine airplane, instrument flying (CFII), helicopter.

certified flight instructor: instrument (CFII) Flight instructor rated to teach instrument flight (flight by instruments only, with no outside visual references).

checkride Flight test an applicant for a pilot's license must take with either an FAA or designated examiner. For each new rating (classification), another flight test must be taken.

Class A Airspace between 18,000 and 60,000 feet MSL over the 48 U.S. states. IFR clearances are required for all aircraft operating in Class A airspace. Formerly called the positive control area.

Class B Airspace area around the busiest U.S. hub airports, typically to a radius of 20 nautical miles and up to 10,000 feet above ground level (AGL). Operations within Class B airspace require an ATC clearance and at least a private-pilot certificate (local waivers available), radio communication, and an altitude-reporting (mode C) transponder. Formerly called terminal control area (TCA).

Class C Airspace area around busy U.S. airports (other than Class B). Radio contact with approach control is mandatory for all traffic. Typically includes an area from the surface to 4,000 feet AGL out to 5 miles and from 1,200 to 4,000 feet AGL to 10 miles from the airport. Formerly called airport radar service area (ARSA).

Class D Airspace around an airport with an operating control tower, typically to a radius of 5 miles from the surface to 2,500 feet AGL. Radio contact with the control tower required prior to entry. Formerly called airport traffic area (ATA).

Class E General controlled airspace comprising control areas, transition areas, Victor airways, the continental control area, and so on.

Class F International airspace designation not used in the United States.

Class G Uncontrolled airspace, generally the airspace from the surface up to 700 or 1,200 feet AGL in most of the United States, but up to as high as 14,500 feet in some remote western and sparsely populated areas.

classic-sport aircraft Aircraft that meet the requirements of new light-sport aircraft rulings, but were initially built as certified aircraft.

clearance Formal instructions from air traffic control authorizing a specific route or action (climb or descend, entry into controlled airspace). Pilots may deviate from an ATC clearance in an emergency or when compliance would threaten the safety of the flight.

comm radio Communications radio.

commercial pilot Holder of an FAA commercial pilot certificate. Minimum requirements: age 18, minimum of 250 flight hours (and other subrequirements), a commercial written test, and a commercial flight test. The certificate allows a pilot to fly for compensation or hire, often in a wide variety of commercial general aviation operations, including sightseeing, aerial application, glider towing, and flight instruction. This classification does not necessarily imply flying for a scheduled airline.

common traffic-advisory frequency (CTAF) Radio frequency, also called the UNICOM frequency, used by all traffic at an airport without an operating control tower to coordinate approaches, landings, takeoffs, and departures. Pilots announce their positions, intentions, and actions in the traffic pattern for the benefit of other traffic.

consensus standards Light-sport aircraft construction standards as established by the ASTM.

controlled airspace Generic term including all airspace classes in which ATC services are available, but does not imply that all flight is under ATC control. VFR aircraft may operate without ATC contact in most controlled airspace as long as weather conditions permit pilots to see and avoid other aircraft.

coordinated universal time (UTC) Primary time zone standard used for aviation and other international needs.

course Intended path of your aircraft to reach a specific destination.

cross-country Flight of at least 75 miles from the home airport.

crosswind Wind that comes from a side of an aircraft, pushing it off course.

cumulus Clouds with vertical development as opposed to layered, stratus-type clouds—thunderheads, for example.

datum line Initial point in an aircraft used for calculating the center of gravity.

dead reckoning As applied to flying, this term refers to the navigation of an aircraft by means of computations based on airspeed, course, heading, wind direction, and speed, ground speed, and elapsed time.

density altitude (performance altitude) Measurement of air density, which can affect the performance of an aircraft.

dew point Temperature at which moisture condenses into a liquid.

Direct User Access Terminal System (DUATS) Permits pilots with a personal computer to obtain preflight weather data and to file flight plans. Toll-free service is available to all pilots with a current medical certificate.

downwind Standard traffic-pattern leg where traffic flies parallel to the landing runway in the direction opposite that of landing. Airplanes usually land into the wind. In this leg of the pattern, the aircraft has the wind behind it, thus the plane is flying "downwind."

drag Effect of air over the surface of an airplane, reducing its forward movement.

drift angle Angle of difference between the heading and the track.

dry In terms of renting an airplane, the pilot pays for the fuel directly and tops off the tanks when done. See also *wet*.

elevator Aircraft control surface hinged to the rear of the left and right horizontal stabilizers of the aircraft tail. Changes the aircraft pitch attitude to nose up or nose down, as during climb or descent. Controlled by pushing or pulling on the control yoke or stick.

emergency locator transmitter (ELT) Radio transmitter activated automatically by the impact of an accident. Emits a warbling tone on the international emergency frequencies of 121.5 MHz, 243 MHz, and (on newer models) 406 MHz. ELT signals can be received by nearby FAA facilities, aircraft overhead, and SARSATs (search-and-rescue satellites).

experimental aircraft Aircraft that is built primarily (majority or at least 51 percent) by the owner.

Federal Aviation Administration (FAA) Department of Transportation's agency for aviation. In addition to regulating airports, aircraft manufacturing and parts certification, aircraft operation, and pilot certification ("licensing"), the FAA operates air traffic control, purchases and maintains navigation equipment, certifies airports, and aids airport development, among other activities.

Federal Aviation Regulations (FARs) Commonly used term for the rules and regulations covering every aspect of aviation. Divided into parts covering specific subjects (see also *Parts 61*, *141*, *142* and *Parts 91*, *121*, *125*, *135*).

final Last leg of the traffic pattern where the aircraft is aligned to fly straight in to the landing runway.

first-class medical Certification that allows a pilot to exercise the privileges of the airline transport pilot (ATP) certificate for six months. If not renewed, certification drops down to second-class medical, then to third-class medical (see also *second-class medical* and *third-class medical*).

fixed-base operator (FBO) Airport-based business that parks, services, fuels, and may repair aircraft. Often rents aircraft and provides flight training. The term was coined to differentiate FBOs from businesses or individuals without an established place of business on the airport.

flaps Hinged surfaces on the inboard rear of wings, deployed to increase wing curvature (and thus, lift), primarily used to control angle of descent and decrease landing touchdown speeds.

flight following ATC radar surveillance of VFR flights at pilot request over water or desolate areas. Facilitates search and rescue when needed. This service is provided only if the controller is not too busy with IFR traffic.

flight instructor Someone who provides flight training. See also *certified flight instructor (CFI)*.

flight plan Record of aircraft number, type, and equipment, estimated time of departure and time en route, route and altitude to be flown, amount of fuel and number of persons aboard, home base and contact phone number, and other information, filed by radio, telephone, computer, or in person with flight service stations.

flight service station (FSS) Air traffic facilities that provide pilot briefing, en route communications, VFR search and rescue services; assist lost aircraft and aircraft in emergency situations; relay ATC clearances; originate notices to airmen (NOTAMs); broadcast aviation weather and NAS information; receive and process IFR flight plans; and monitor NAVAIDs. At selected locations, FSS provides en route flight advisory service (EFAS), takes weather observations, issues airport advisories, and advises the Customs and Immigration Department of transborder flights.

flight standards district office (FSDO) FAA field office serving an assigned geographical area and staffed with flight standards personnel who serve the aviation industry and the general public on matters relating to the certification and operation of air carrier and general aviation aircraft. Activities include general surveillance of operational safety, certification of airmen and aircraft, accident prevention, investigation, enforcement, and so on.

flight watch Shortened term used in air/ground contacts to identify the flight service station providing en route flight advisory service (EFAS).

fly the patch Flying around an airport.

fuselage Main body of the aircraft.

general aviation (GA) Ninety-two percent of U.S. aircraft and more than 65 percent of U.S. flight hours flown by other than major and regional airlines or the military.

Global Positioning System (GPS) Space-based radio positioning, navigation, and time-transfer system. The system provides highly accurate position and velocity information, and precise time, on a continuous global basis, to an unlimited number of properly equipped users.

go-around Rejected landing that becomes a takeoff so you can go around the traffic pattern again for another landing.

heading Direction in which you must point the aircraft nose.

headwind Wind that comes from in front of an aircraft, slowing it down.

hypoxia Effect of insufficient oxygen to the body. Dangerous when it interferes with a pilot's ability to think and function properly.

IFR flight plan Mandatory filing before a flight under instrument flight rules. Based on flight plan information, ATC can issue (immediately before departure) an IFR clearance to enter clouds or low visibility conditions for instrument rather than visual flight.

instrument flight rules (IFR) Rules of the road for flights permitted to penetrate clouds and low visibility conditions that must rely on cockpit flight instruments and radio navigation. The aircraft must be appropriately equipped and pilots must be qualified and current for IFR flight. Flight plans and ATC clearances are required. Flights are monitored and traffic separated by air traffic control, usually by radar.

instrument landing system (ILS) Precision instrument-approach system located at the runway ends, which utilizes radio transmitters that provide precise descent and course guidance to the runway, permitting aircraft to land during periods of low ceilings or poor visibility.

knot One nautical mile per hour, the most common measure of aircraft speed. One hundred knots equal 115 statute miles per hour. (For miles per hour, multiply knots by 1.15.)

light-sport aircraft (LSA) Aircraft that complies with the limitations of the new light-sport aircraft designations (see Appendix A for sport flying rules).

long-range navigation (LORAN) Electronic navigational system by which hyperbolic lines of position are determined by measuring the difference in the time of reception of synchronized pulse signals from two fixed transmitters. Loran A operates in the 1,750 to 1,950 kHz frequency band. Loran C and D operate in the 100 to 110 kHz frequency band.

magneto Component that supplies electrical spark to the engine for combustion of gas in the cylinders. Most aircraft have two magnetos for safety.

marginal VFR Weather occurring with less than 3,000-foot ceiling and/or five miles visibility, but above the required 1,000 ft. and three miles visibility.

mean sea level (MSL) or **above mean sea level (AMSL)** Altitude expressed as feet above sea level, rather than above ground level (AGL). To ignore varying terrain elevations, all navigational altitudes and barometric altimeters are based on height above mean sea level. Only radar altimeters, which measure the distance between the aircraft and the ground at low altitudes, indicate actual height above the ground.

military operations area (MOA) Airspace assignment of defined vertical and lateral dimensions established outside Class A airspace to segregate certain military activities from IFR traffic and to identify for VFR traffic where these activities are conducted.

mode C Transponder operating mode that also reports aircraft altitude by transmitting data from an encoding altimeter.

nautical mile (NM) See *knot*.

N-numbers Refers to U.S.–registered aircraft numbers, which begin with "N." Canadian numbers begin with "C" or "CF"; German numbers with "D"; United Kingdom numbers with "G"; French numbers with "F"; Japanese numbers with "JA," and so on.

nontowered airport Airport without a control tower, which comprises the majority of the 13,000 airports in the United States. Only 722 airports have control towers. Nontowered airports are far from being "uncontrolled." Pilots follow traffic pattern procedures and self-announce positions and intentions using the common traffic advisory frequency (CTAF), usually called the UNICOM frequency.

notice to airmen (NOTAM) Notice containing information (not known sufficiently in advance to be publicized by other means) concerning the establishment, condition, or change in any component (facility, service, procedure, or hazard in the national airspace system) when the timely knowledge is essential to personnel concerned with flight operations.

Parts 61, 141, 142 Parts of Federal Aviation Regulations (FARs) covering pilot certification and flight school operations: the pilot certification and standard flight school (Part 61), the integrated curriculum type school (Part 141) requiring slightly fewer flying hours, and a new Part 142 program allowing replacement of more flight time with advanced flight simulators.

Parts 91, 121, 125, 135 Parts of Federal Aviation Regulations (FARs) covering noncommercial operations (Part 91), major scheduled air carriers (Part 121), commuters (Part 125), and nonscheduled carriers and air taxis (Part 135).

pilot in command (PIC) Person who has the final authority and responsibility for the operation and safety of the flight; has been designated as PIC before or during the flight; and holds the appropriate category, class, and type rating, if appropriate, for the conduct of the flight.

pilot weather report (PIREP) Report of meteorological phenomena encountered by aircraft in flight.

pilotage Navigation by ground reference from point to point.

pitot tube Tube or opening for gathering flowing air pressure for use by the airspeed indicator.

pressure altitude Indicated altitude when the altimeter is set to 29.92 in. Hg (inches of mercury).

private pilot Designation of a pilot certified to fly passengers for personal transportation and business. Certification requires the pilot to be at least 17 years old (16 years old for a glider or hot air balloon), to have a minimum of 40 hours of flight experience and training (35 hours under Part 141), and to pass at least a third-class medical exam, a written exam, and a flight test. May not fly for hire or compensation but may share expenses equally with passengers.

prohibited area Designated airspace where aircraft flight is prohibited.

recreational pilot Designation of a pilot with less training than a certified private pilot. To be certified, a recreational pilot must be at least 17 years old. Privileges are limited to flight within 50 nautical miles of base, carrying no more than one passenger, using airports without towers, and flying during daylight hours, only, unless restrictions are removed through further training. The recreational pilot may not share expenses. Few new pilots currently choose the recreational-pilot certificate.

restricted area Airspace which (when "active" or "hot") usually excludes civilian aircraft. Examples: airspace for rocket flights, for practice air-to-air combat, or for ground-based artillery practice. Temporary restricted areas are established for events such as forest fires, natural disasters, or major news stories. Flight through a restricted area may be authorized by the controlling agency or by the FAA.

rpm Revolutions per minute. Defines how fast the engine crankshaft is turning.

rudder Aircraft control surface attached to the rear of the vertical stabilizer (fin) of the aircraft tail. Forces the tail left or right, correspondingly yawing the aircraft right or left. Rudder movement coordinates with the banking of wings to balance a turn. Controlled by left and right rudder (foot) pedals.

second-class medical Certification that allows a pilot to exercise the privileges of a commercial pilot certificate for compensation or hire for one year. Then, if not renewed, certification drops down to third-class medical (see also *third-class medical*).

sectional aeronautical chart (SAC) Designed for slow- or medium-speed aircraft for use during visual navigation. Topographic information on these charts features elevations of land surfaces and a judicious selection of visual checkpoints for VFR flight. Aeronautical information includes visual and radio aids to navigation, airports, controlled airspace, restricted areas, obstructions, and related data.

see-and-avoid Describes the FAA requirement that all pilots be ultimately responsible for their separation from other aircraft when visual conditions permit spotting traffic. Even IFR flights when operating in visual weather conditions or VFR flights being issued radar advisories are responsible for visual scanning to see-and-avoid other traffic.

single-engine land (SEL) Airplane class rating on a pilot certificate, meaning the pilot can fly single-engine aircraft that take off and land on the ground rather than water.

skin Covering of an airframe.

slip or sideslip Aircraft control technique. With the wings banked one way and the rudder deployed for the opposite turn, an aircraft flies slightly sideways, increasing drag to make it descend faster without increasing forward speed. Also, one of two control configurations used to neutralize the wind's effect in crosswind landings, allowing the rudder to counteract the turning effect of banking into a crosswind.

solo Flight performed alone. After initial flight training, qualified student pilots are permitted to undertake some flights to build experience and confidence without a flight instructor on board. Soloing requires a written endorsement from the student's flight instructor and a third-class medical certification, or, for sport pilots, a valid driver's license. The first solo, a major event for any pilot, includes traditionally three takeoffs and landings at the student's home airport. Once the pilot certificate is endorsed, the student may fly solo without further endorsement.

spin Descending corkscrew flight pattern that develops when the wings lose lift. An aircraft must stall for a spin to occur. A spin is usually the result of "crossed" flight controls (uncoordinated rudder) causing residual lift on one wing during the stall.

SP/LSA ruling FAA ruling that regulates sport pilots and light-sport aircraft.

sport flying Flying light-sport aircraft for recreation. Pilots require a sport-pilot certificate and aircraft must conform to the requirements of light-sport aircraft as defined by the FAA.

sport pilot (SP) Designation of a pilot certified to fly only light-sport aircraft. Must be at least 17 years old. Privileges are expanded by training and endorsements in the sport-pilot logbook (see Appendix A).

sport-pilot knowledge test Written component of the sport-pilot certification test.

sport plane (SP) Aircraft conforms to the regulations established for light-sport aircraft (LSAs).

squawk Noun: Radio transmission of the radar transponder onboard an aircraft. Verb: ATC instruction to the pilot to set one of 4,096 possible codes to identify the aircraft on controller radar. All VFR flights squawk code 1200 except when receiving radar advisories or when instructed otherwise by ATC.

stall Purely an aerodynamic event—nothing to do with engine operation. Occurs when lift-producing airflow over the wings is disrupted or lost because the angle of the wings to the airflow (angle of attack) is too high. Most commonly occurs when a pilot doesn't maintain sufficient airspeed in a climb or turn. Student pilots are trained in stall prevention, recognition, and recovery.

standard rate turn Turn of three degrees per second.

tachometer Instrument that measures the revolutions per minute (RPMs) of an engine.

taildragger Aircraft with fixed (nonretractable) tail gear.

tailwind Wind that comes from behind an aircraft, speeding it up.

taxi To operate an aircraft on the ground under its own power.

temporary flight restriction (TFR) No-fly zone that can be established for a few hours (or semipermanently, despite its name) by the FAA through the NOTAM system to prohibit all air traffic in a defined area. Often used for reasons of national security: presidential movements, nuclear facilities, large sporting events, shuttle launch and landing, and the like. Any aircraft violating the airspace is subject to interception and escort by military jet fighters.

terminal area Airspace in which approach control service or airport traffic control service is provided.

terminal radar service area (TRSA) Radar service that assists with traffic sequencing in some Class D airspace. Pilot participation is voluntary.

tetrahedron Device normally located at an airport without a tower. Used as a landing direction indicator. The small end of a tetrahedron points in the direction of landing.

third-class medical Certification that allows a pilot to exercise the privileges of a recreational or private-pilot certificate. Requires examination by an FAA-designated aviation medical examiner (AME) for general health, eyesight, and hearing. Valid for three years (pilots younger than 40) or two years (age 40+). Allowed, but not required, for a sport-pilot certificate. Not valid for flying for compensation or hire.

touch-and-go Operation by an aircraft that lands and departs on a runway without stopping or exiting the runway.

tower Terminal facility that uses air/ground communications, visual signaling, and other devices to provide ATC services to aircraft operating in the vicinity of an airport. Authorizes aircraft to land or take off at the airport controlled by the tower or to transit the Class D airspace area. May also provide approach control services (radar or nonradar).

track Plane's actual path over the ground.

traffic pattern Imaginary standard rectangular flight pattern around the landing runway at an airport. Includes a 45-degree or crosswind entry to the rectangle, with downwind, base, and final legs as sides of the rectangle. Ninety-degree left-hand turns around the rectangle are standard (nonstandard right-hand traffic pattern is noted in Airport/Facility Directory) with downwind flown at a specified altitude, usually 1,000 or 1,500 feet above the airport elevation. At airports with a control tower, the pattern may be modified or shortcut according to ATC instructions.

trailing edge Rear side of an aircraft's control surface (wing, tail).

transponder Special onboard 1,090 MHz radio transmitter used to enhance and code an aircraft's radar return. When activated by ground radar, it transmits a return signal which controllers can use to identify and tag the flight on their computerized video display radar screen. Paired with an altitude encoder, a mode C transponder also transmits the aircraft's altitude. All aircraft flying in Class B airspace or higher than 10,000 feet are required to have mode C transponders.

uncontrolled airspace Also known as Class G airspace. That portion of the airspace that has *not* been designated as Class A, Class B, Class C, Class D, and Class E airspace.

UNICOM Common, multipurpose radio frequency used at most nontowered airports as the common traffic advisory frequency (CTAF). The Aircraft Owners and Pilots Association (AOPA) coined the term (derived from the words "universal communications") in the 1950s. UNICOM is also used by a fixed-base operator for general administrative uses, such as fuel orders and parking instructions. Originally 122.8 MHz universally, UNICOM now includes 122.7, 123.0, and other frequencies.

vertigo Spatial disorientation caused by not seeing a horizon.

VFR flight plan Voluntary filing for cross-country flights under visual flight rules (VFR). For search and rescue use only. It has no air traffic control role.

VHF omnidirectional range (VOR) Ground-based radio navigation aid. More than 1,000 VORs electronically define Victor airways and jet airways, "highways in the sky." Most IFR and many VFR flights follow airway routes.

visual flight rules (VFR) Defined set of FAA regulations and "rules of the road" covering operation of aircraft primarily by visual reference to the horizon (for aircraft control) and see-and-avoid procedures (for traffic separation). VFR is used by more than 70 percent of all flights.

VOR Means very high frequency omnidirectional range. A ground-based electronic navigation aid transmitting VHF radio signals in all directions.

vortices Circular patterns of air created by the movement of an airfoil through the air when generating lift. Vortices from medium to heavy aircraft can be of extremely high velocity and hazardous to smaller aircraft.

wake turbulence Turbulent air condition caused by small, tornado-like horizontal whirlwinds trailing an aircraft's wingtips (wingtip vortices). Wake turbulence associated with larger aircraft flying at slow speeds (as on takeoff or landing approach) is the most severe and can cause loss of control for smaller aircraft following close behind. Controllers use defined separation standards to avoid the problem for takeoff, landing, approach, and departure operations.

warning area Airspace of defined dimensions extending from 3 nautical miles outward from the coast of the United States, which contains activity that may be hazardous to nonparticipating aircraft. The purpose of such warning areas is to warn nonparticipating pilots of the potential danger. A warning area may be located over domestic or international waters, or both.

wet In terms of renting an airplane, the cost of fuel is included in the rental fee. See also *dry*.

wide-area augmentation system (WAAS) Enhancement to the GPS system providing greater navigation accuracy and system integrity, and permitting the GPS to be used for precision instrument approaches to most airports.

wind-correction angle (crab angle) Difference between the course and the heading.

wind shear Large changes in either wind speed or direction at different altitudes, which can cause sudden gain or loss of airspeed. Especially hazardous when aircraft airspeeds are low on takeoff or landing.

world aeronautical charts (WACs) Standard series of aeronautical charts, covering land areas at a size and scale convenient for navigation by moderate speed aircraft. Topographic information includes cities and towns, principal roads, railroads, distinctive landmarks, drainage, and surface elevations. Aeronautical information includes visual and radio aids to navigation, airports, airways, restricted areas, and obstructions.

yaw Movement around the vertical axis.

yoke Flight control that moves the wings' ailerons and the tail's elevators.

Appendix D

Sport Flying Abbreviations and Acronyms

AC advisory circular

ACAR aircraft communications addressing and reporting system

AD airworthiness directive

ADDS aviation digital data service

ADF automatic direction finder

AFB air force base

AFCS automatic flight control system

A/FD Airport/Facility Directory

AFM aircraft flight manual

AFSS automated flight service station

AGL above ground level

AHRS attitude heading reference system

AIM *Aeronautical Information Manual*

AIRMET airmen's meteorological information

ALD available landing distance

ALS approach-light systems

AME aviation medical examiner

AMSL above mean sea level

AOCC airline operations control center

AOPA Aircraft Owners and Pilots Association

A&P airframe and power-plant mechanic

AP autopilot system

APC approach clearance

APR effective annual percentage rate

APV approach with vertical guidance

ARSA airport radar service area

ARSR air route surveillance radar

ARTCC air route traffic control center

ARTS automated radar terminal system

ASA Aviation Supplies & Academics, Inc.

ASEL airplane, single engine, land

ASES airplane, single engine, sea

ASOS Automated Surface Observing System

ASR airport surveillance radar

ASTM American Society for Testing and Materials

ATA airport traffic area

ATC air traffic control

ATCRBS air traffic control radar beacon system

ATCT airport traffic control tower

ATD along-track (straight-line) distance

ATIS automatic terminal information service

ATP airline transport pilot

avgas aviation fuel

AWC Aviation Weather Center

AWOS Automated Weather Observing System

AWW severe weather forecast alert

BBS bulletin board system

BC back course

BKN broken cloud coverage

CAP Civil Air Patrol

CAT clear-air turbulence

CD controller display

CDI course deviation indicator

CFA controlled firing area

CFI certified flight instructor

CFII certified flight instructor: instrument

CFR Code of Federal Regulations

CH course heading

CPDLC controller pilot data link communications

CTAF common traffic-advisory frequency

CVFP charted visual flight procedure

CVRS computerized voice reservation system

CWA center weather advisory

CWSU Center Weather Service Unit

DA decision altitude

DCP data collection package

DF direction finder

DH decision height

DME distance-measuring equipment

DME/N standard DME

DME/P precision DME

DOD Department of Defense

DP instrument departure procedure

DPE designated pilot examiner

DRT diversion recovery tool

DUATS Direct User Access Terminal System

DVA diverse vector area

DVFR defense visual flight rules

DVRSN diversion

EAA Experimental Aircraft Association

EDCT expect departure clearance time

EFAS en route flight advisory service

ELT emergency locator transmitter

EPE estimate of position error

ETA estimated time of arrival

ETD estimated time of departure

ETE estimated time en route

EU European Union

EWINS enhanced weather information system

FA area forecast

FAA Federal Aviation Administration

FARs Federal Aviation Regulations

FB flyby

FBO fixed-base operator

FCC Federal Communications Commission

FD flight director system

FDC flight data center

FIR flight information region

FISDL flight information services data link

FL flight level

FLIP flight information publication

FO flyover

fpm feet per mile; also feet per minute

FPNM feet per nautical mile

FRME factory remanufactured engine

FSDO flight standards district office

FSS flight service station

GA general aviation

GBAS ground-based augmentation system

GEO geostationary satellite

GLS global landing system

GNSS global navigation satellite system

GNSSP global navigation satellite system panel

GPS Global Positioning System

GSD geographical situation display

GUS ground uplink station

HAT height above touchdown

HDTA high-density traffic airports

Hg mercury, as in "inches of mercury"

HIRL high-intensity runway lights

HIWAS hazardous in-flight weather advisory service

hp horsepower

Hz hertz

IAP instrument approach procedure

IAS indicated airspeed

ICAO International Civil Aviation Organization

IFIM International Flight Information Manual

IFR instrument flight rules

ILS instrument landing system

IM inner marker

IMC instrument meteorological conditions

INS inertial navigation system

IOC initial operational capability

IR IFR military training route

ITWS integrated terminal weather system

kg kilogram

kHz kilohertz

LAA local airport advisory

LAAS local area augmentation system

LAHSO land and hold short operations

LAWRS limited aviation weather-reporting station

LDA localizer-type directional aid

LIRL low-intensity runway lights

LLWAS low-level wind shear alert system

LLWAS NE low-level wind shear alert system network expansion

LNAV lateral navigation

LOC localizer

LOP line of position

LORAN long-range navigation system

LSA light-sport aircraft

Lyc Lycoming engine

MAP missed approach point

MDA minimum descent altitude

MEA minimum en route altitude

METAR meteorological aerodrome report (aviation routine weather report)

MH magnetic heading

MHz megahertz

MIRL medium-intensity runway lights

MLS microwave landing system

MM middle marker

MOA military operations area

MOCA minimum obstruction clearance altitude

mpg miles per gallon

mph miles per hour

MRA minimum reception altitude

MRB magnetic reference bearing

MSA minimum safe altitude

MSAW minimum safe altitude warning

MSL mean sea level

MTOS mountain obscuration

MTR military training route

MVA minimum vectoring altitude

MVFR marginal visual flight rules

MWO meteorological watch office

NACO National Aeronautical Charting Office

NAS national airspace system

NASA National Aeronautics and Space Administration

NAVAID navigational aid

NAVCEN Coast Guard navigation center

NCWF national convective weather forecast

NDB nondirectional radio beacon

NEXRAD next generation weather radar

NFDC National Flight Data Center

NIDS National Institute for Discovery Sciences

NIMA National Imagery and Mapping Agency

nm nautical mile

NMAC near-midair collision

NOAA National Oceanic and Atmospheric Administration

NOTAM notice to airmen

NPA nonprecision approach

NSA national security area

NSW no significant weather

NTAP notices to airmen publication

NTSB National Transportation Safety Board

NTZ no transgression zone

NWS National Weather Service

OAT outside air temperature

OBS omni-bearing selector

ODP obstacle departure procedure

OM outer marker

OVC overcast sky

PAR precision approach radar

PATWAS Pilot's Automatic Telephone Weather Answering System

PC personal computer

PFD personal flotation device

PIC pilot in command

PIREP pilot weather report

POB persons onboard

PPS precise positioning service

PRM precision runway monitor

PTS *Sport-Pilot Practical Test Standards*

RAA remote advisory airport

RAIM receiver autonomous integrity monitoring

RAIS remote airport information service

RCAG remote center air/ground

RCC rescue coordination center

RCLS runway centerline lighting system

RCO remote communications outlet

REIL runway end identifier lights

RLIM runway light-intensity monitor

RMI radio magnetic indicator

RNAV area navigation

RPM revolutions per minute

RVR runway visual range

SAC sectional aeronautical chart

SAM system area monitor

SAR search and rescue

SARSAT search and rescue satellite

SCT scattered cloud coverage

SDF simplified directional facility

SEL single-engine land

SFL sequenced flashing lights

SFR special flight rules

SIAP standard instrument approach procedure

SID standard instrument departure

SIGMET significant meteorological information

SKC clear sky condition

SM statute mile

SMGCS surface movement guidance control system

SNR signal-to-noise ratio

SOP standard operating procedure

SP sport plane; also sport pilot

SPC storm prediction center

SPE sport-pilot examiner

SPI sport-pilot instructor

SP/LSA sport plane/light-sport aircraft

SPS standard positioning service

STAR standard terminal arrival

STMP special traffic management program

STOH since top overhaul

STOL short takeoff and landing

SWSL supplemental weather service locations

TA traffic advisory

TAA terminal arrival area

TAC terminal area chart

TACAN tactical air navigation

TAF terminal aerodrome forecast

TAS true airspeed

TC true course

TCA terminal control area

TCAS traffic alert and collision avoidance system

TCH threshold crossing height

TD time difference

TDWR terminal Doppler weather radar

TDZL touchdown zone lights

TEC tower en route control

TFR temporary flight restriction

TH true heading

TIBS telephone information briefing service

TIS traffic information service

TLS transponder landing system

TPP terminal procedures publications

TRSA terminal radar service area

TSO technical standard order

TTAE total time airframe and engine

TWEB transcribed weather broadcast

TWIB terminal weather information for pilots system

UFO unidentified flying object

UHF ultrahigh frequency

UNICOM universal communications

UPAC Ultralight Pilot Association of Canada

USUA United States Ultralight Association

UTC coordinated universal time

UWS urgent weather SIGMET

V_{H} maximum continuous power

V_{MINI} instrument flight minimum velocity

V_{NE} never-exceed velocity

V_{NEI} instrument flight never-exceed velocity

V_{REF} reference landing approach velocity

V_{SO} stalling velocity

V_{Y} velocity for best rate of climb

V_{YI} instrument climb velocity

VAR magnetic variation

VASI visual approach slope indicator

VDA vertical descent angle

VDP visual descent point

VFR visual flight rules

VGSI visual glide slope indicator

VHF very high frequency

VIP video integrator processor

VMC visual meteorological conditions

VNAV vertical navigation

VOR VHF (very high frequency) omnidirectional range

VOR-DME VHF (very high frequency) omnidirectional range with distance-measuring equipment

VORTAC VHF omnidirectional range/tactical air navigation

VOT VOR test facility

VR VFR military training route

VSI vertical speed indicator; also visual slope indicator

VV vertical visibility

WA AIRMET

WAAS wide-area augmentation system

WAC world aeronautical chart

WCA wind correction angle

WFO weather forecast office

WMO World Meteorological Organization

WMS wide-area master station

WMSC weather message switching center

WMSCR weather message switching center replacement

WP waypoint

WRS wide-area ground reference station

WS SIGMET

WSO weather service office

WW severe weather watch bulletin

Index

A

B

C

G

H

I

J-K

L

M

N

O

T

U

V

W

X-Y-Z